Making false confessions a real problem

Secret interrogation still the norm

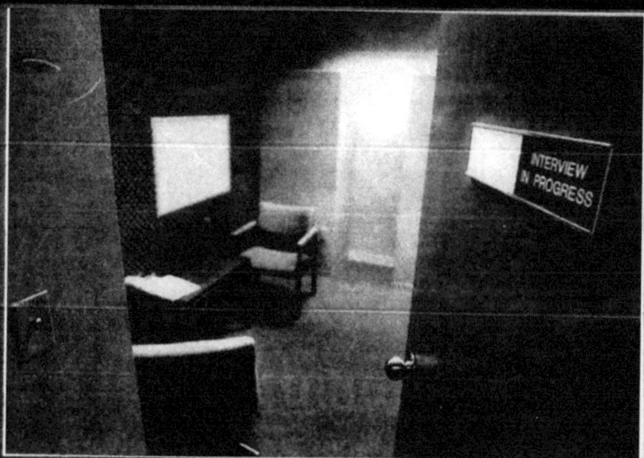

WALTER MICHOT/HERALD STAFF

ON THE RECORD: This Coral Springs interrogation room is a South Florida exception: Interrogations are videotaped in their entirety.

"This is a prime example of what mishandling that can be done by law enforcement in an unmonitored, unreported interrogation

"For decades, we have seen false confession after false confession lead to tragic wrongful convictions of the innocent while serious criminals go undetected. The courts have done little to respond to abuses in the interrogation room; if anything they have eroded constitutional protections, such as the right to remain silent.

Police, in false confessions, are too quick to identify a suspect, and will often subject a suspect to interrogations lasting several hours, Leo said. These interrogations are seldom taped, and police, it is later learned, have made threats or lied about evidence they had.

In Chicago, the center of a false-confession maelstrom that led to a moratorium on executions, The Chicago Tribune last year found at least 247 murder cases with incriminating statements that were thrown out by courts or which failed to secure convictions.

And in April, a judge acquitted a 16-year-old boy who spent more than a year behind bars awaiting trial for murder. The teen-ager had confessed to stabbing a woman who, it turns out, was never stabbed at all. The judge suggested that the zeal of police and prosecutors clouded their judgment.

Judge rules investigators coerced confession, overturns conviction

Many of us wonder how someone could confess guilt to something they had never done, especially something this horrific. As a matter of fact, it's not that unusual.

At least a half-dozen confessed killers who were charged with murder have been determined to be unquestionably innocent.

Frenzy

POLICE

CULTURE

Last year, according to court testimony, a man falsely confessed to Niagara Falls police that he murdered Clarkson resident John Montstream. The man, identified only as "Juan," told police he admitted to the crime after hours of questioning "because I thought that's what you guys wanted me to say.' ""

coerced into convicting themselves

But the newfound ability to match bodily fluids or hair to a suspect's unique genetic code, known as DNA testing, has exposed false confessions around the nation, freeing dozens of inmates previously thought to be guilty beyond question.

One analysis of 44 proven false-confession cases revealed that more than a third of the interrogations lasted six to 12 hours, many lasted between 12 and 24 hours, and the aver-

System 'running amok'

Interrogation method 'oppressive,' judge says

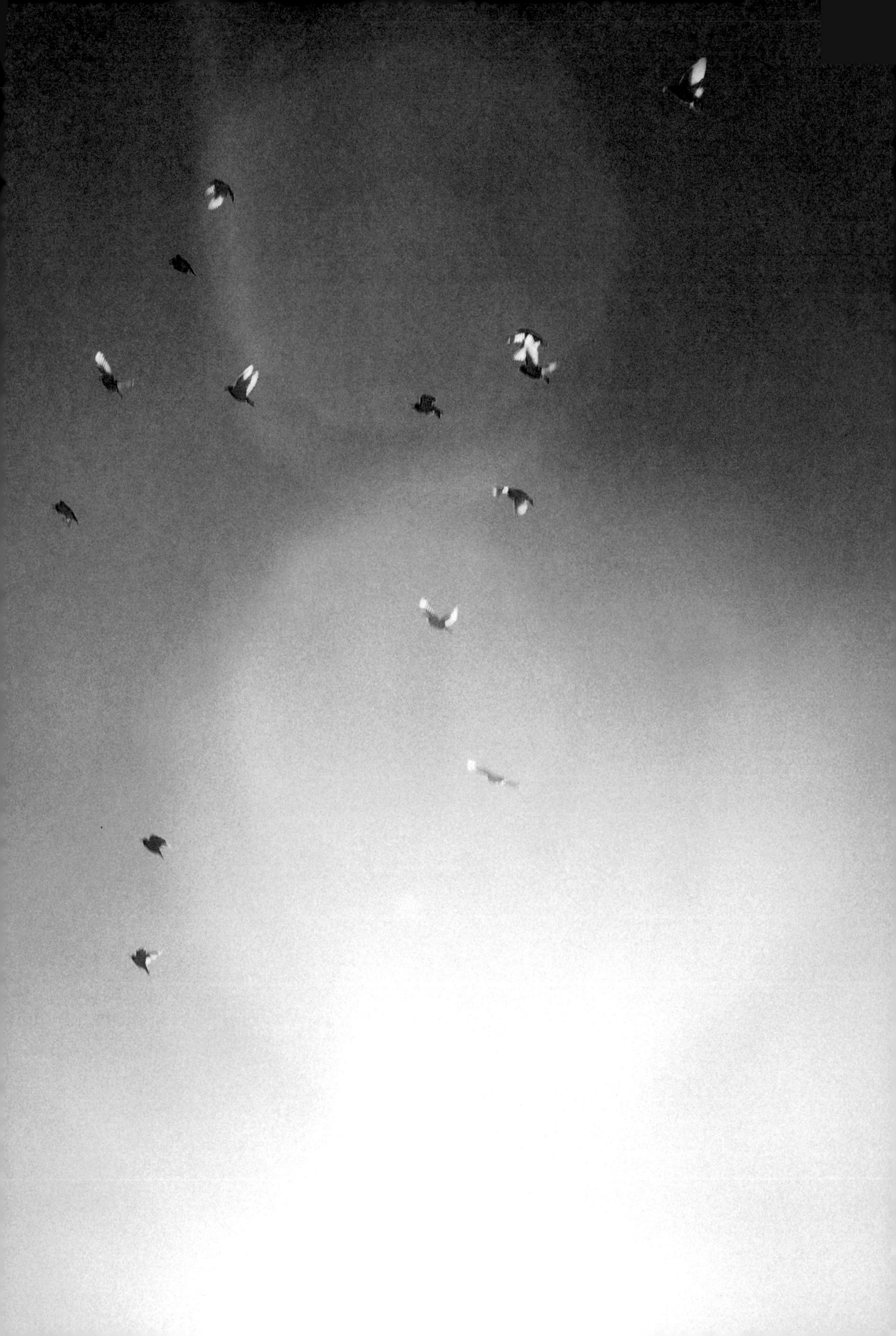

Breaking Point | Robin Dahlberg

KEHRER

“If you didn’t commit a crime, why the hell would you admit that you did?”

“Forum in Focus, Wrongfully imprisoned,”
The Journal News, Sept. 24, 2006

“Intuition holds that the innocent do not make false confessions. What on earth could be the motive?”

David K. Shipler, “Why do Innocent People Confess?” The New York Times, Feb. 23, 2012

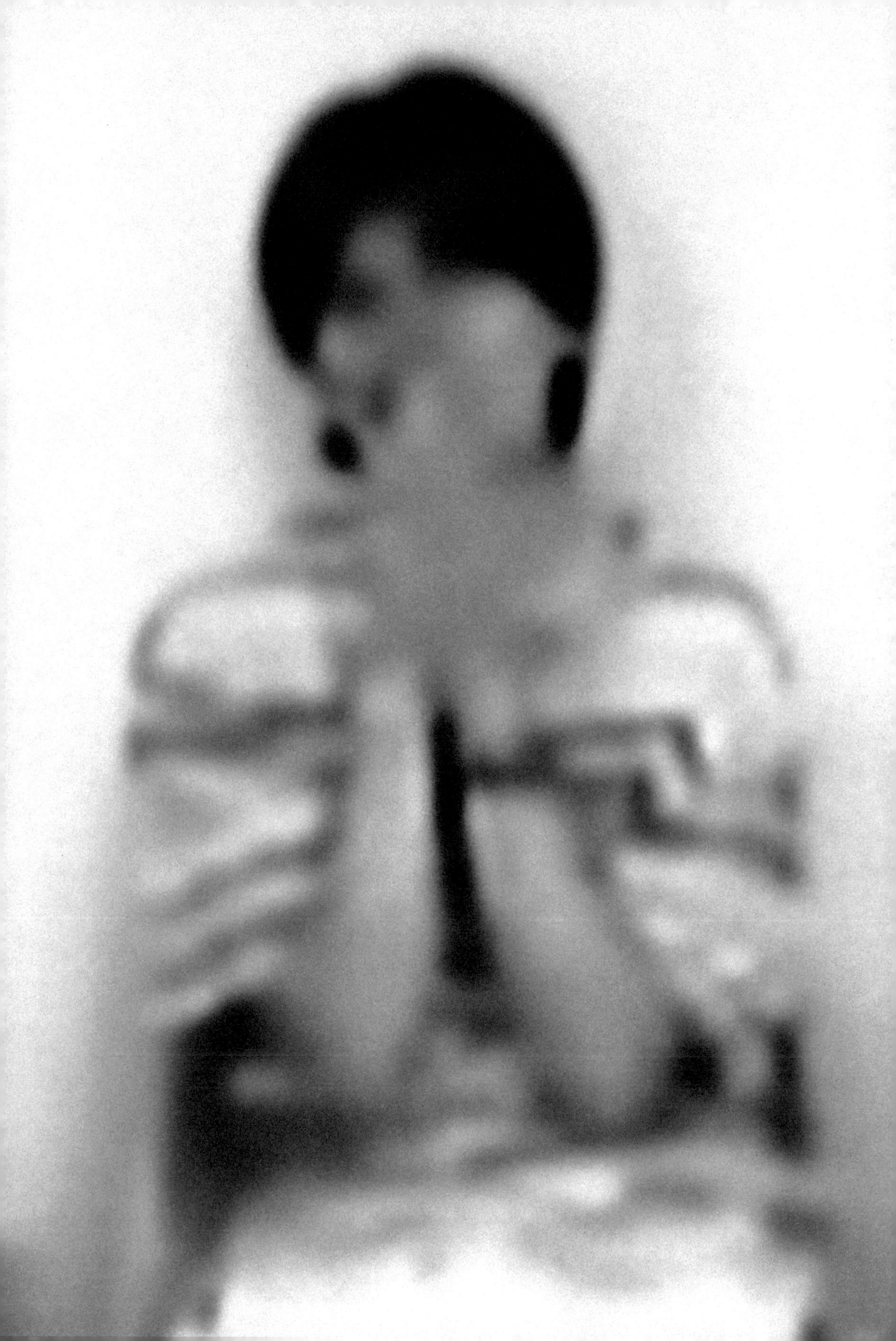

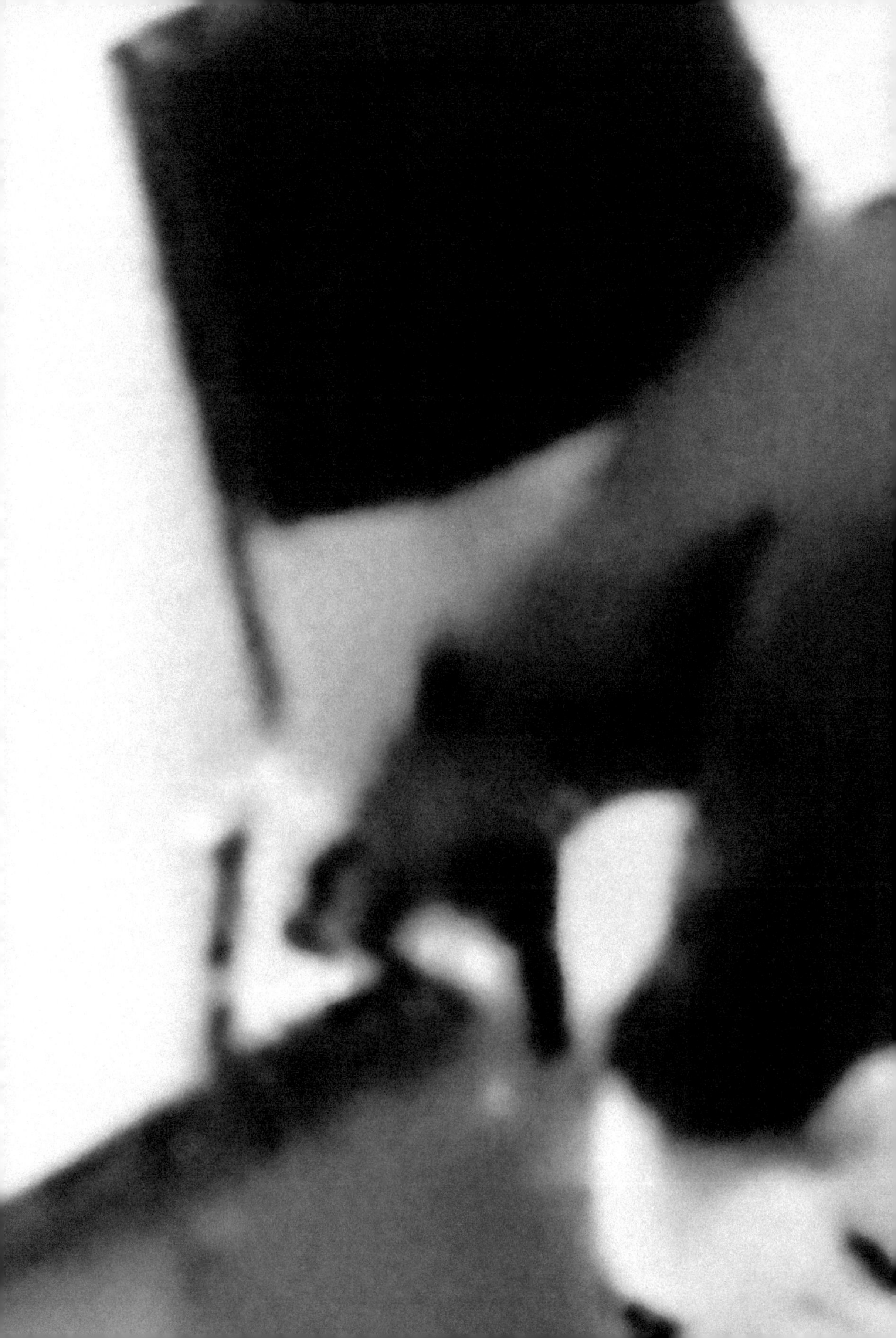

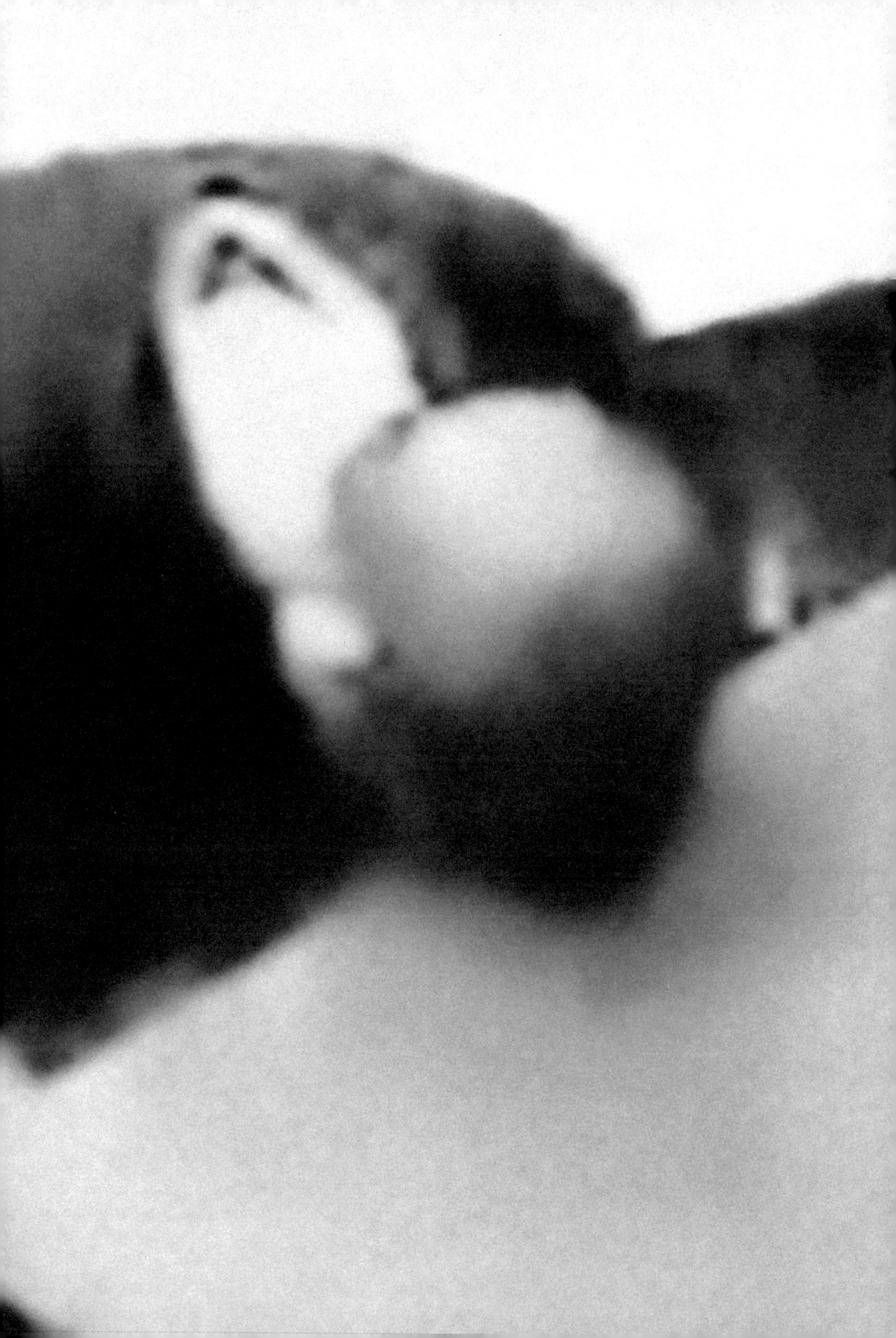

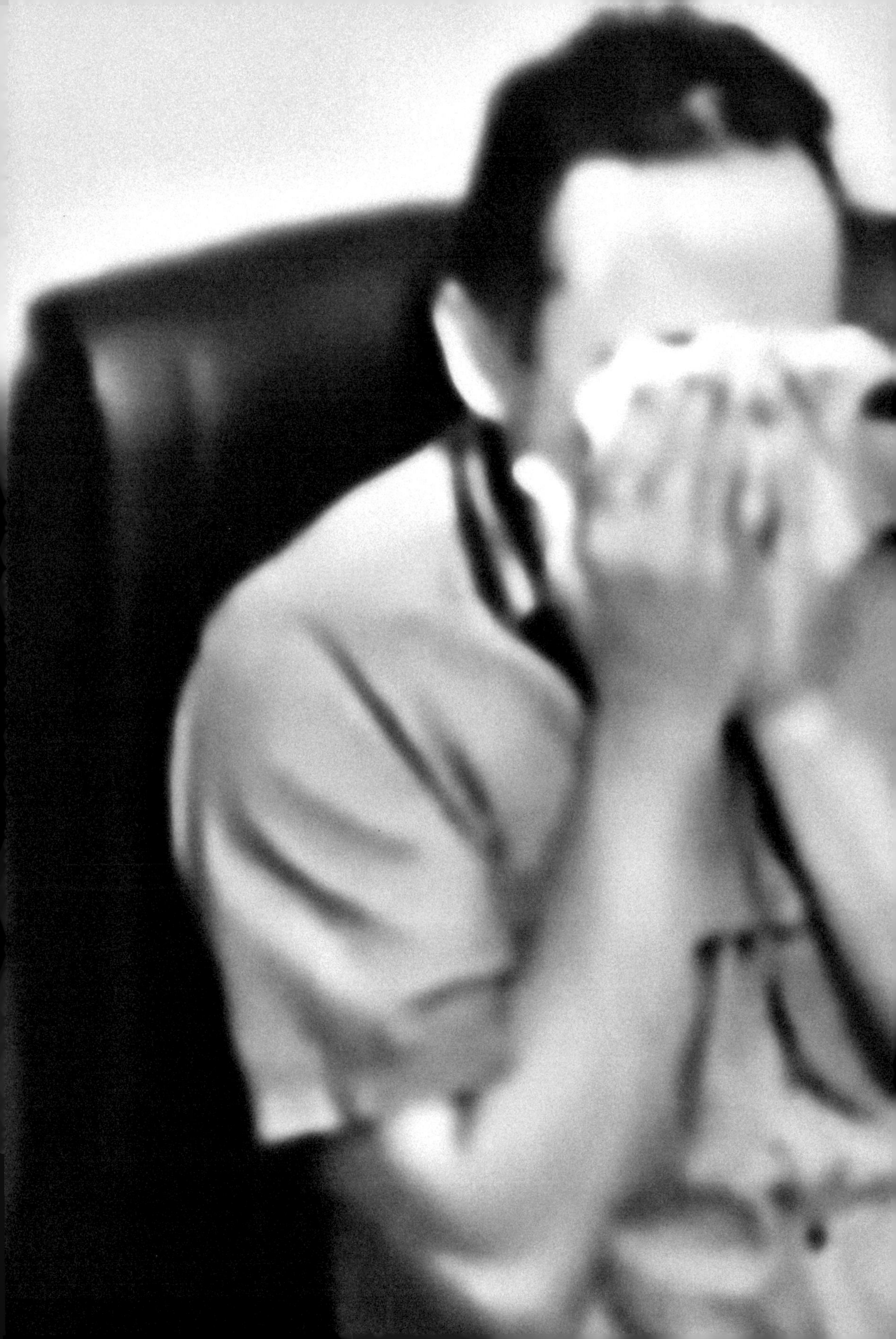

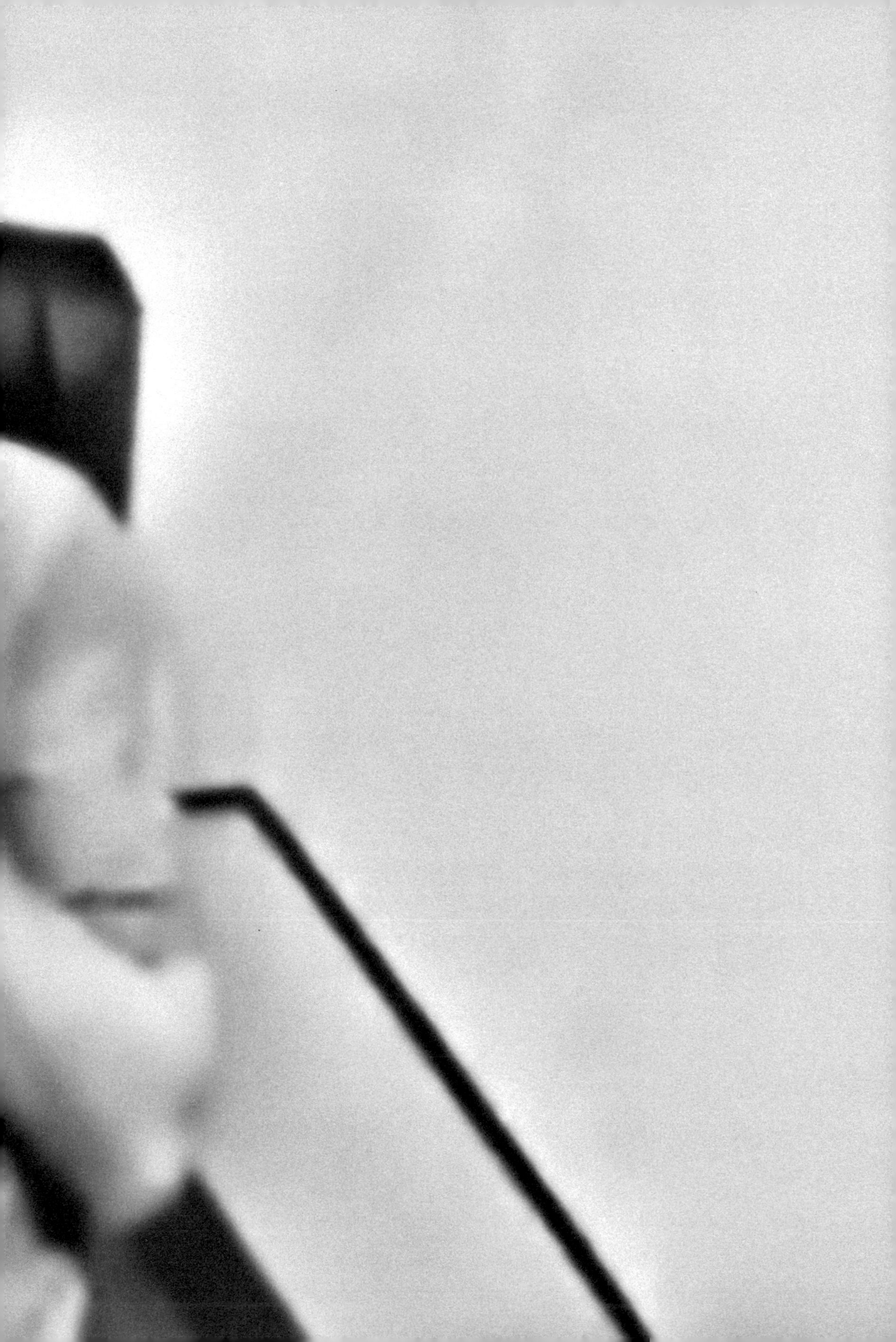

Raymond Santana

I decided to lie and
tell them what they wanted to hear.

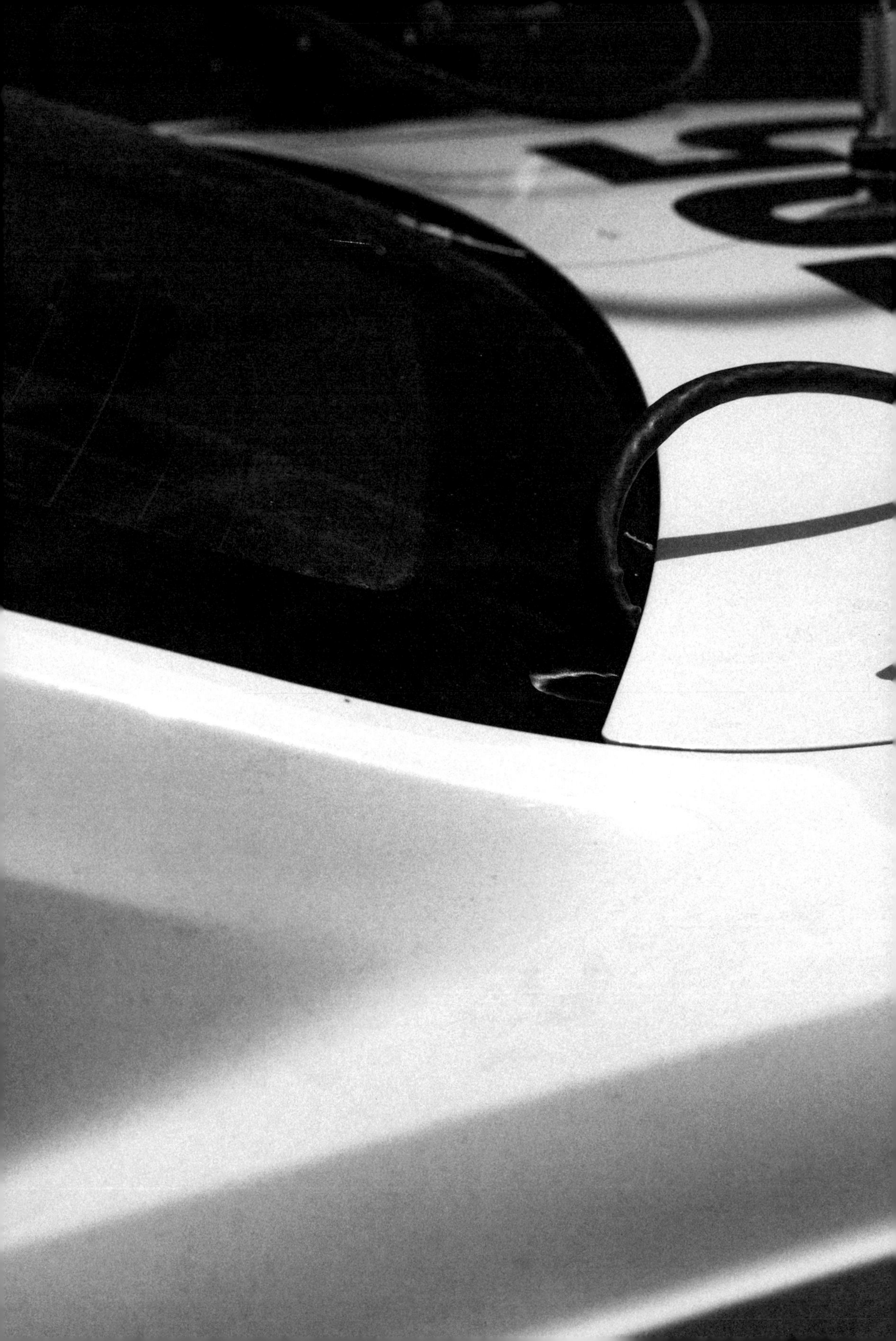

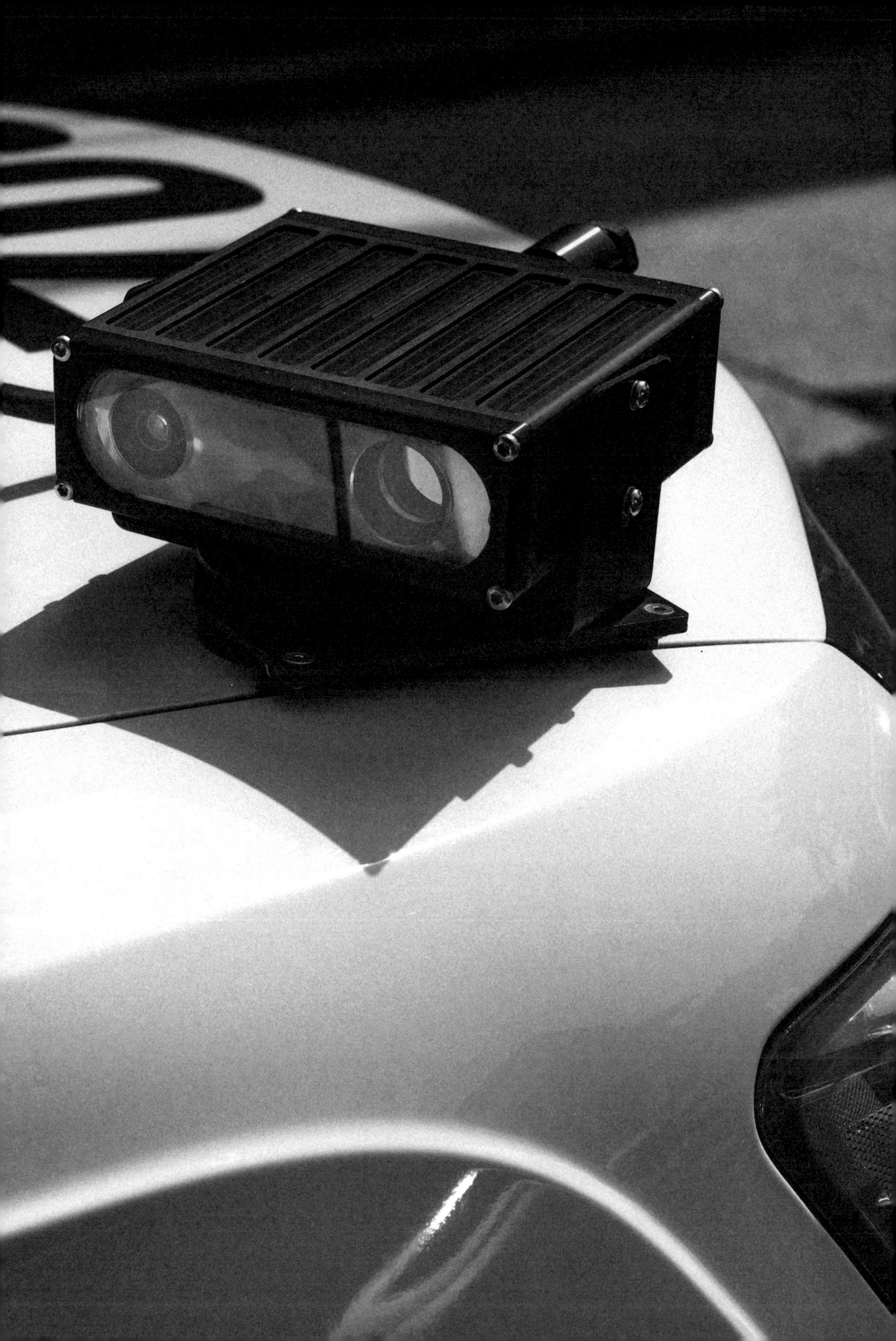

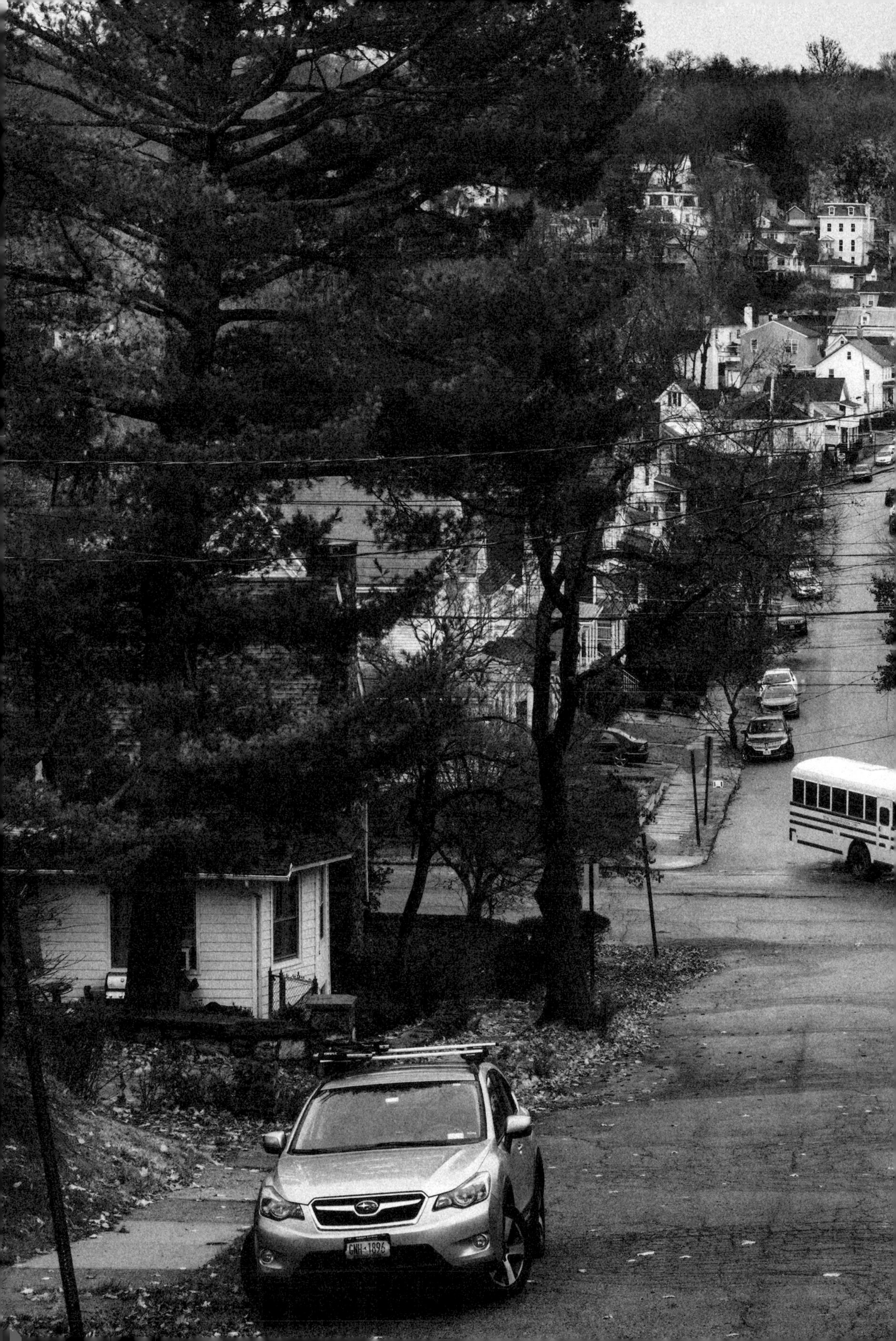

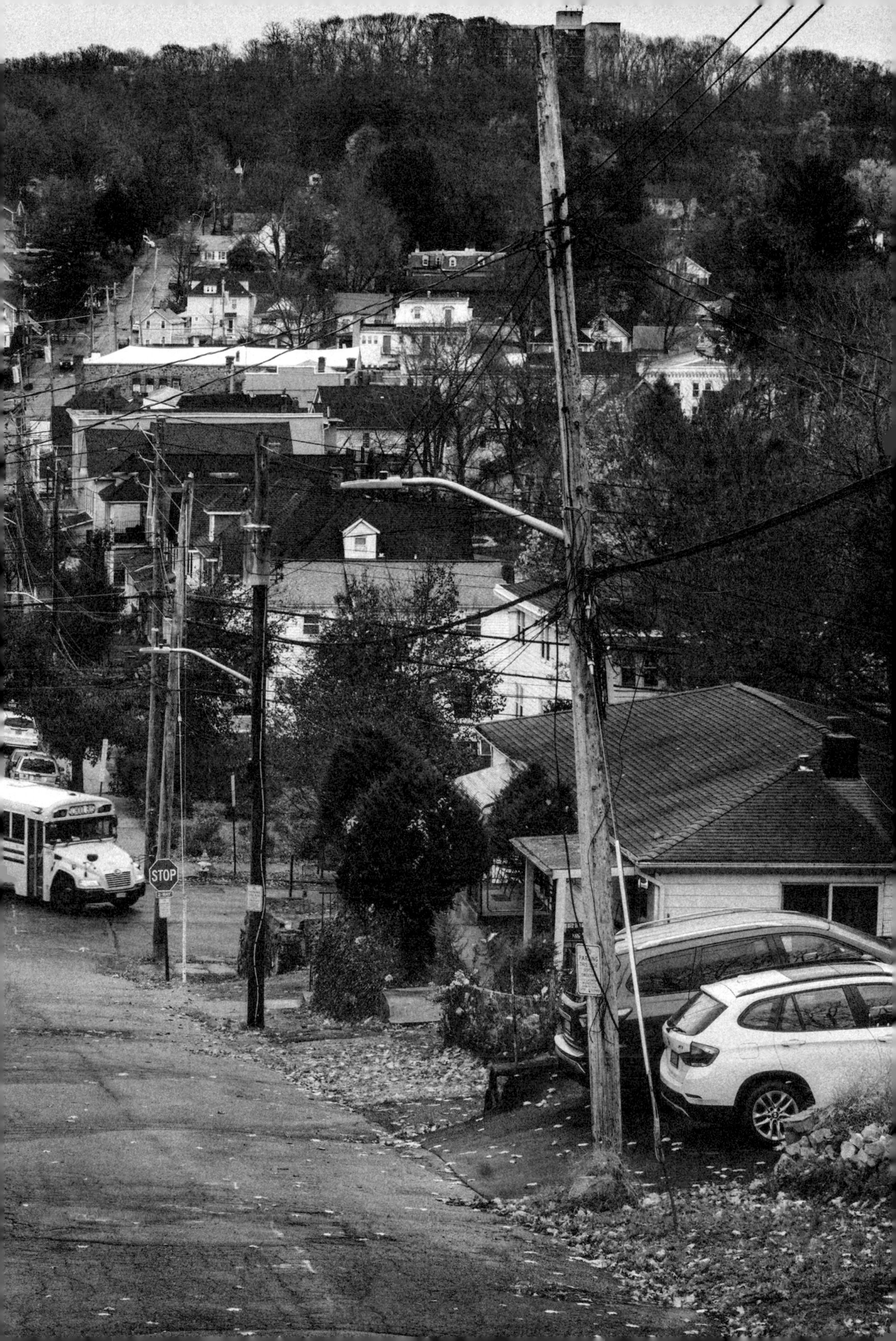
STOP

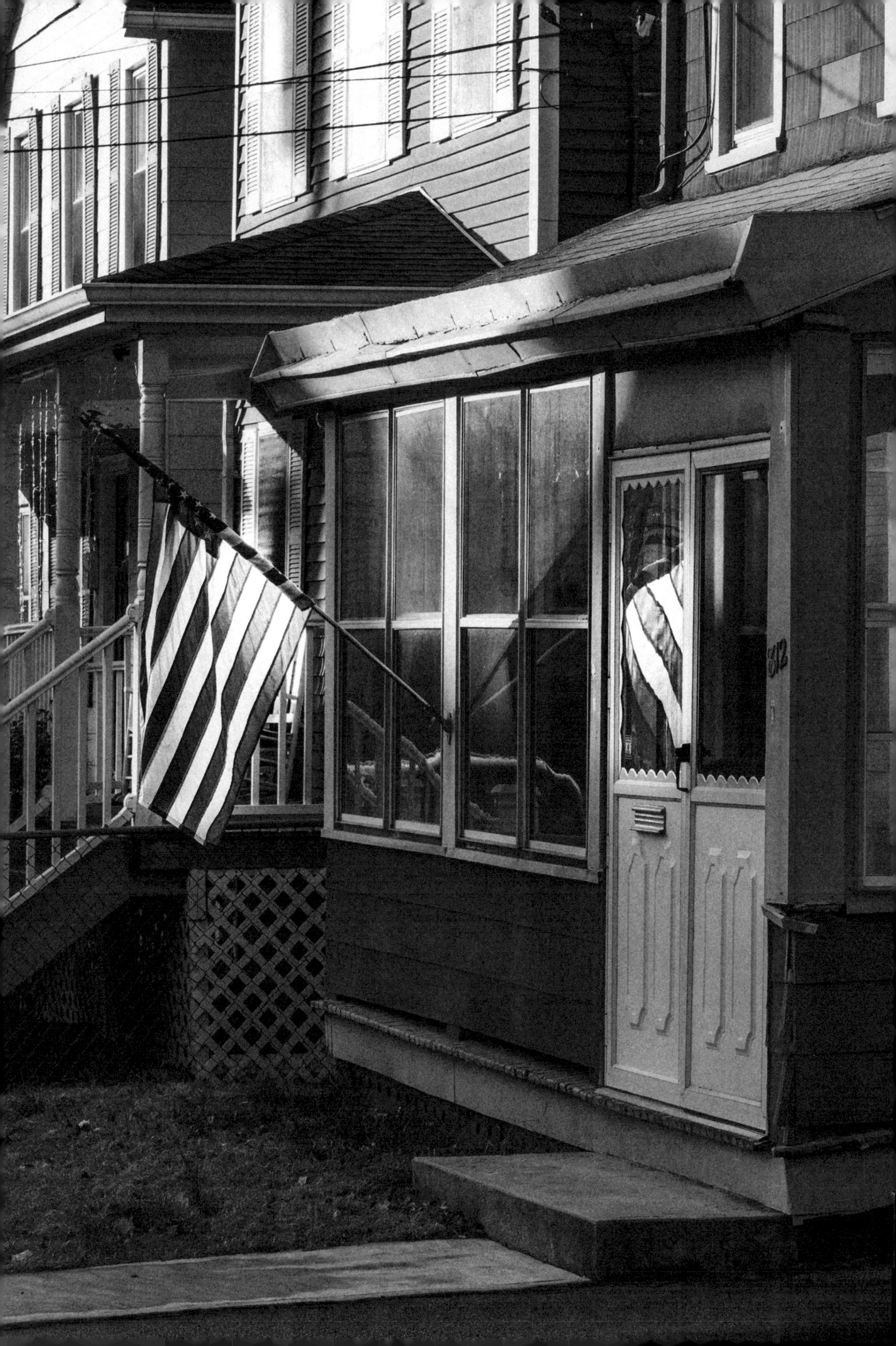

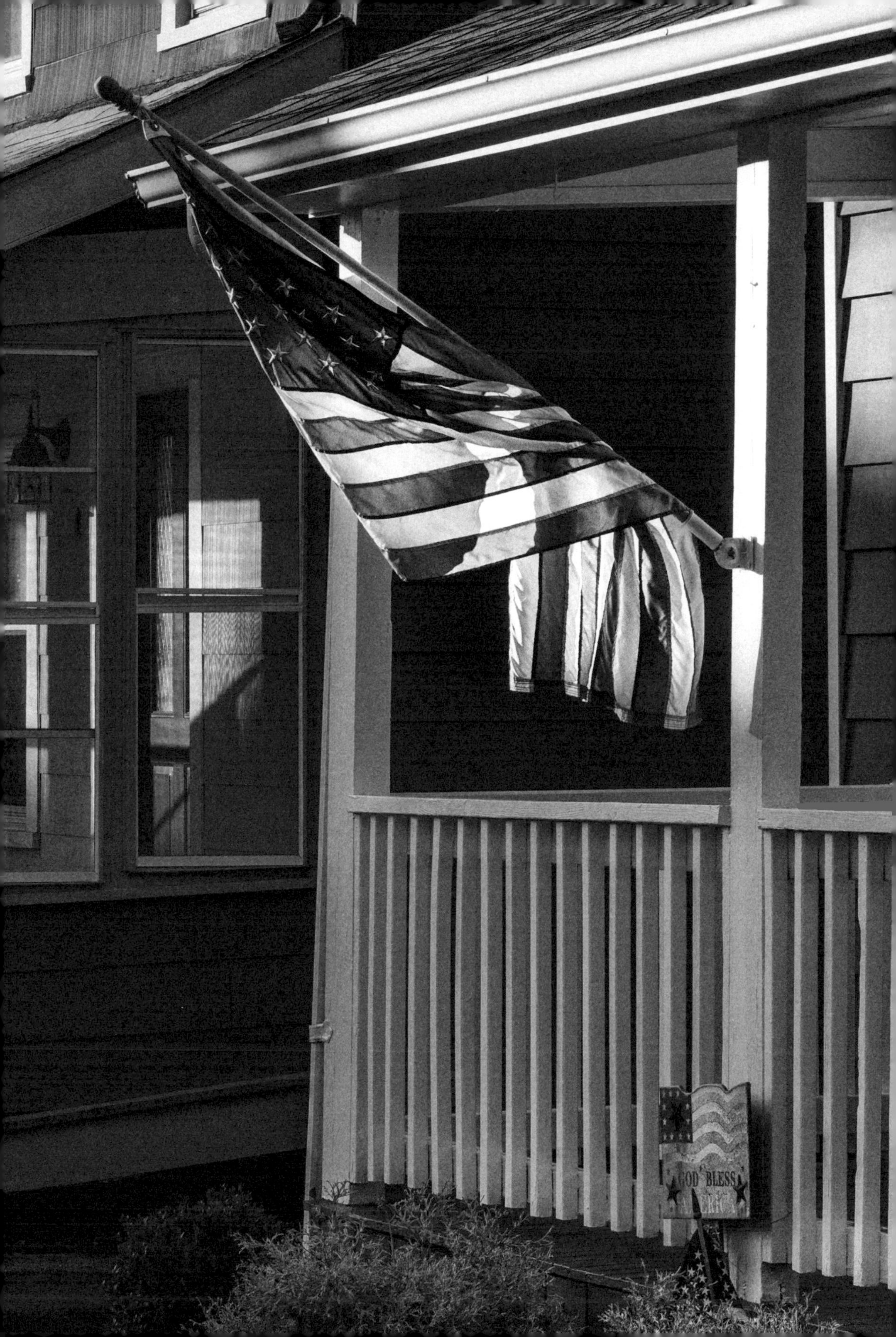
GOD BLESS

Jeffrey Deskovic, Vanessa Gathers, Byron Halsey, Eddie Lowery, Christopher Ochoa, and Raymond Santana were each subjected to coercive police interrogations during which they confessed to crimes that they did not commit.

All of them were convicted, sentenced to lengthy prison terms, and subsequently exonerated.

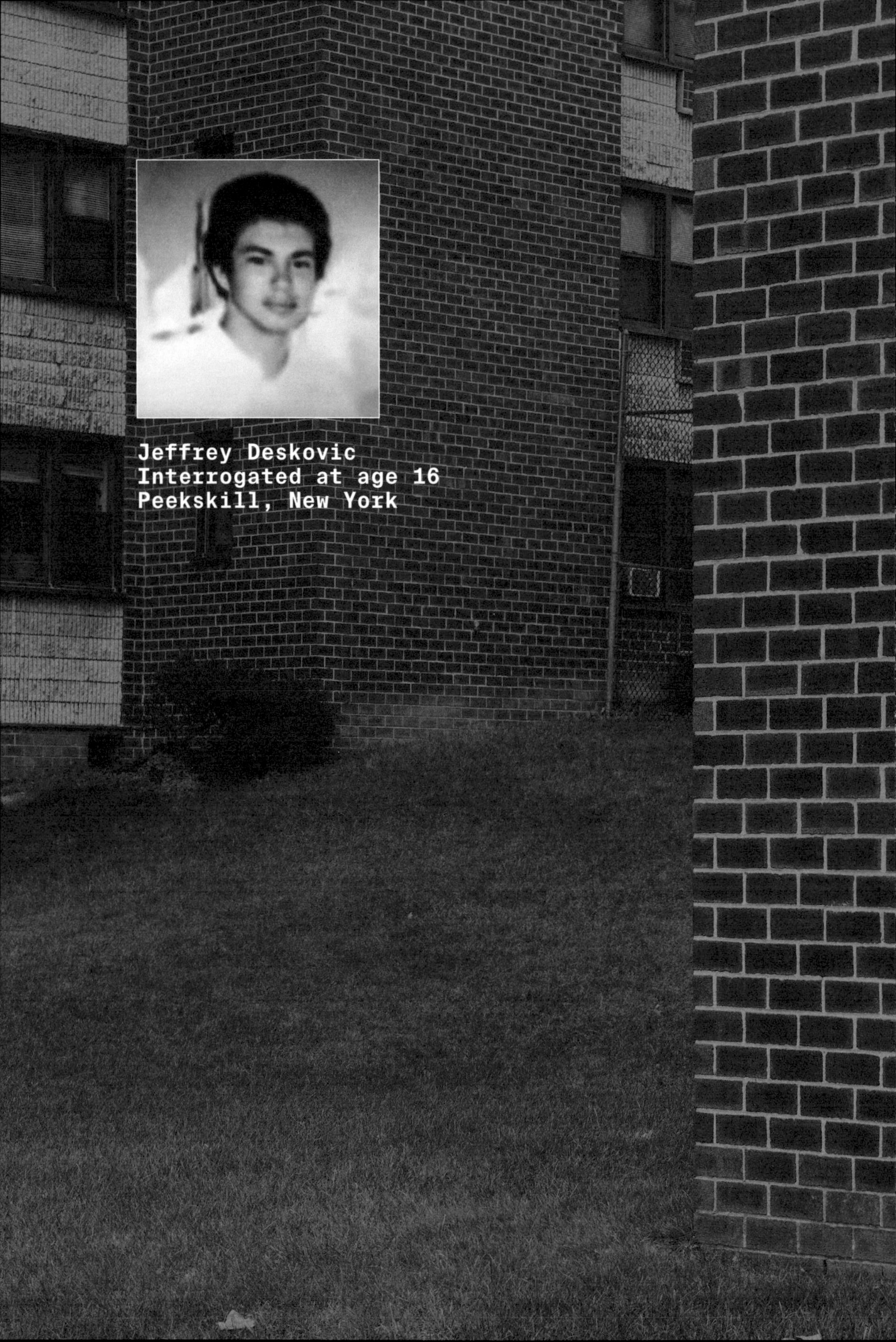

Jeffrey Deskovic
Interrogated at age 16
Peekskill, New York

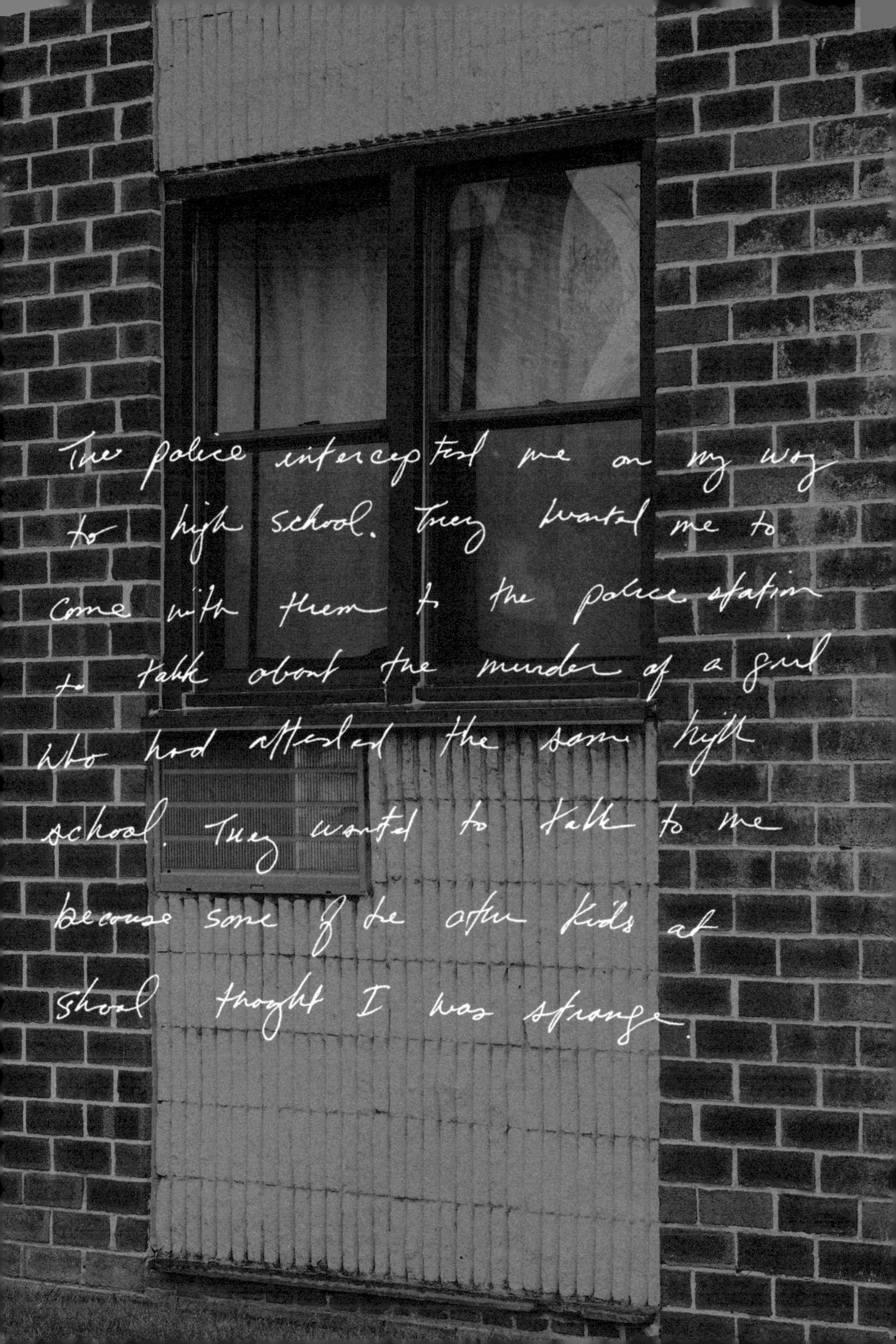
The police intercepted me on my way
to high school. They wanted me to
come with them to the police station
to talk about the murder of a girl
who had attended the same high
school. They wanted to talk to me
because some of the other kids at
shool thought I was strange.

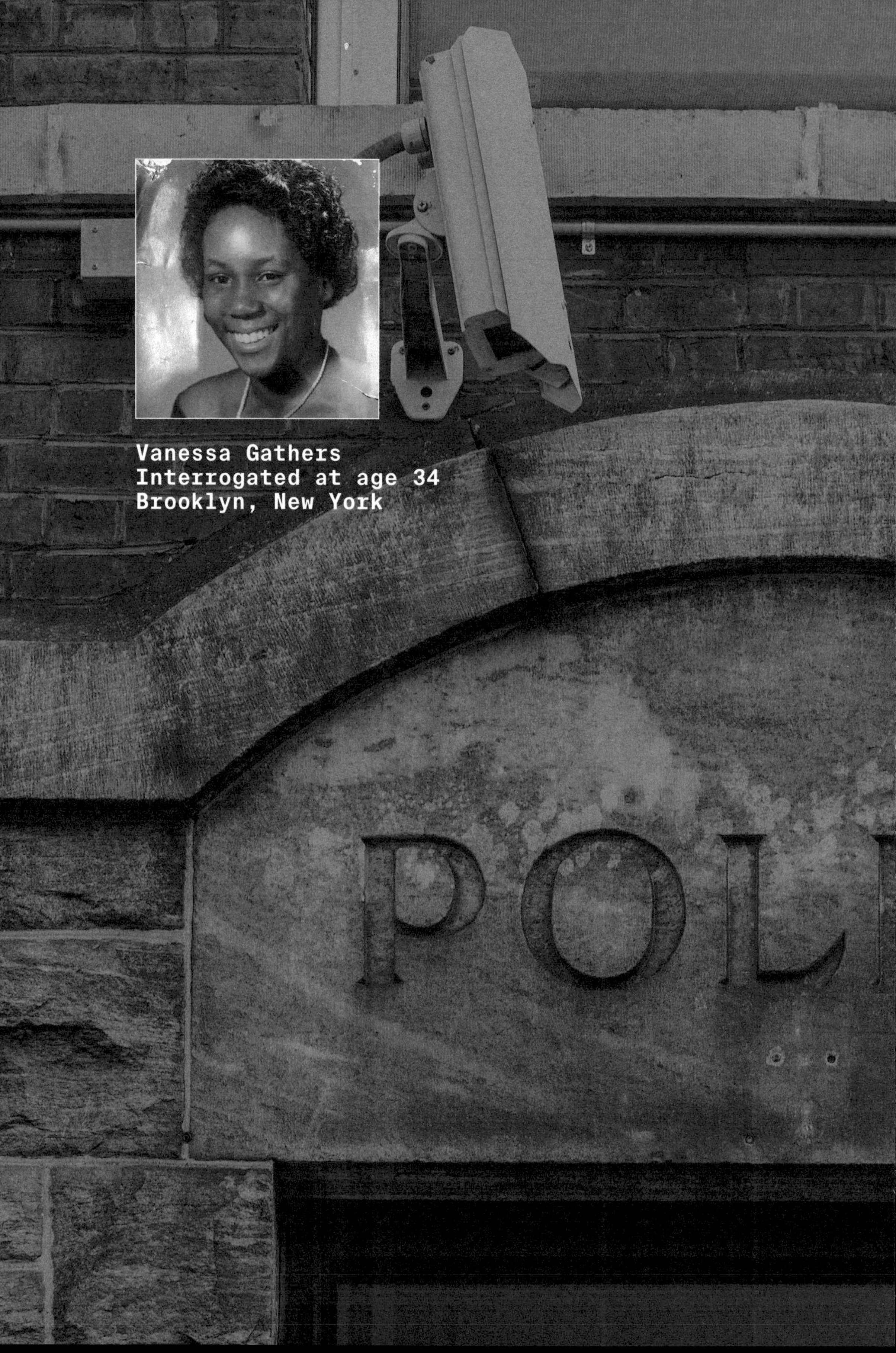

Vanessa Gathers
Interrogated at age 34
Brooklyn, New York

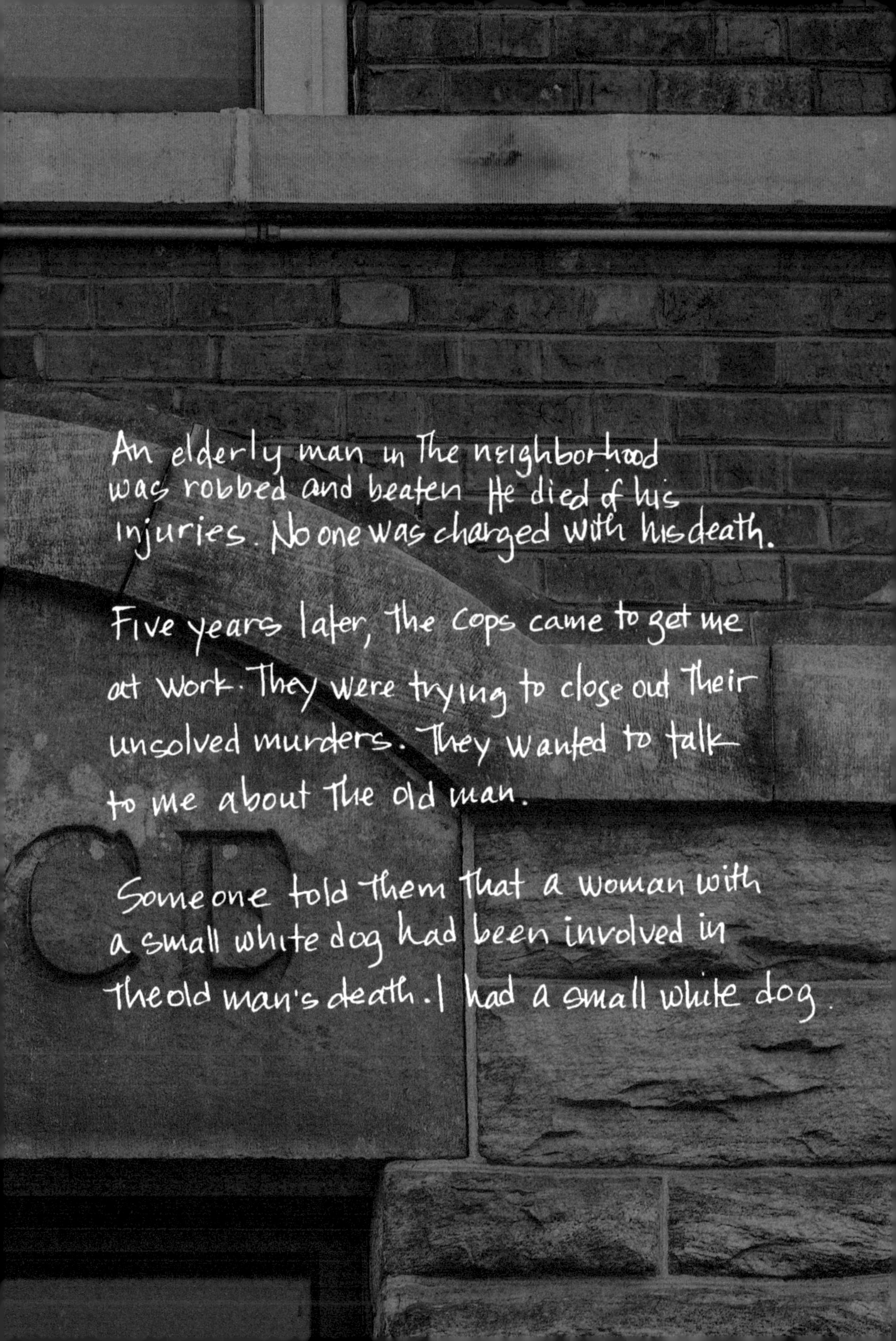

An elderly man in the neighborhood was robbed and beaten. He died of his injuries. No one was charged with his death.

Five years later, the cops came to get me at work. They were trying to close out their unsolved murders. They wanted to talk to me about the old man.

Someone told them that a woman with a small white dog had been involved in the old man's death. I had a small white dog.

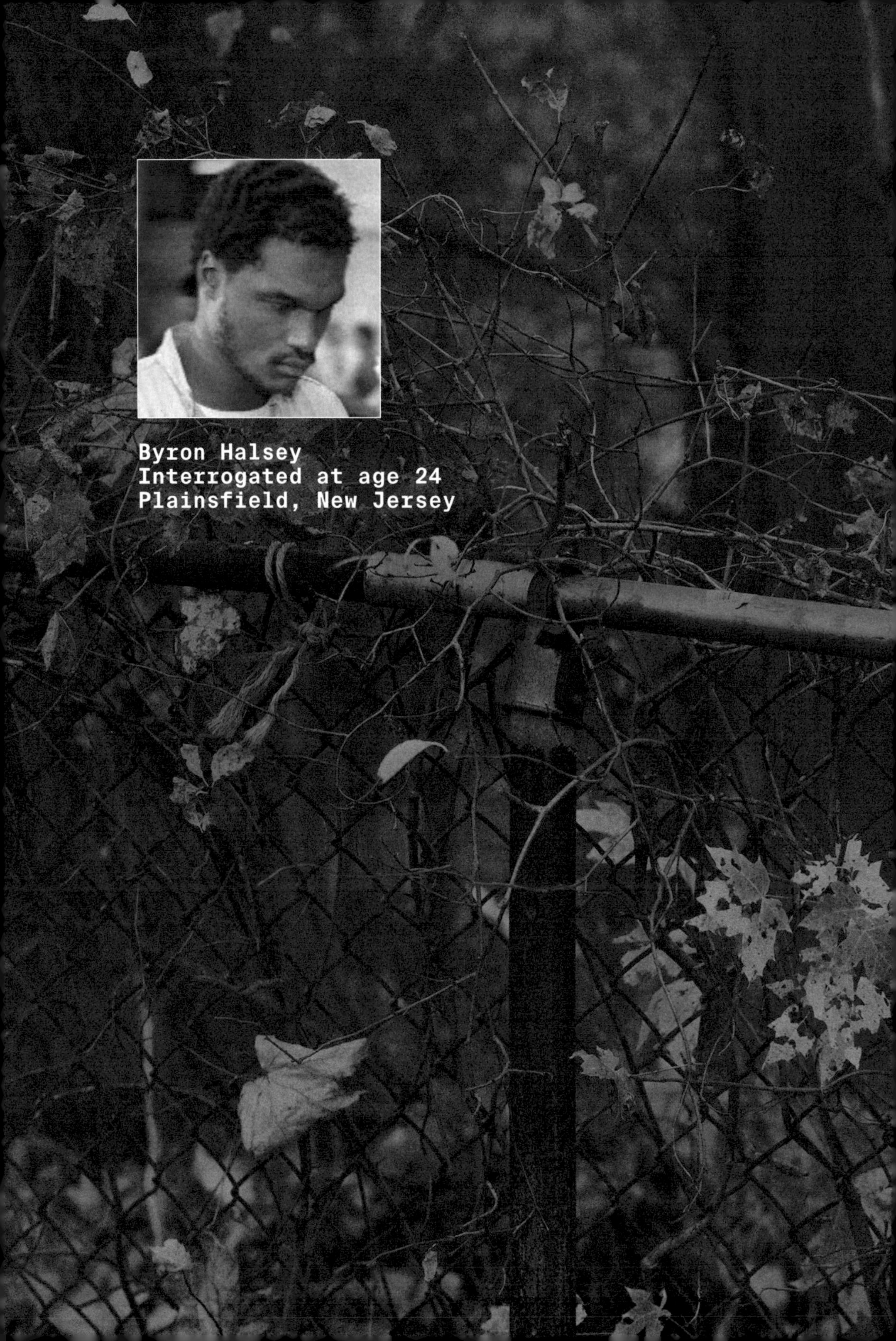

Byron Halsey
Interrogated at age 24
Plainsfield, New Jersey

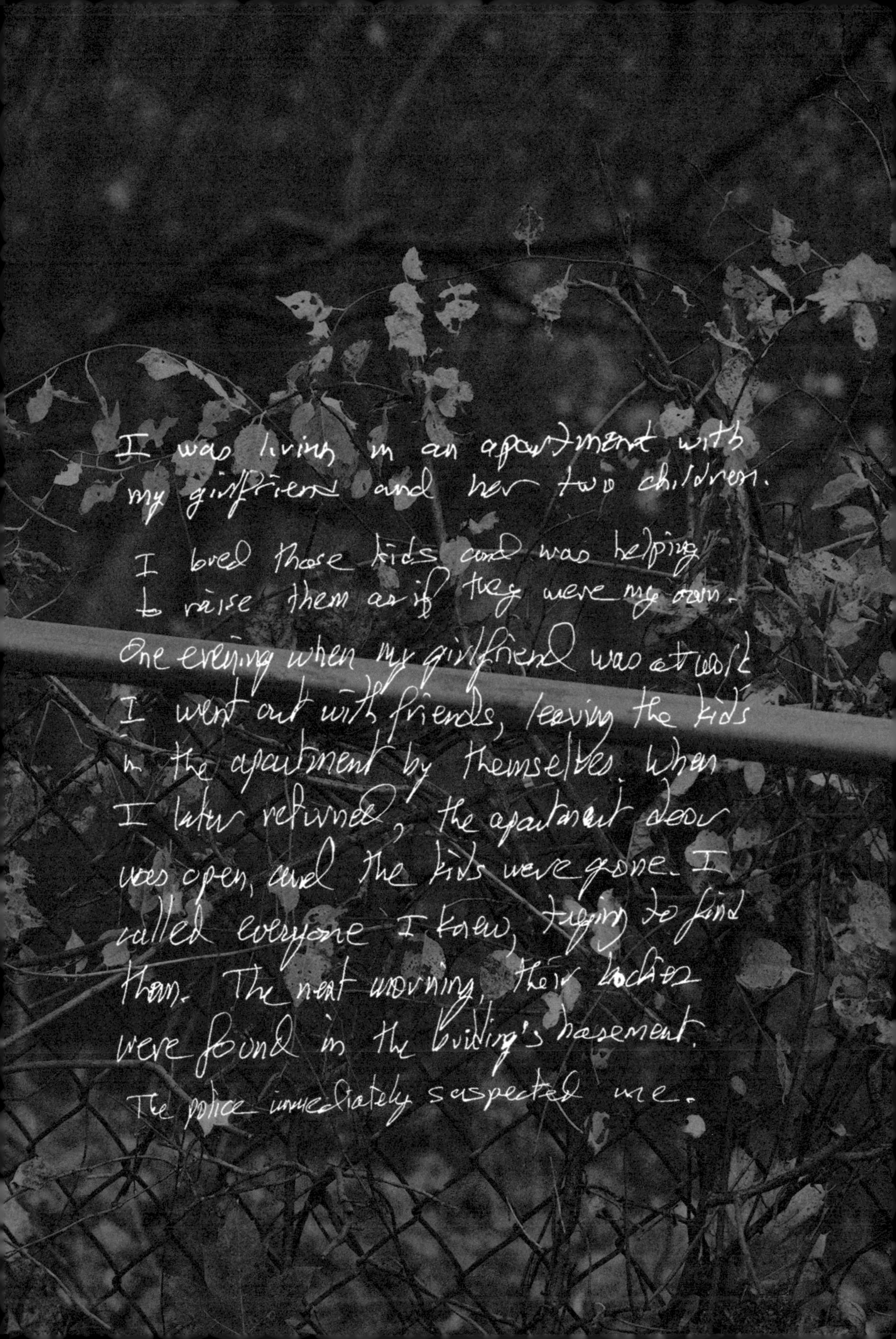
I was living in an apartment with
my girlfriend and her two children.
I loved those kids and was helping
to raise them as if they were my own.
One evening when my girlfriend was at work
I went out with friends, leaving the kids
in the apartment by themselves. When
I later returned, the apartment door
was open, and the kids were gone. I
called everyone I knew, trying to find
them. The next morning, their bodies
were found in the building's basement.
The police immediately suspected me.

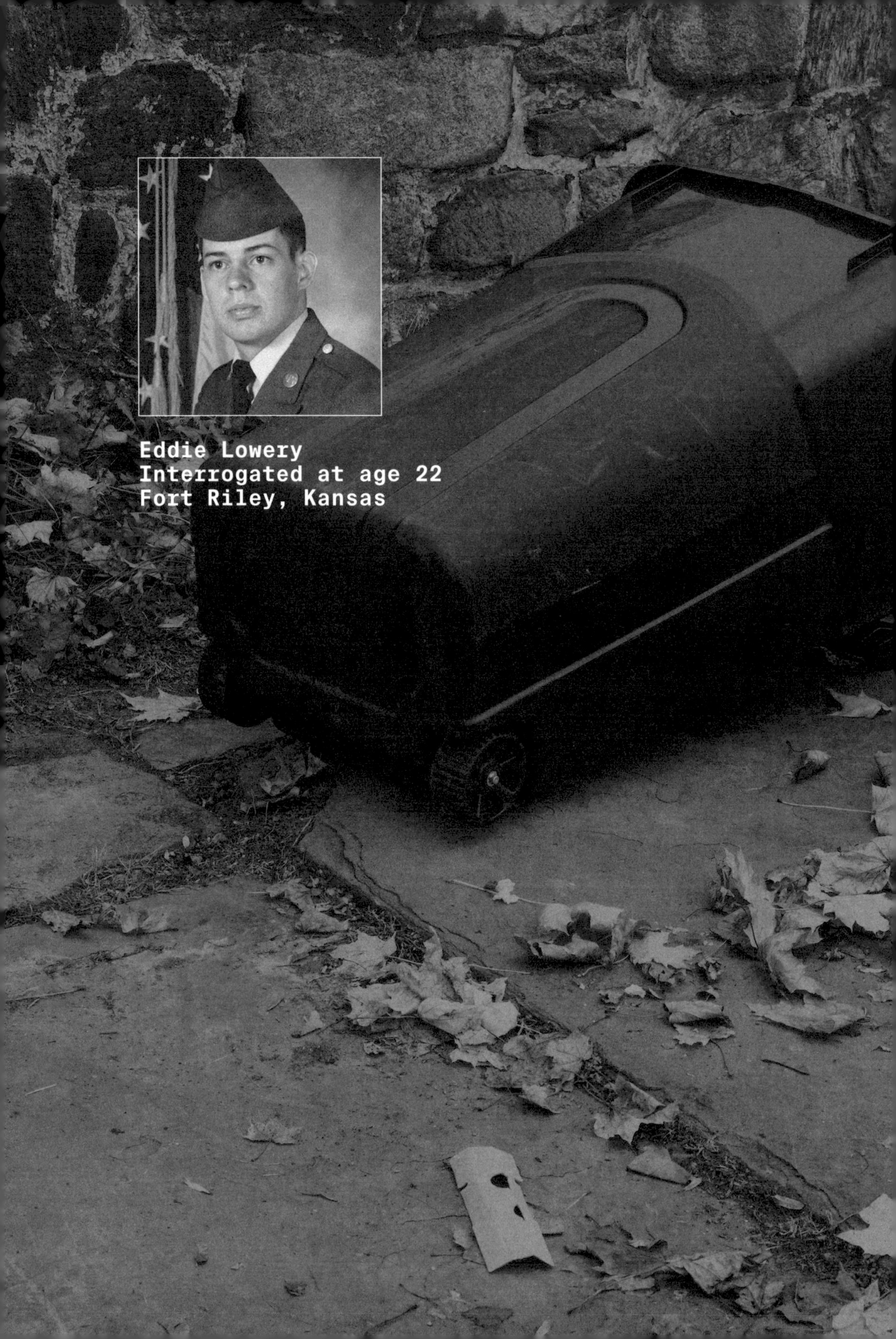

Eddie Lowery
Interrogated at age 22
Fort Riley, Kansas

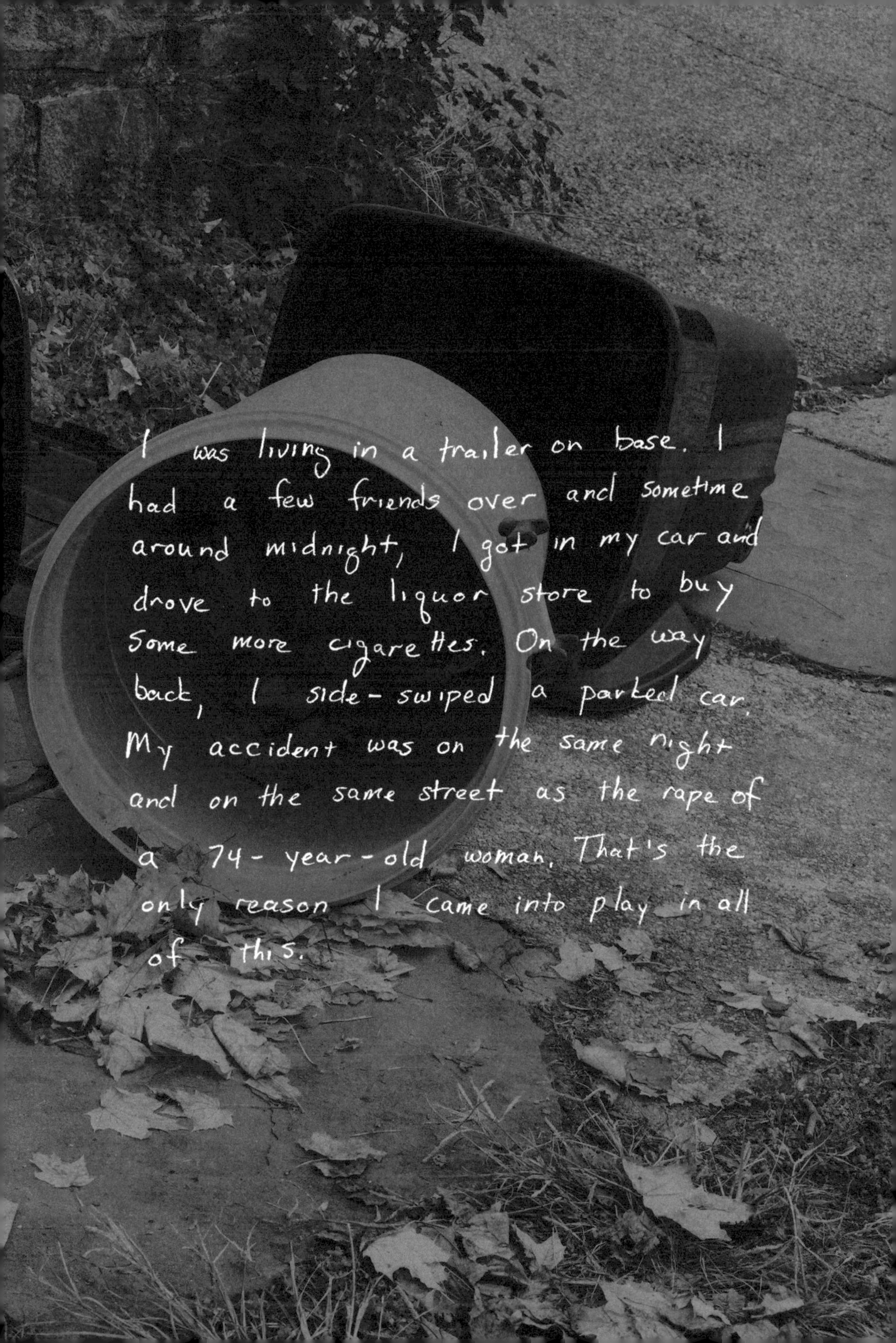
I was living in a trailer on base. I had a few friends over and sometime around midnight, I got in my car and drove to the liquor store to buy Some more cigarettes. On the way back, I side-swiped a parked car. My accident was on the same night and on the same street as the rape of a 74-year-old woman. That's the only reason I came into play in all of this.

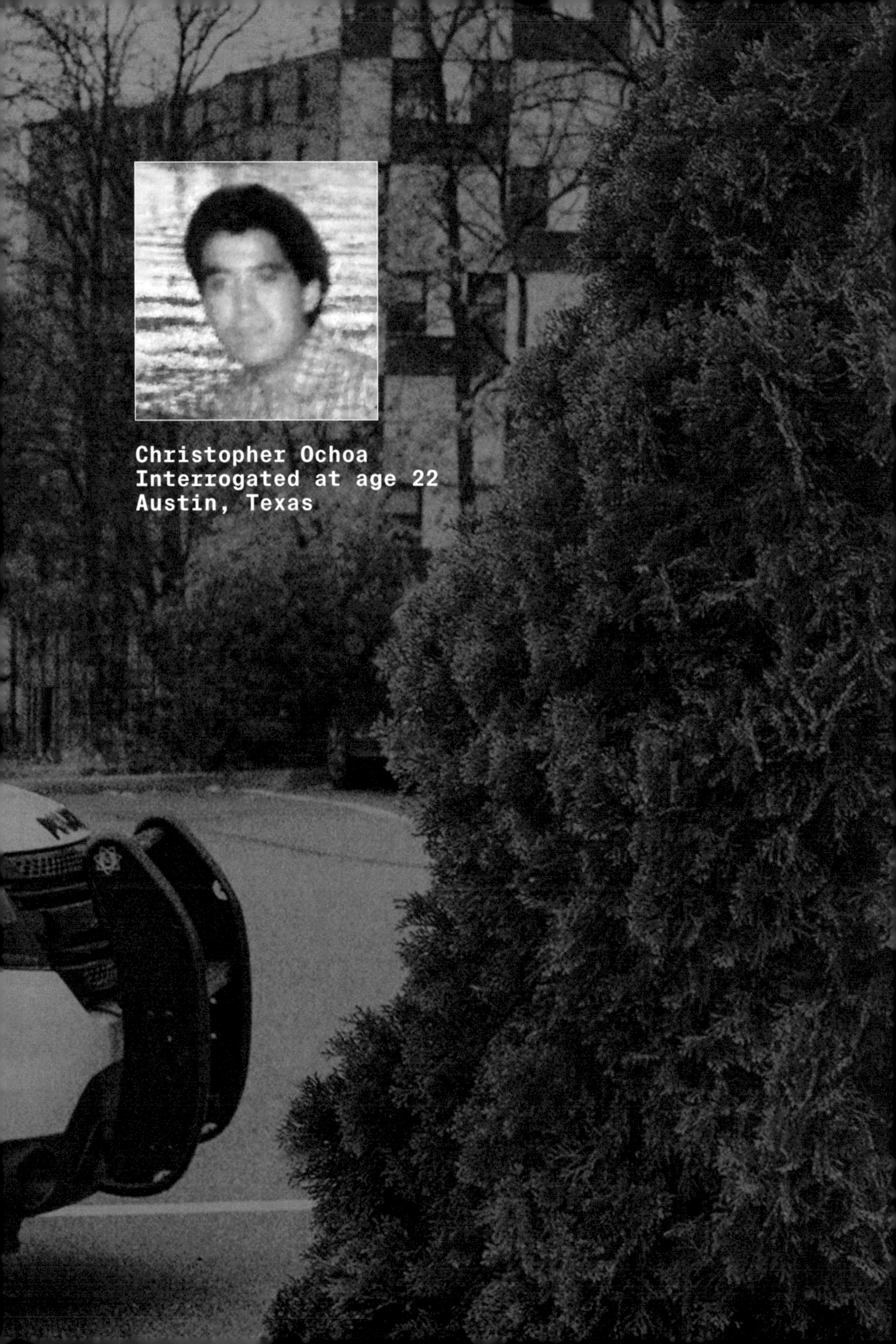

Christopher Ochoa
Interrogated at age 22
Austin, Texas

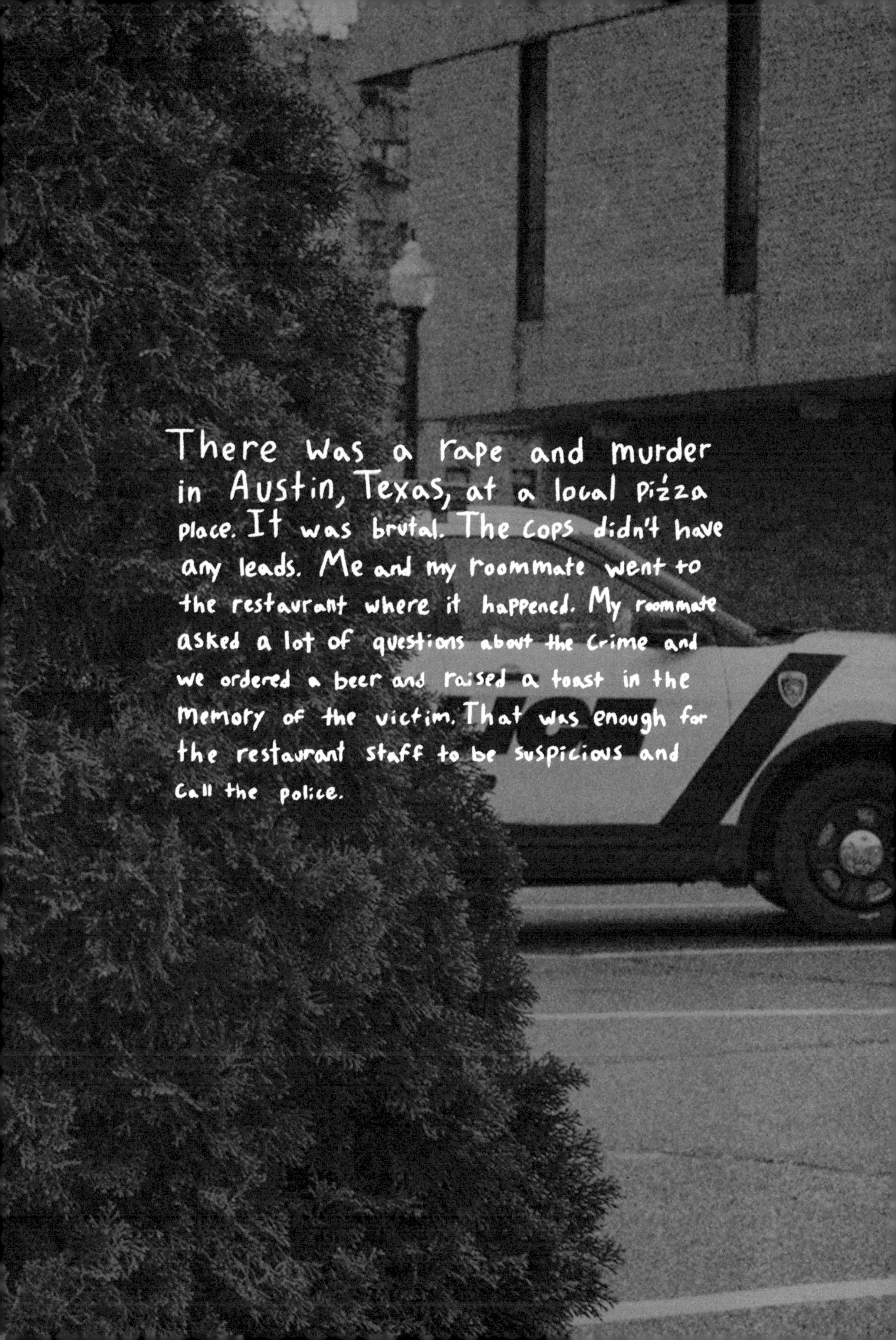

There was a rape and murder in Austin, Texas, at a local pizza place. It was brutal. The cops didn't have any leads. Me and my roommate went to the restaurant where it happened. My roommate asked a lot of questions about the crime and we ordered a beer and raised a toast in the memory of the victim. That was enough for the restaurant staff to be suspicious and call the police.

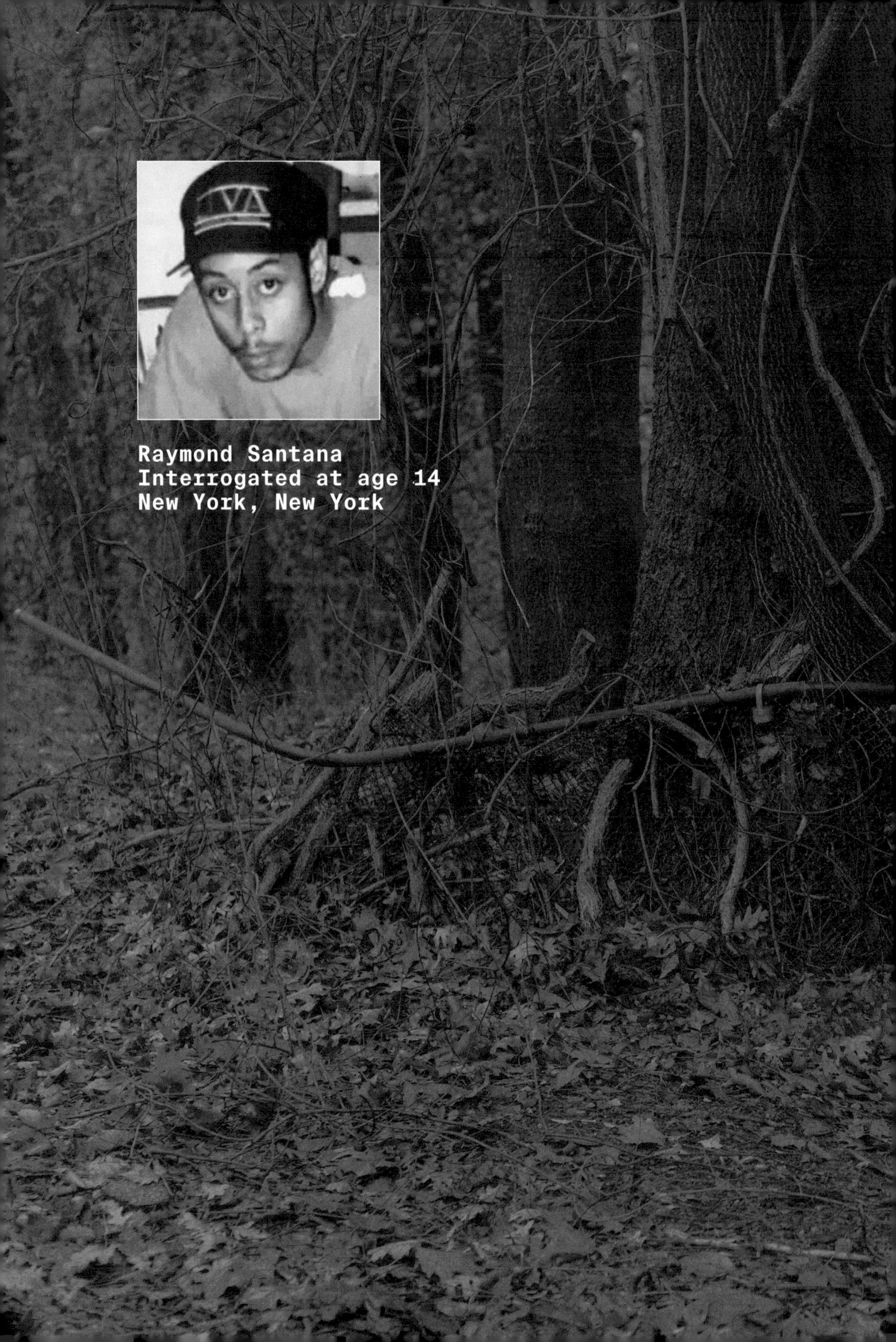

Raymond Santana
Interrogated at age 14
New York, New York

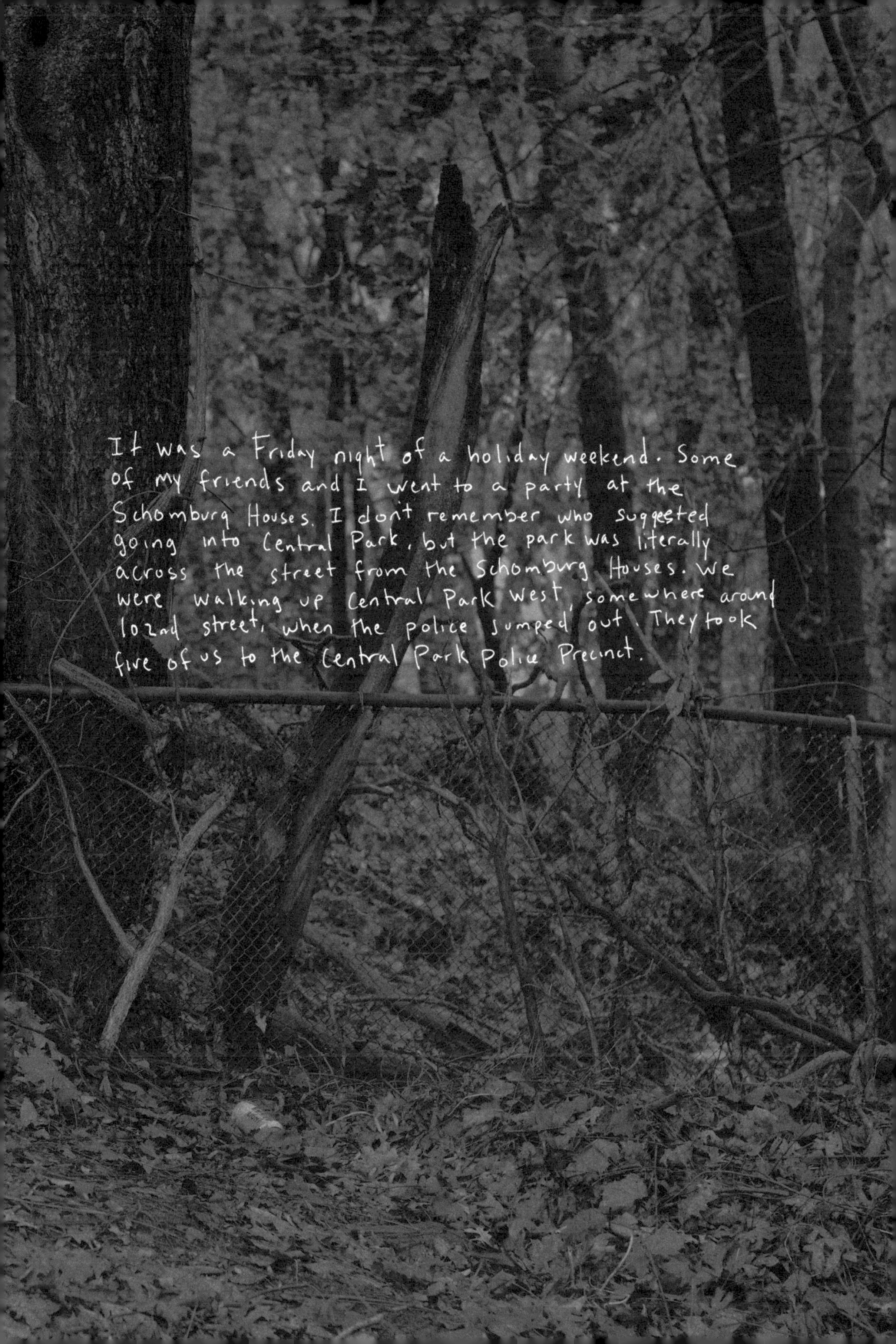
It was a Friday night of a holiday weekend. Some
of my friends and I went to a party at the
Schomburg Houses. I don't remember who suggested
going into Central Park, but the park was literally
across the street from the Schomburg Houses. We
were walking up Central Park West, somewhere around
102nd street, when the police jumped out. They took
five of us to the Central Park Police Precinct.

Christopher Ochoa

Vanessa Zathers

I had never been in trouble with the law.
Never even gone to the principal's office.

I was very naive.

I had never been in this type of experience.
I didn't know my rights. I didn't
understand.

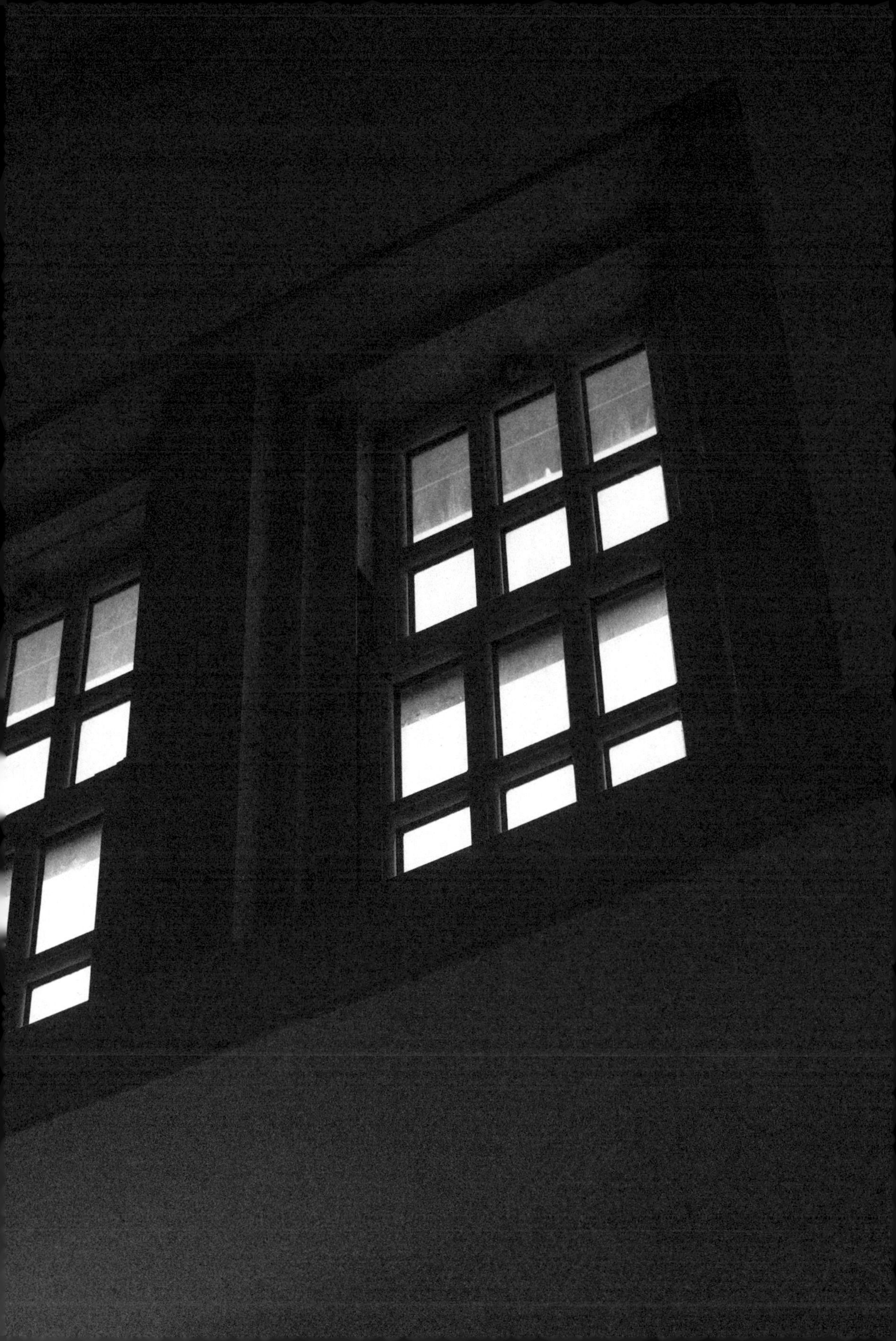

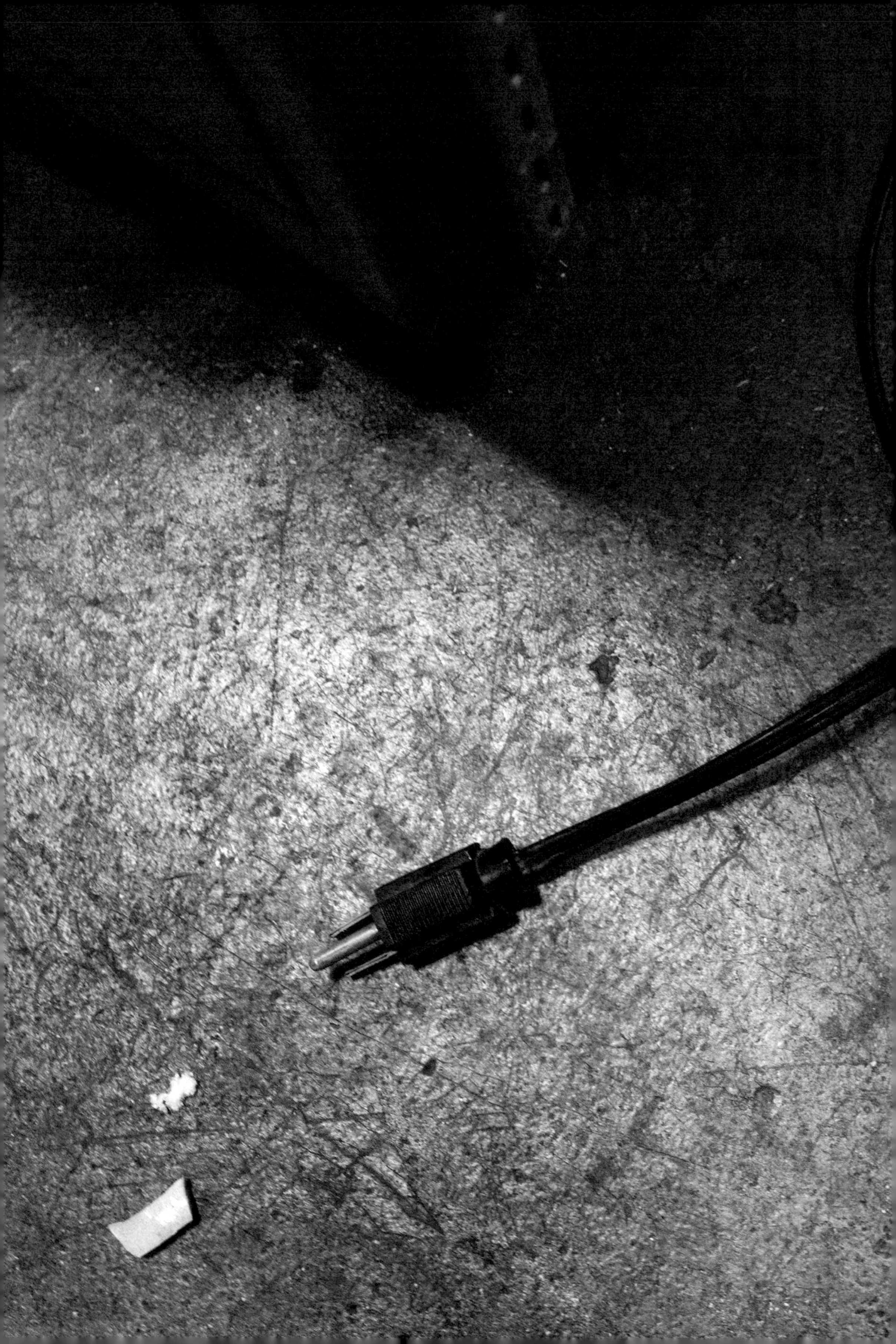

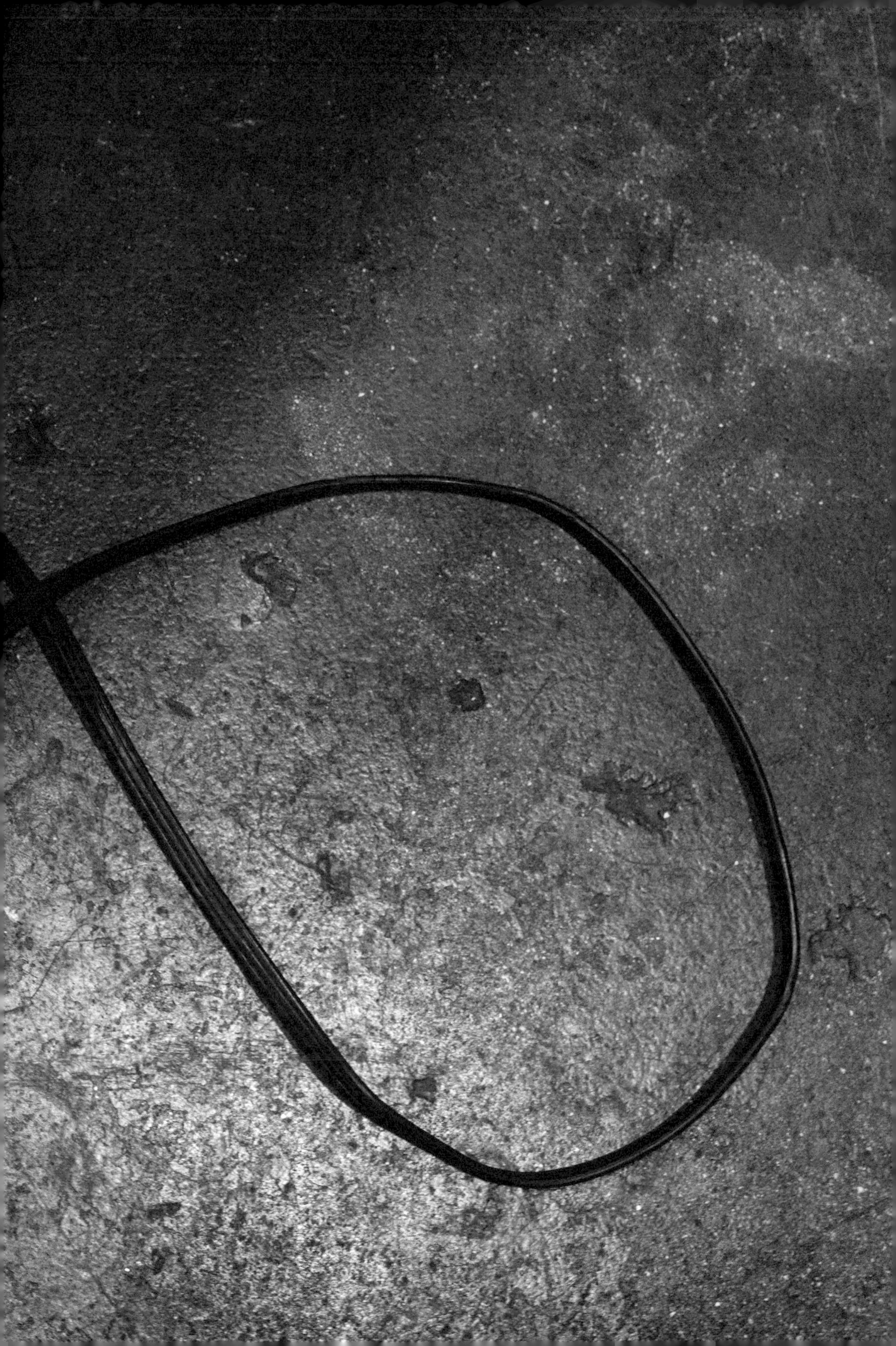

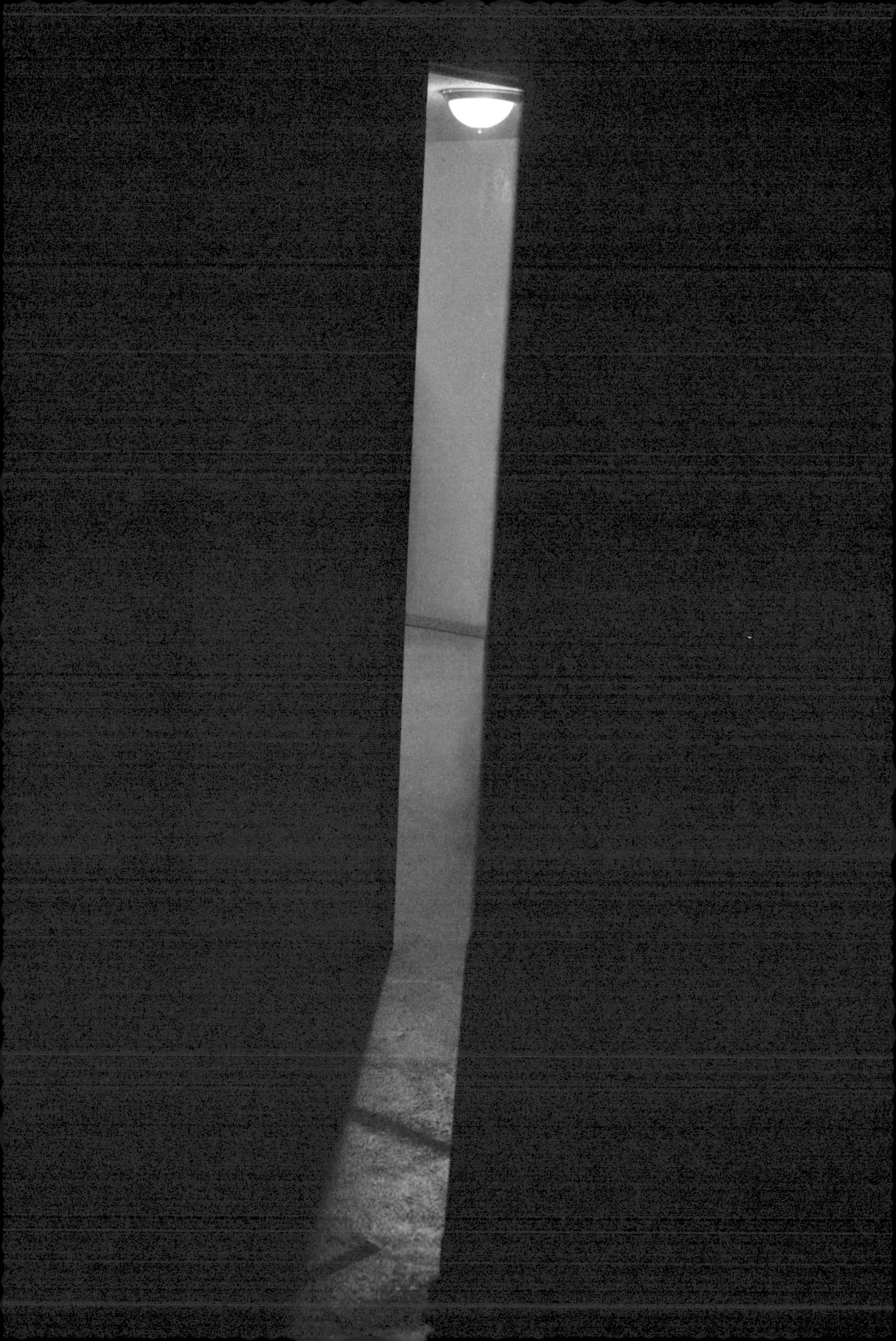

The detective was this tall guy
with this dark mustache, this
dark hair with these glasses.
Smoked cigarettes. A couple of
times he blew smoke in my direction.

I am a kid. He's a grown man.

He slammed his fist on the table.
"Do you know what they call me
on the streets? They call me the
BOOGIE MAN."

Raymond Santana

Christopher Ochoa

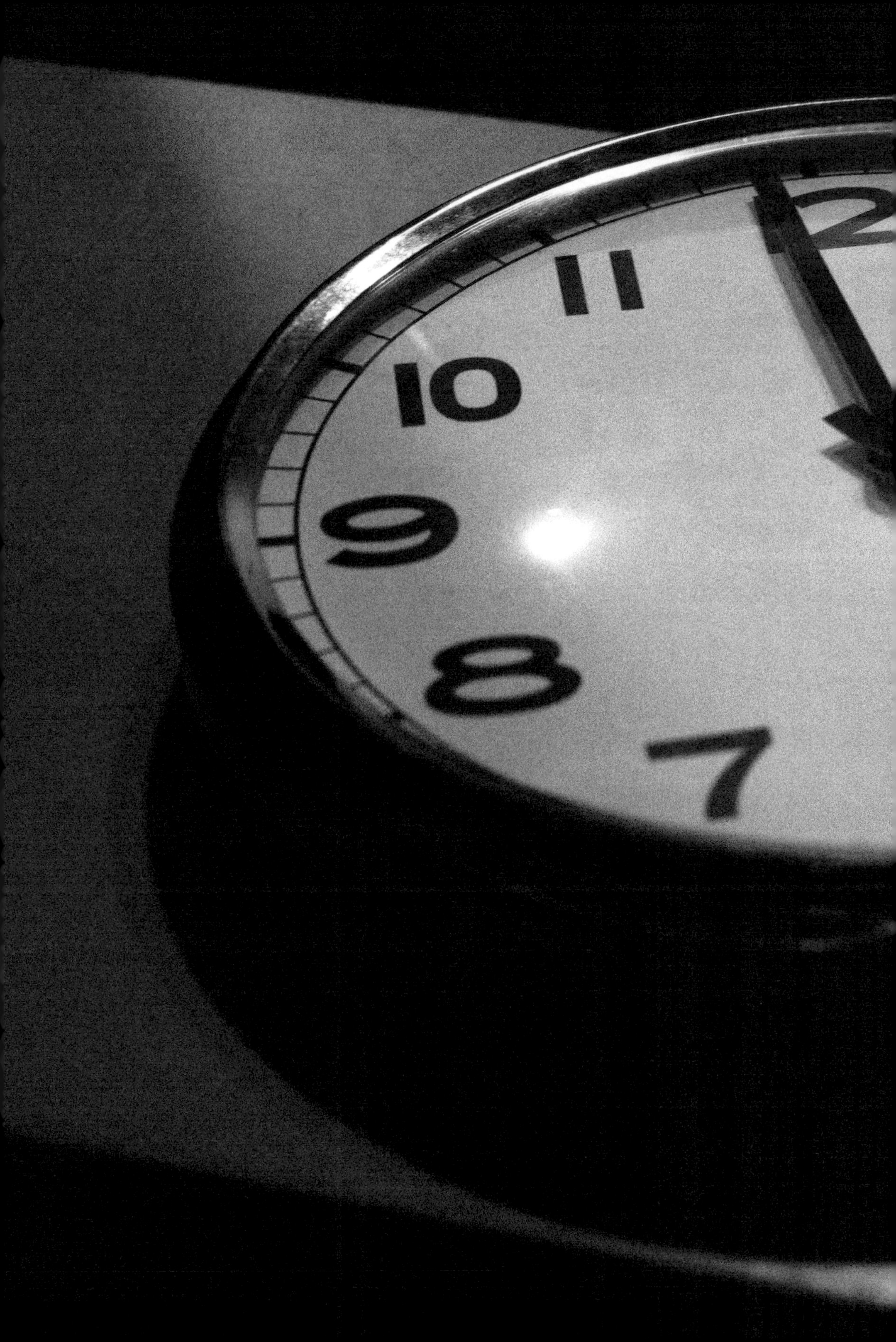

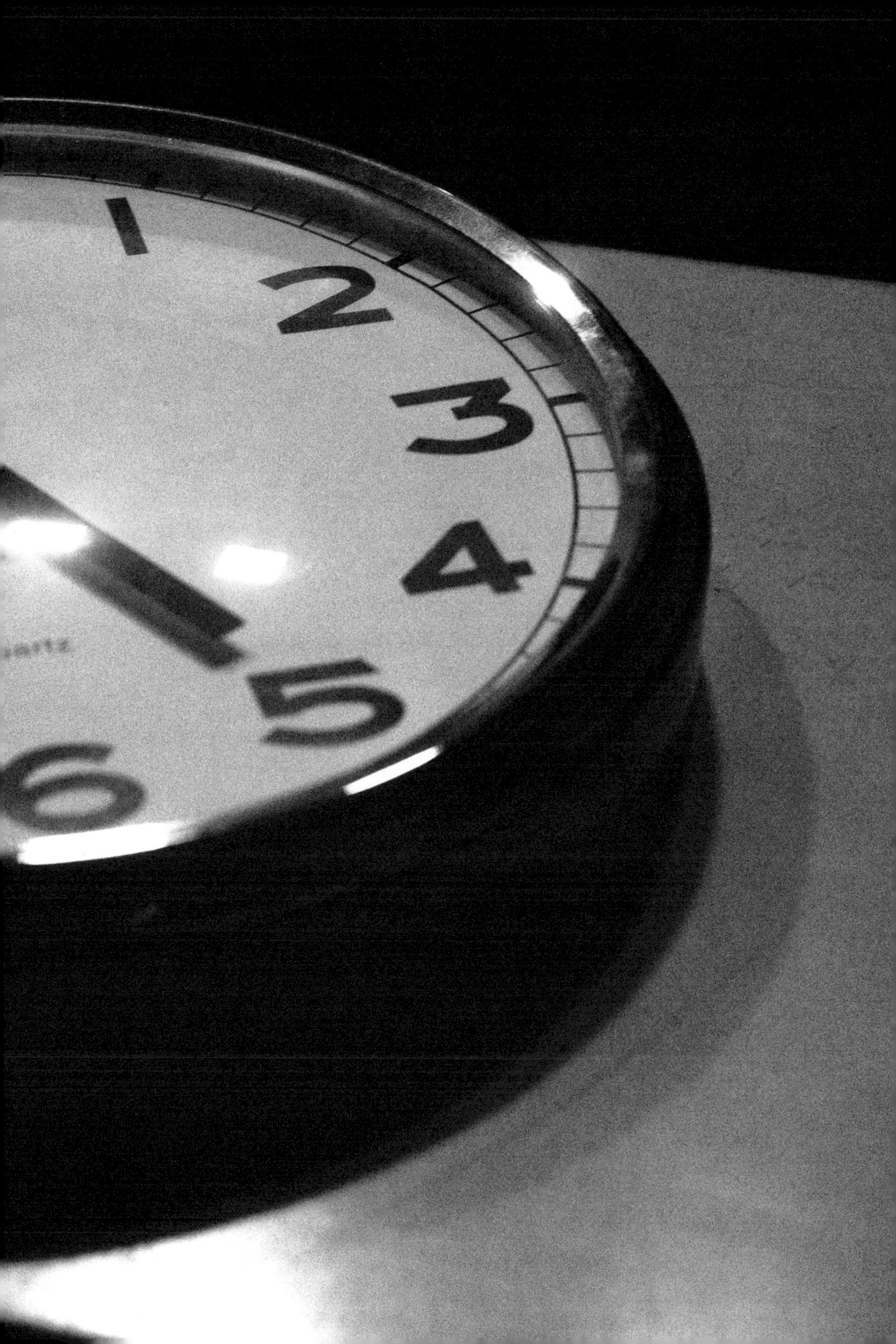

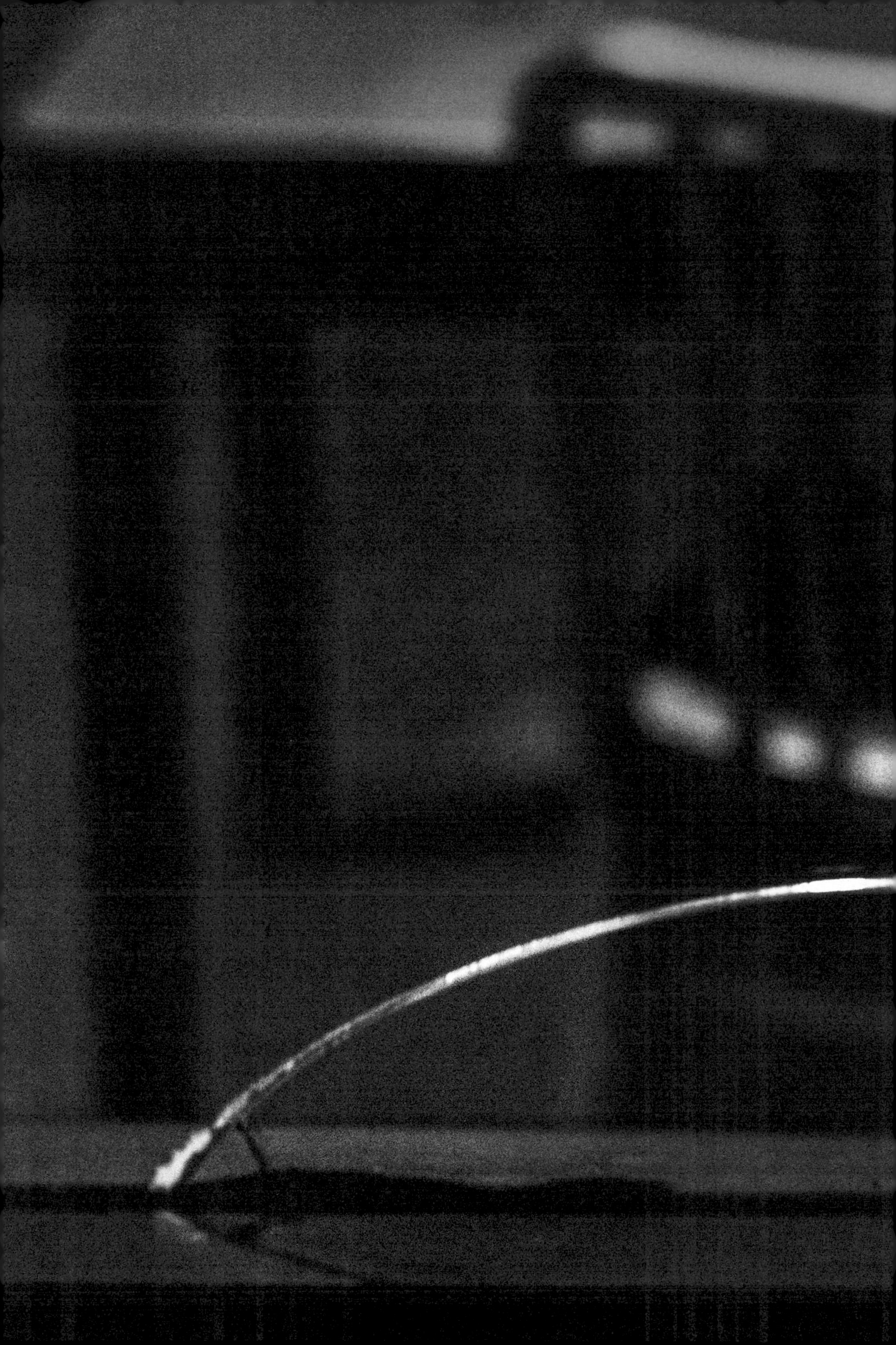

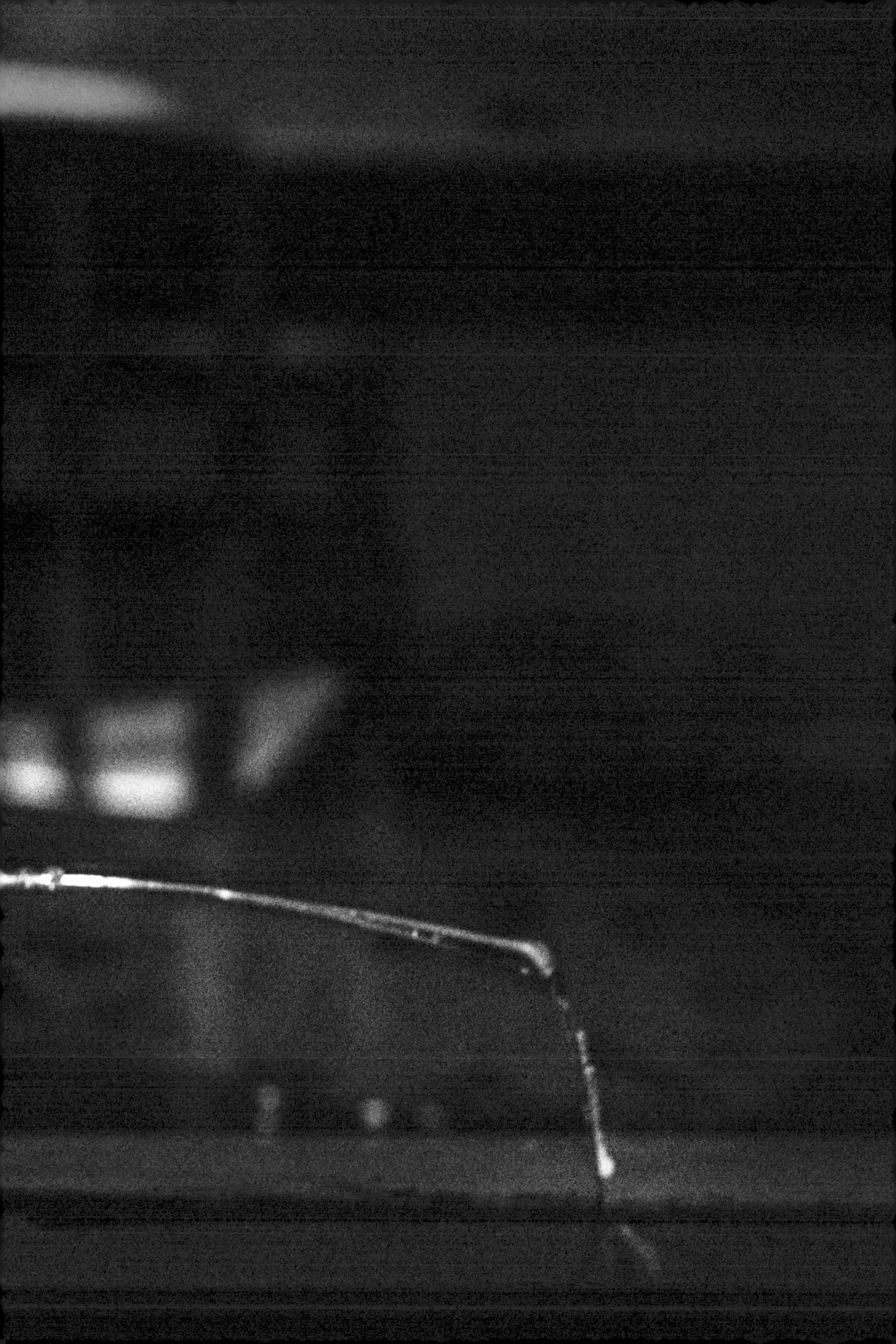

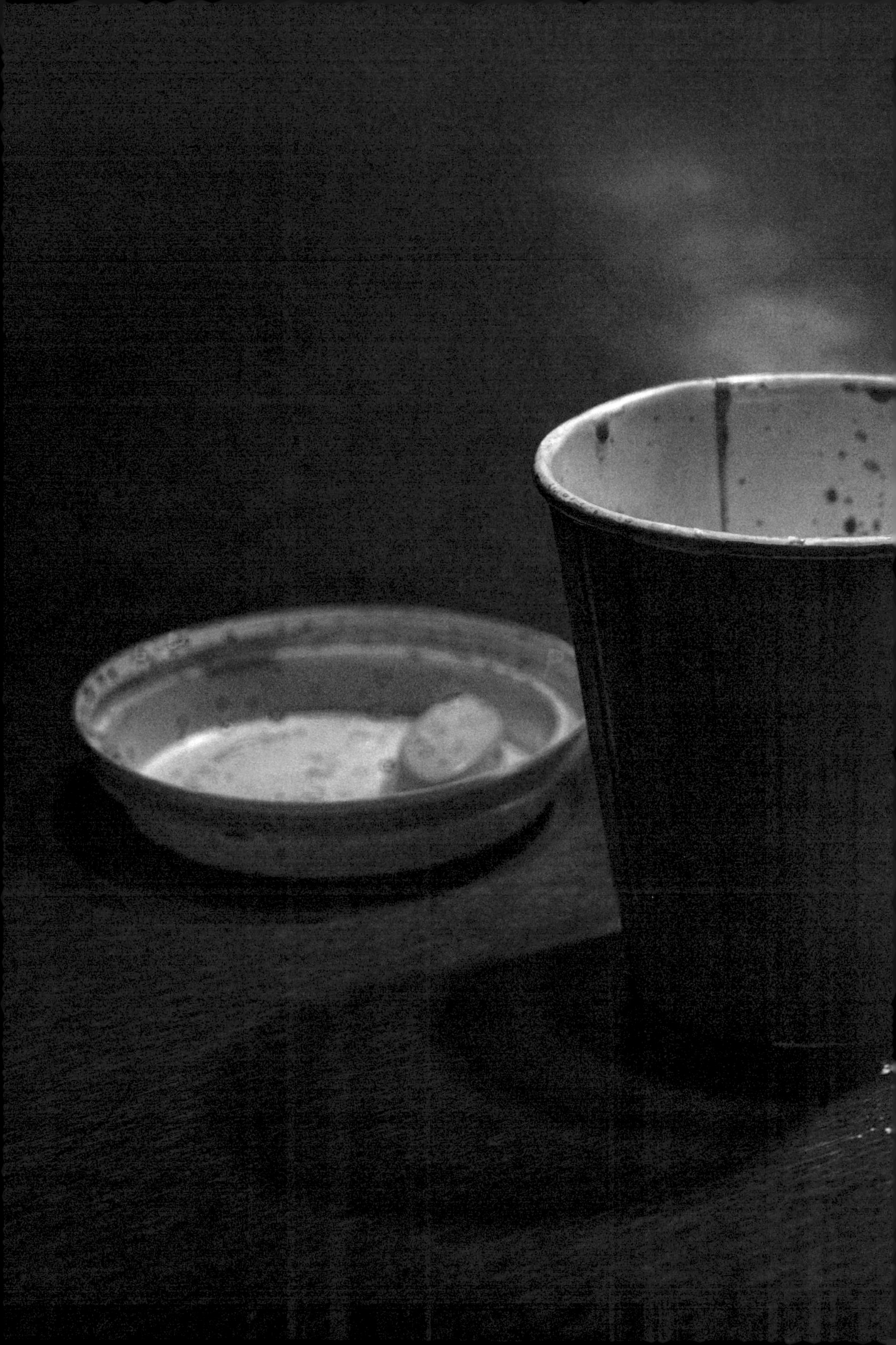

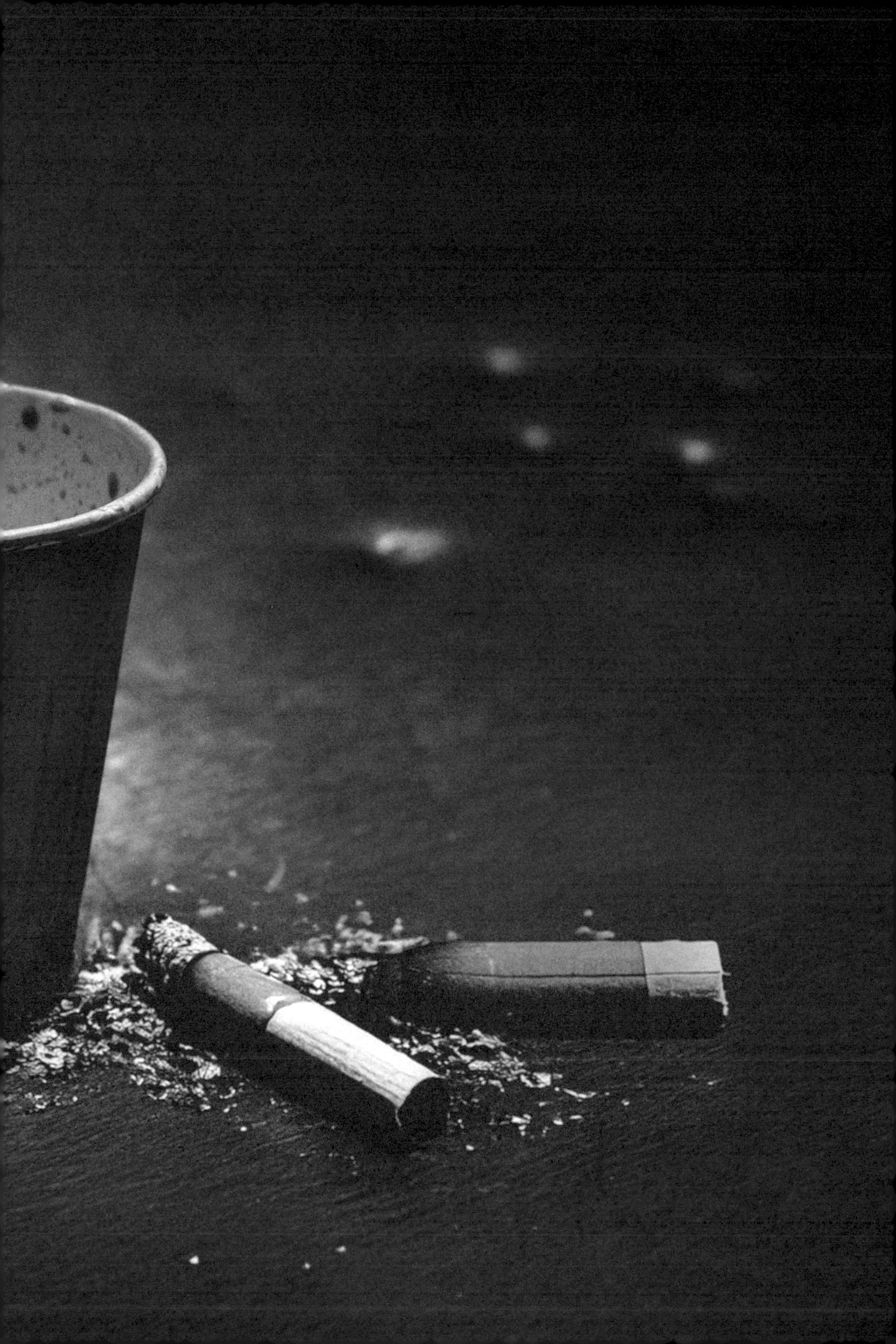

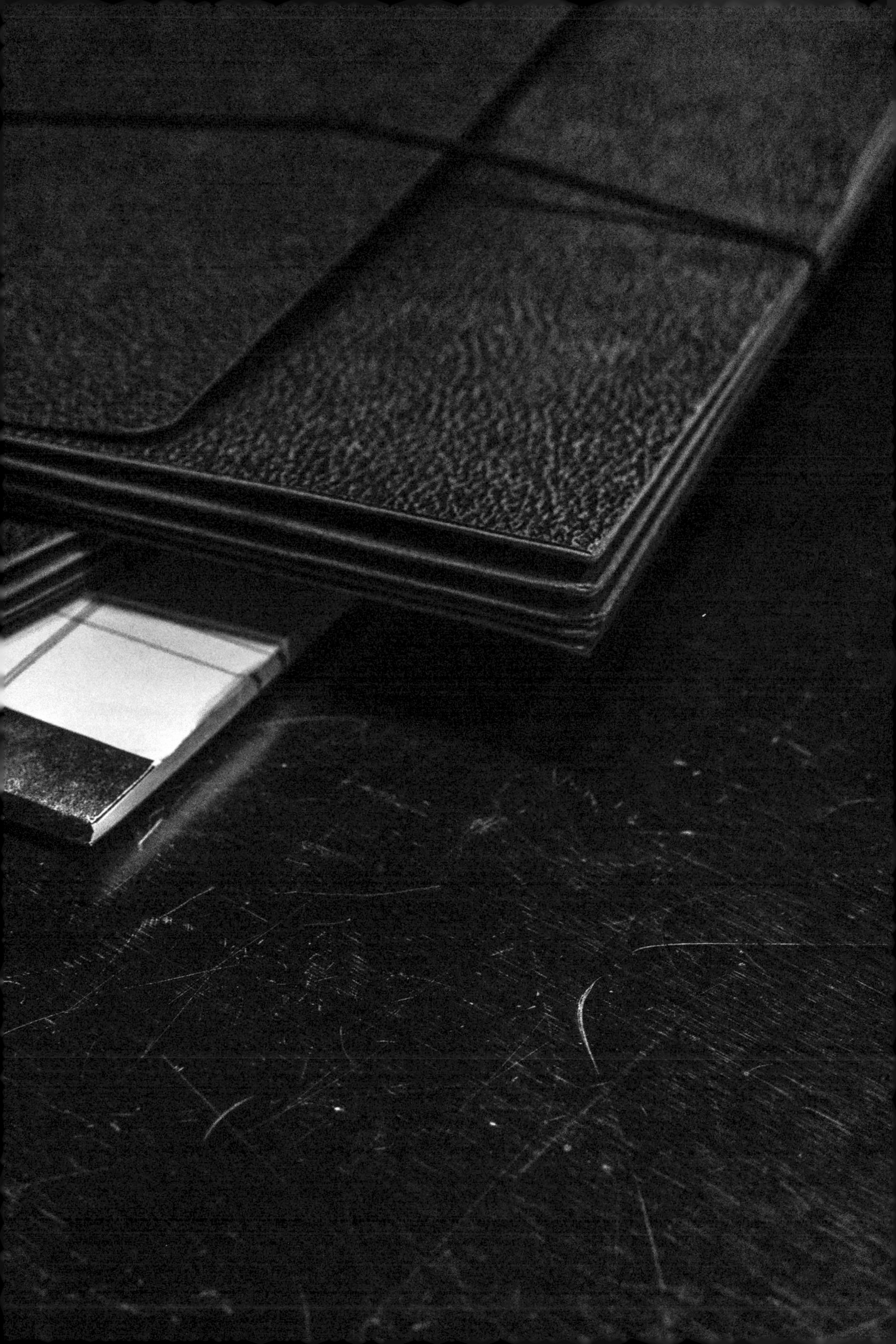

Christopher Ochoa

Eddie Lowery

Byron Halsey

Raymond Santana

"Do you think I can have an attorney?"

"No, no, no, you don't need a lawyer," they told me. "We are just asking you questions. That's all."

Asking for a lawyer wasn't even on my mind. I am trying to get out of here. I am trying to answer the questions and get out of here.

It never even occured to me to ask for a lawyer. I'm 14 years old. What's a lawyer?

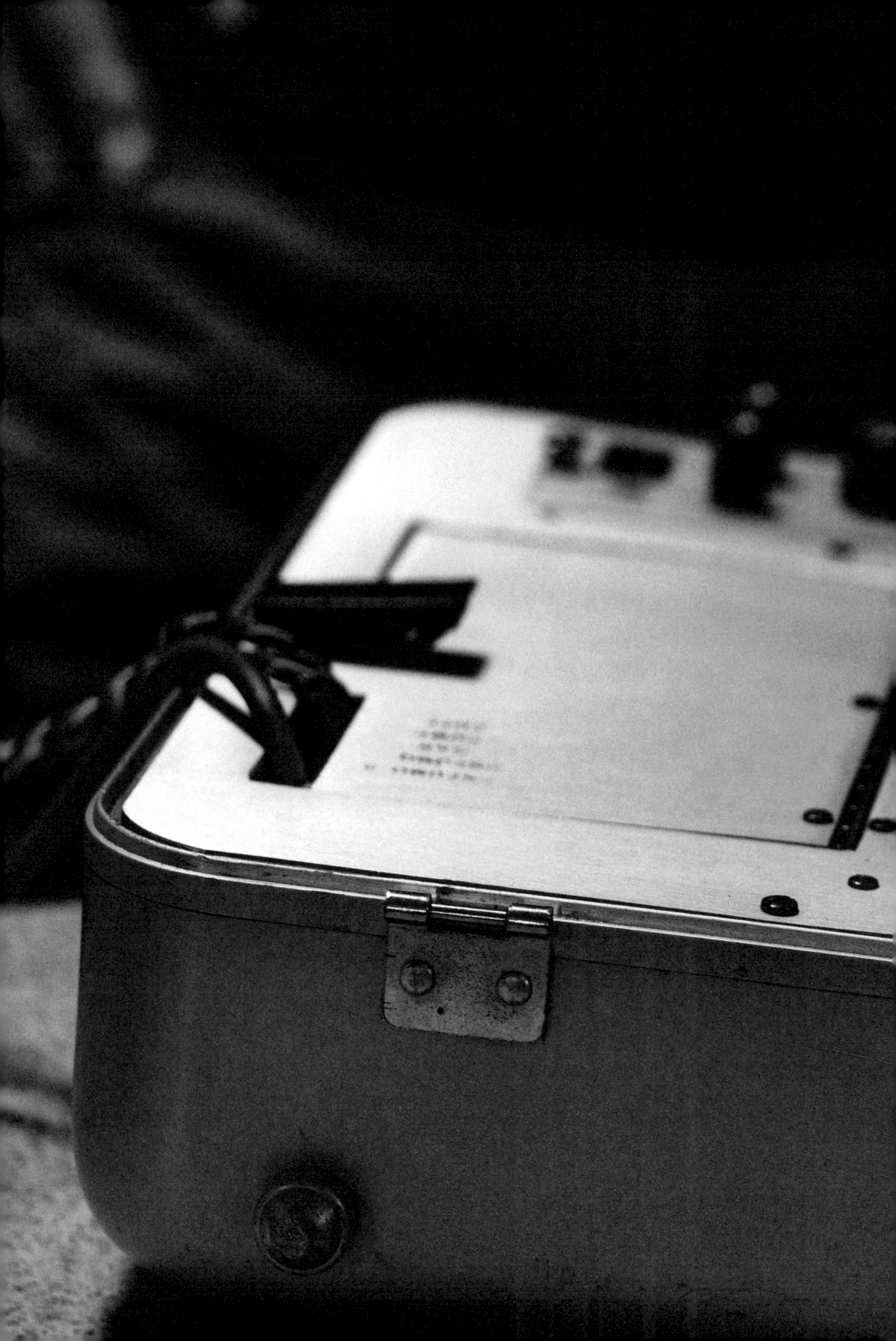

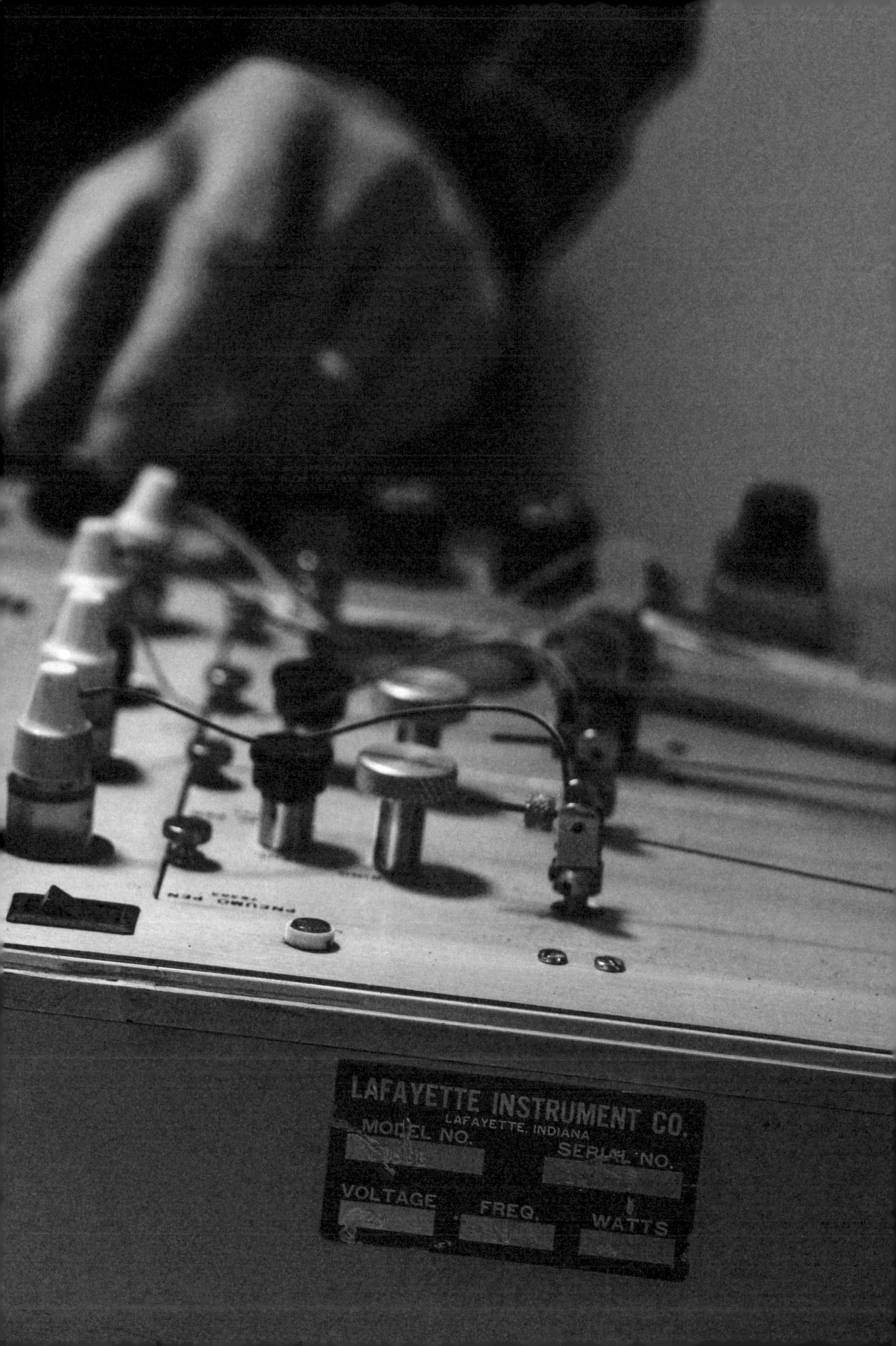
LAFAYETTE INSTRUMENT CO.
LAFAYETTE, INDIANA
MODEL NO.
SERIAL NO.
VOLTAGE
FREQ.
WATTS

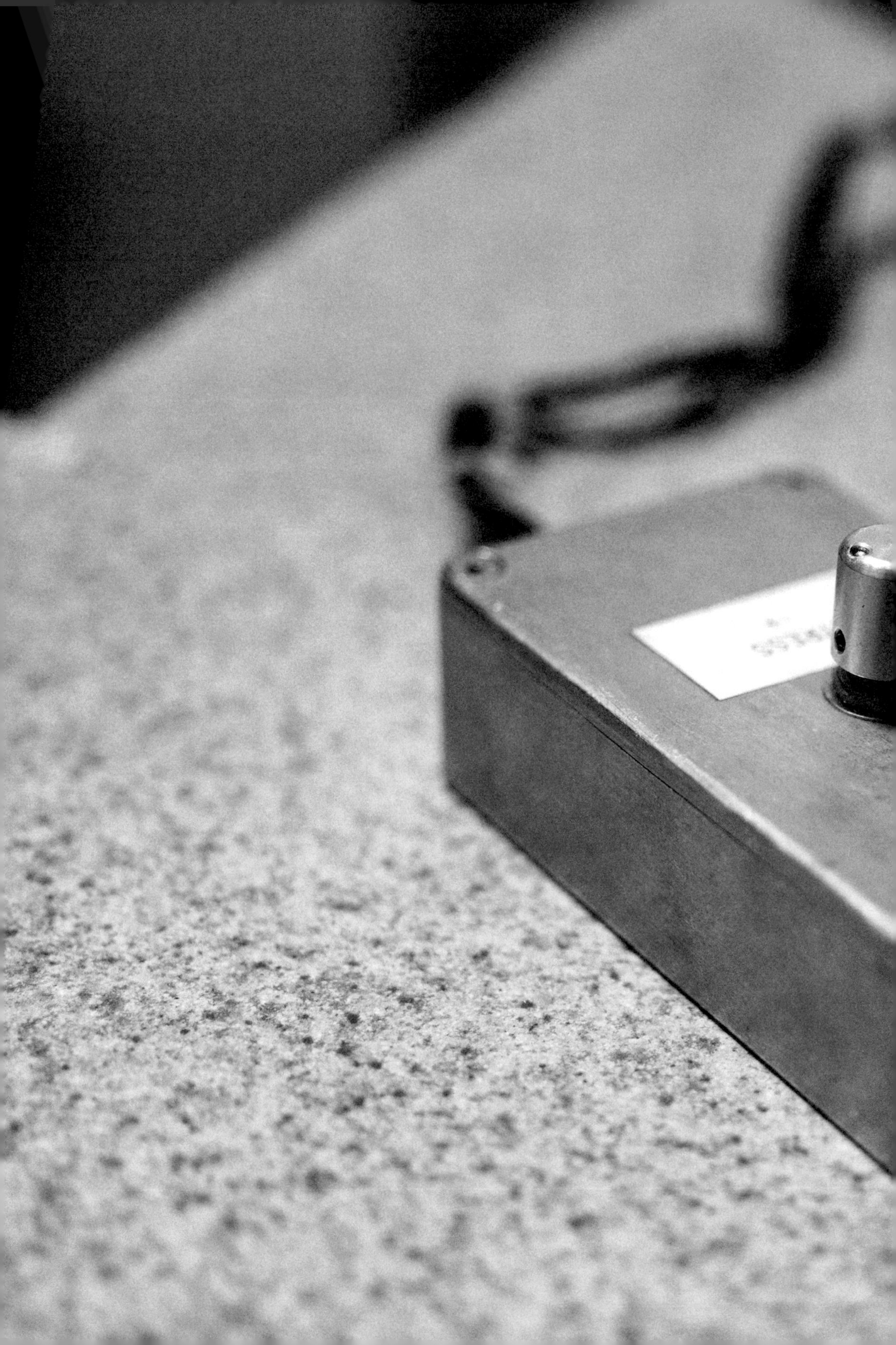

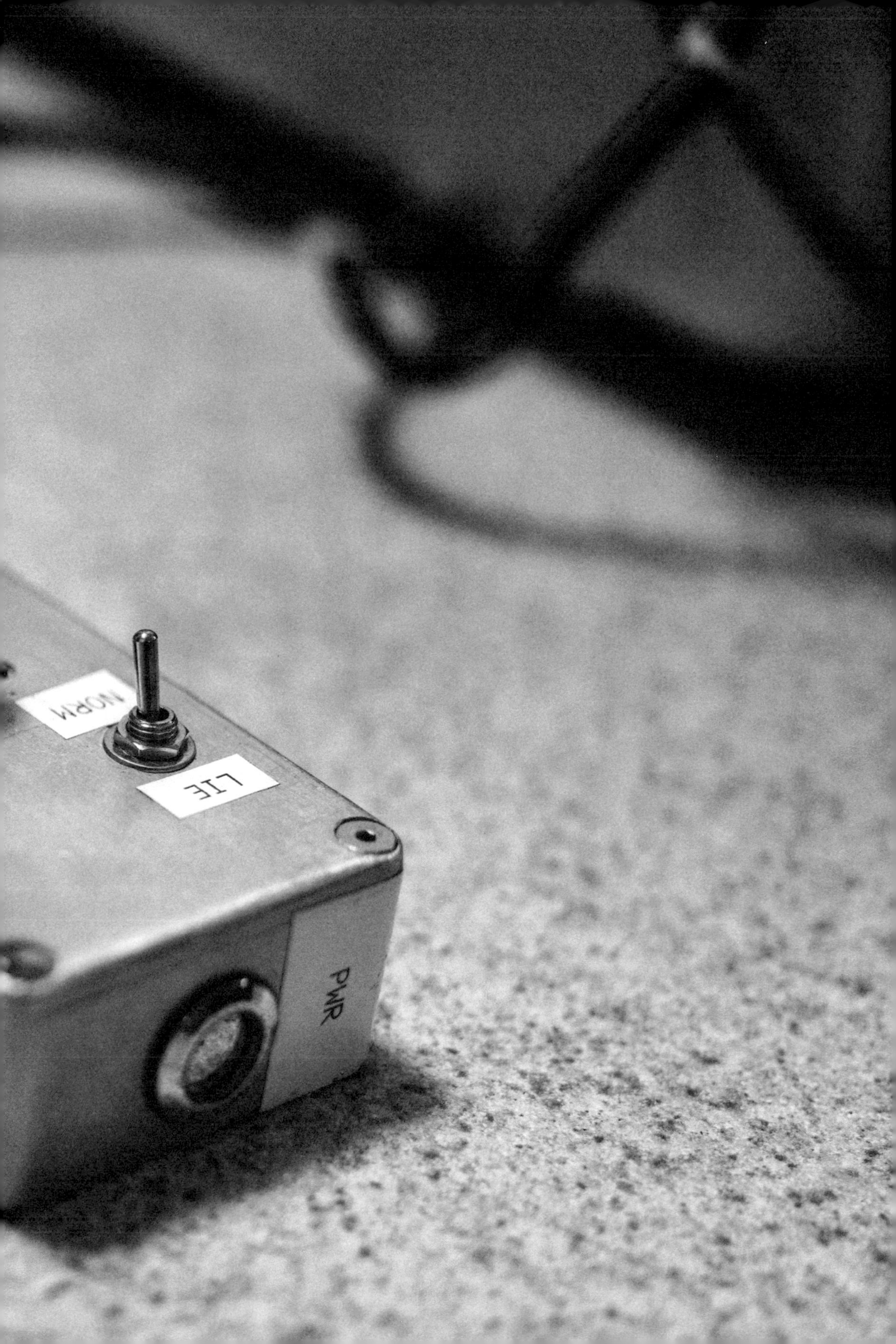
NORM
LIE
PWR

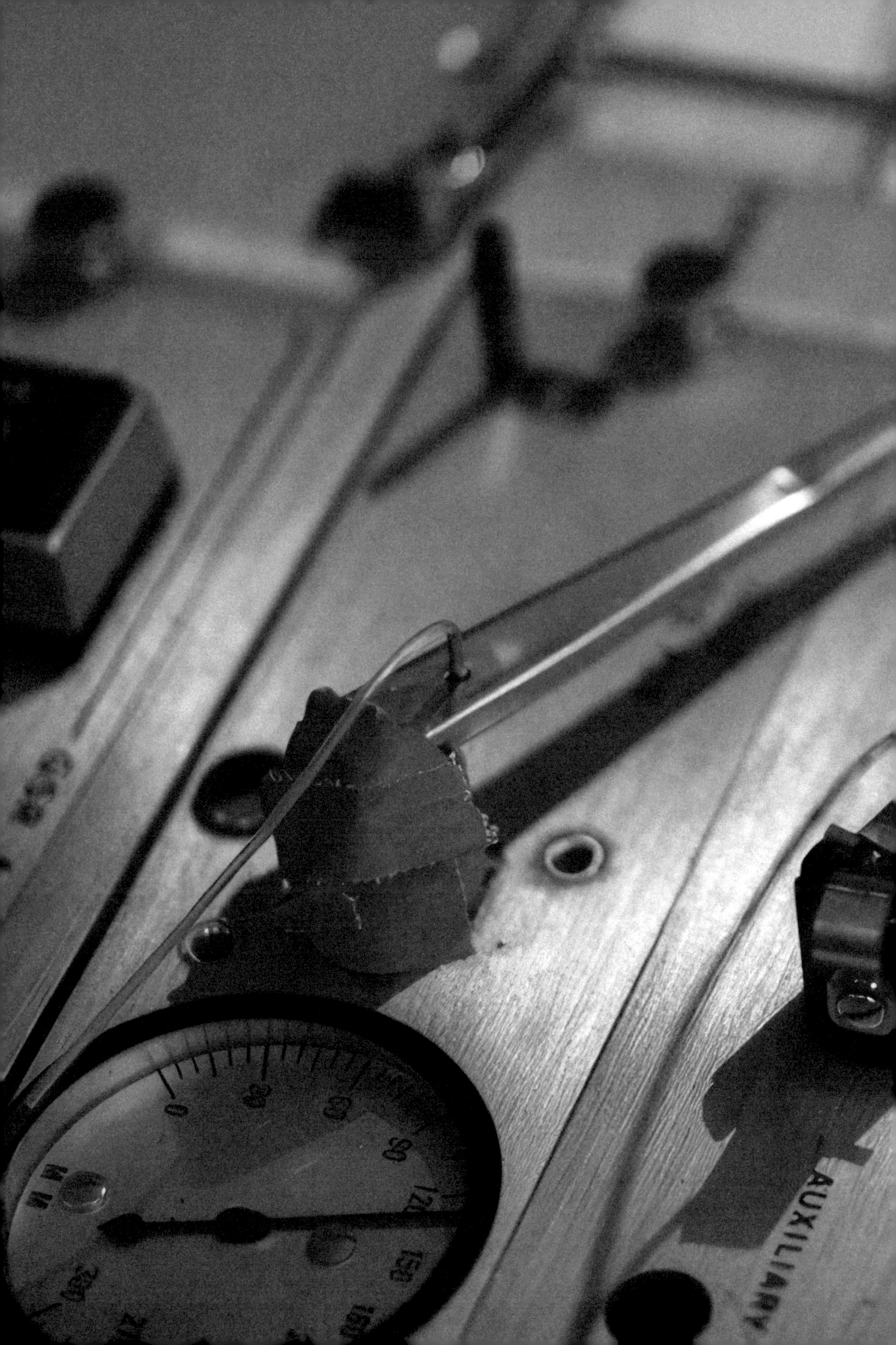
AUXILIARY

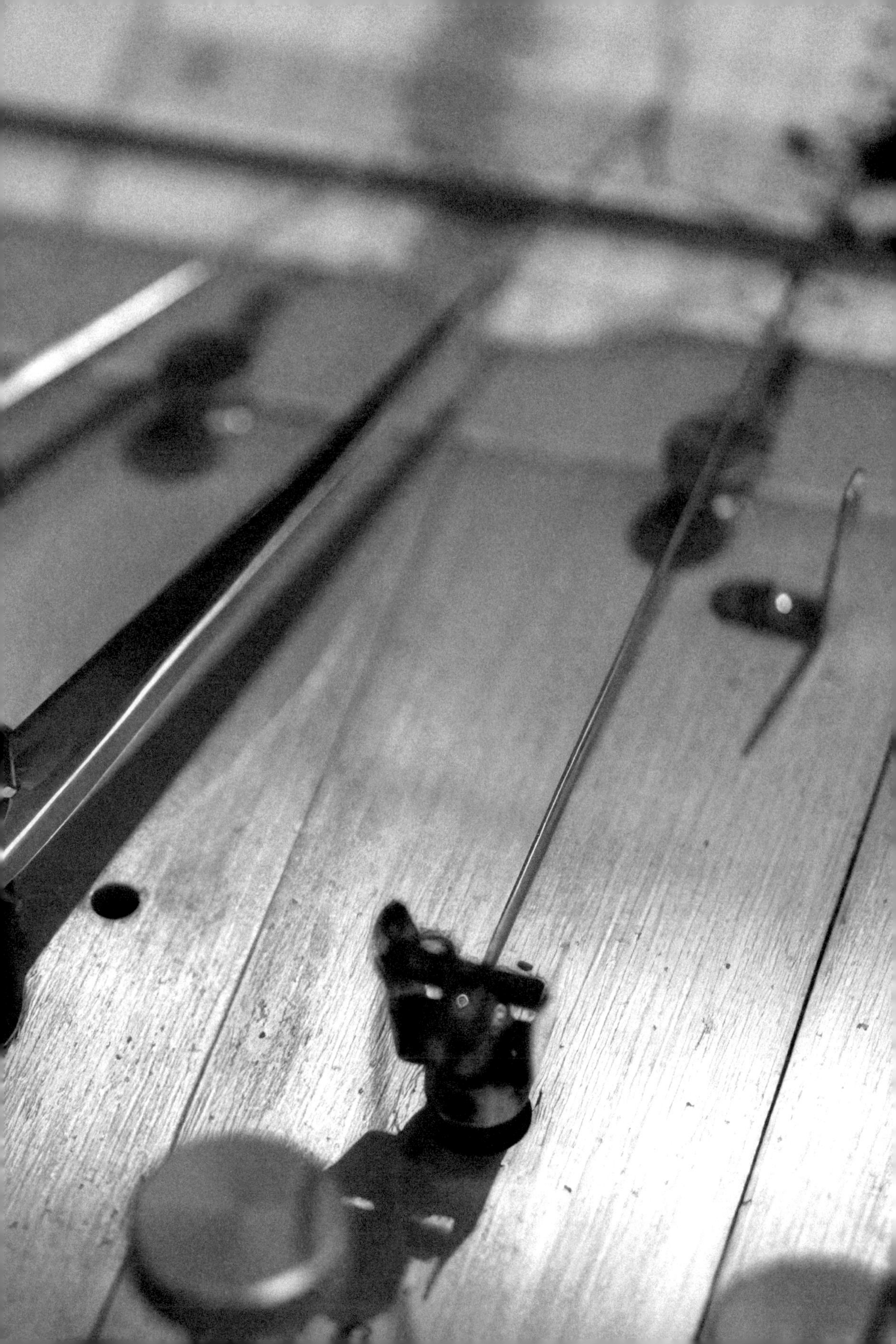

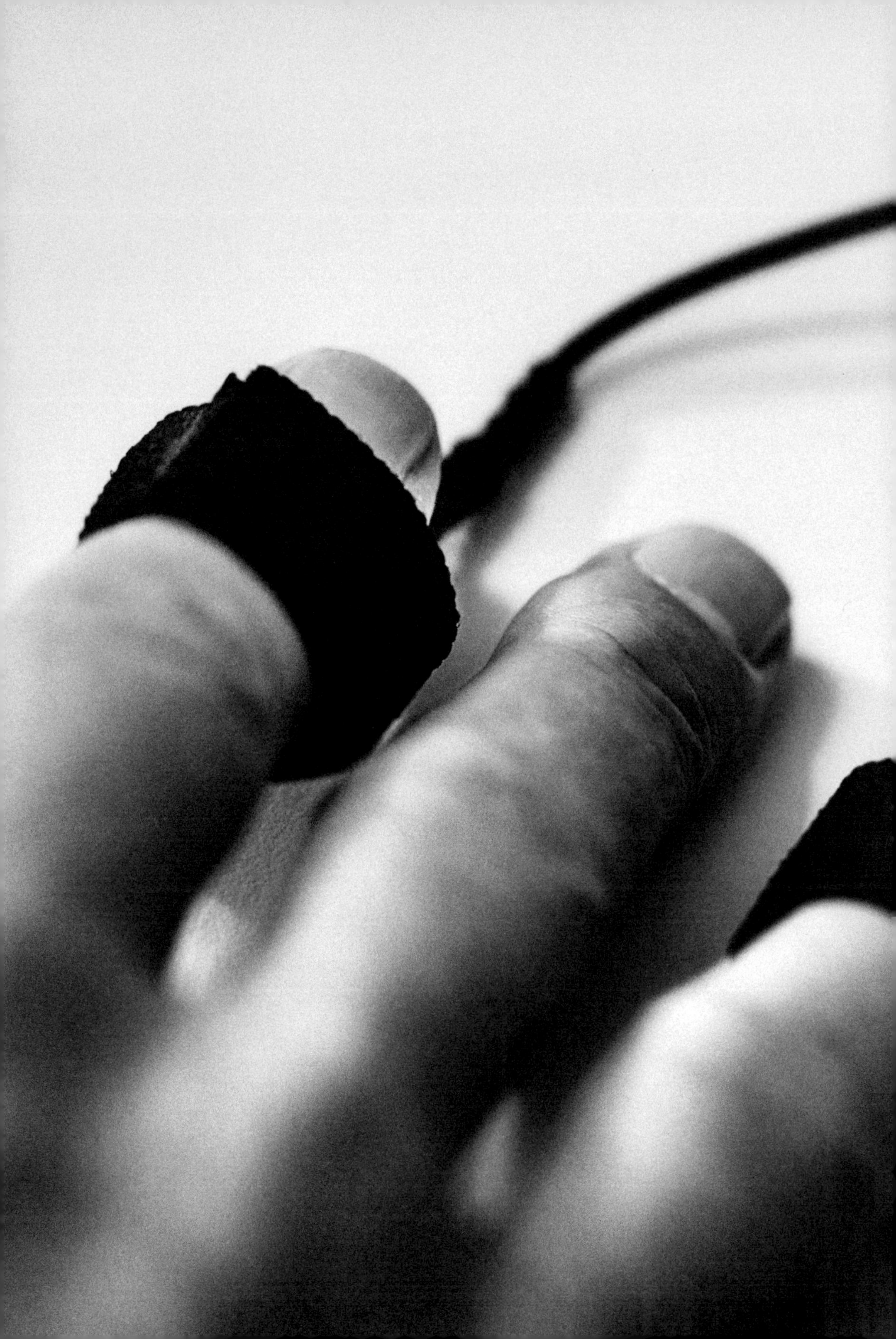

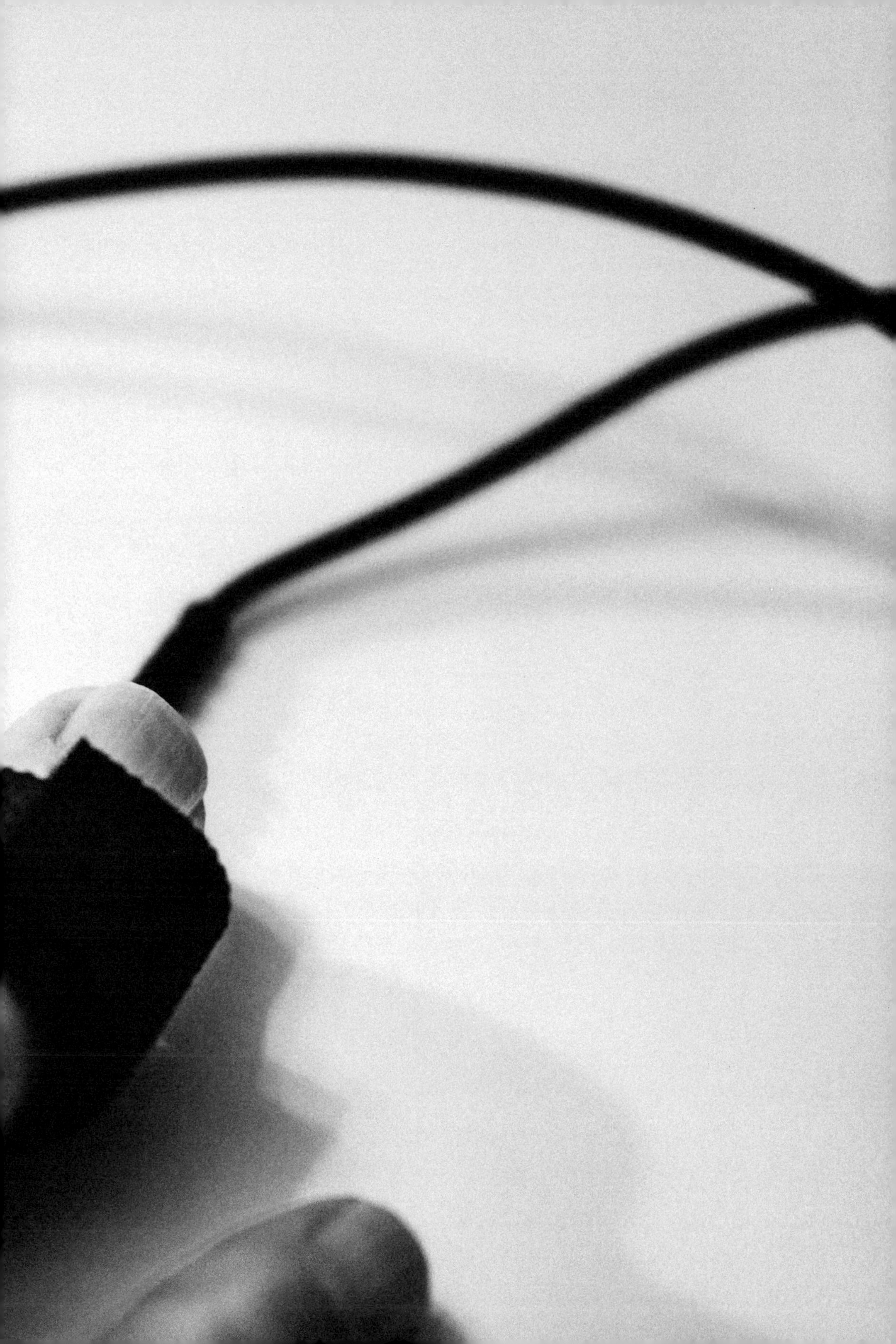

Byron Halsey

After the polygraph, the detective says he wanted to take me back to the police station and clear up a few things. At that point, I realized that this isn't going the way I thought it was going to go. They weren't letting me go home.

..

cd[redacted].txt

TRANSCRIPTION

OF

RECORDING ON

DVD

LABELED

"COMMONWEALTH V. [redacted] DISC 2"

D

Q, (By Det. [redacted]) You're just a kid yourself, right? Hmm? Because you're only 16; right?

A. Mm-hmm.

Q.(By Det. [redacted]) That's pretty young for a junior, isn't it?

A. (INAUDIBLE).

Q. (By Det. [redacted]) Yeah. I think that's young.

Q. (By Sgt. [redacted]) okay. I'm sorry about the interruption. I just want to say for the record, the recorder stopped, but it started up again. so, we're good. okay. so once again, you're in there at nine. He's healthy and awake. You go back at eleven, he's not. The only problem with that is that there's no reason for him to have died. Right? Because he's healthy. He doesn't have asthma. He doesn't have bronchitis. He ate. He's been changed. what happened to him?

A. I don't know.

Q, (By Sgt. [redacted]) You do know. Because there's no scientific reason for him to

have died. He’s not going to hold his breath.
He’s not going to smother himself, we’ve already
said that. The blanket wasn’t over his face.
His face wasn’t in the mattress. There’s no
reason for him to have died.
well, let me change that. There’s one
reason for him to have died. No natural reason.
No natural reason.

Q. (By Det. [redacted]) Now, I’ve got to
tell you, you’re still a kid, right. You’re only
16. And by law you’re still, still considered a
child. (INAUDIBLE) a little differently than it
would in a couple of days, actually, because
you’ll be 17. But right now it’s, they really
just want to help you. okay. Rehabilitate you.
And from what I see of your   From the condition
of your apartment, and what I’ve seen of your
mother, it seems like a lot of pressure’s put on
you to take care of not only your own child, but
the children of your mother. And she’s only
what? 14 years older than you. Right? And I
think she puts a lot of pressure on you to take
care of the kids. And that’s -- that’s a pretty
D

big responsibility at your age. so we're here today, because we're trying to get to the bottom of this, to get you and your family help, to possibly protect people from something tragic happening again. Do you understand that?
A. Yes.
Q. (By Det. [redacted]) It's tragic. [redacted]'s no longer with us. There's not a whole lot to be said about that, I guess. You know the autopsy was performed this morning, [redacted], so we know some things now that we didn't know. The truth is sometimes hard to admit especially when we hurt somebody that we love. The fact is that your story just doesn't add up.
Q. (By Sgt. [redacted]) Do you have any other half brothers in the city or any other siblings?
A. I have another sister.
Q. (By Sgt. [redacted]) Another sister. where is she?
A. (INAUDIBLE).
Q. (By Sgt. [redacted]) That's it. You have no other brothers or sisters? No?
D

5

A. (INAUDIBLE).
Q. (By Sgt. [redacted]) Your dad's side. But from your mom, you have no other -- no other siblings. okay. I just want to go over once again, your mother knows you're here. Your mother was here earlier, and then we went and got you. okay. And I spoke with you and your mother yesterday. And do you still feel comfortable speaking to us without her or what?
A. I'm fine.
Q.(By Sgt. [redacted]) You're fine. Are I you sure? okay. I think she went to pick up your brother, but we can call her if you'd like, it's up to you. But she was already here, she can come back. It's up to you.
Q. (By Det. [redacted]) Is your father in Worcester?
A.(INAUDIBLE).
Q. (By Sgt. [redacted]) All right. So getting back to [redacted], we've got a problem here. We've got a big problem. Because you're in the room with him, and [redacted] was in the room with him. And [redacted] ends up dead. somebody hurt that

D

baby and we need to know who it was, and we're going to find out who it was. Either the hard way or the easy way. You can tell us what happened, and we can get you some help, or we can do it the hard way, go all the way around, go to the autopsy, bring in the doctors, prove what happened, and then tell the judge how uncooperative you were. It's up to you. How do you want this to go?
A. I'm telling you everything.
Q. (By Sgt. [redacted]) No, you're not. stop. Don't lie to me. Because that baby's dead and there's no reason for him to be dead. He was healthy. He was full. He was clean. And now he's dead.
Q. (By Det. [redacted]) Do you get angry at your mom when she's laying in bed telling you to change your baby's diaper? Hmm?
A. (INAUDIBLE).
Q. (By Sgt. [redacted]) Because your mother keeps having babies that you have to take care of; right? It's not fair to you. It's not fair to you. You're a kid. You should be able to be a kid. Right? Is it too much pressure for you

7

to take care of that baby? I would think it would be--Right?
A. (INAUDIBLE).
Q. (By Sgt. [redacted]) You've been taking care of babies for a long time, haven't you? Because your mother has kids that you have to take care of every day. Not your kids. Hers. Right? Why should you take care of her kids? Does that make you angry? sometimes. Now you have one, and that's way too much to bear, isn't it?
Q. (By Det. [redacted]) That would make anybody angry, your mother's laying in bed and telling you to get a diaper, put a diaper on her kid.
Q. (By Sgt. [redacted]) Do this, do that. Feed them. Take care of them?
Q. (By Det. [redacted]) Do you and [redacted] ever get to go out by yourselves? Does your mom ever volunteer to take care of [redacted]? No. so that it's a one-way street. Huh? You're doing all the work and she's laying in bed. Would that be correct? we need you to answer verbally, I'm sorry.

8

A. Yes.
Q. (By Sgt. [redacted]) Now, I need you to tell me what happened to [redacted] this morning. I will tell you this, that I had a medical investigation conducted on [redacted] this morning. And I know how he died, which is why we are in here. I need you to tell me so we can get you some help, I know it's not easy, but once you let it go, it will be fine. What did you do to [redacted]?
A. (INAUDIBLE) to check on him His face (INAUDIBLE).
Q. (By Sgt. [redacted]) His face was what? I'm sorry. I didn't hear.
Q. (By Det. [redacted]) I'll get some tissues.
Q. (By Sgt. [redacted]) Now, you say that you're going to tell me the truth. Just make sure that's what you do, okay. Because I know the truth.
A. when I went to check on him (INAUDIBLE). I didn't want to tell (INAUDIBLE)
Q. (By Sgt. [redacted]) You didn't want to

9

tell who?

Q. (By Det. [redacted]) His face was in the mattress?
A. (INAUDIBLE).
Q. (By Det. [redacted]) okay. That's not [illegible] strong [illegible] on the mattress? [illegible] didn't fall down
A. (INAUDIBLE).

Q: (By Sgt. [redacted]) No, you're not, ever. hell

but twice, he was on his back. You told

10

Detective [redacted] he was on his back. Now I let

A: (INAUDIBLE) know why. Do you know why?

11

Q: (By Sgt. [redacted]) Think about it.

happened, [redacted] was in the mattress. Oh,

12

we're done here. Oh, okay, thank you. Yeah,

dies. Either you're a liar or you just got the

13

worst luck in the world. How do you think a

Q: (By Sgt. [redacted]) That's why you

smothered him, didn't you?

have died in your care. It's kind of hard to

14

believe at this point. [redacted] just out the

from here. Two babies have died under your care

15

in suspicious circumstances, right? Where do you

Q: (By Sgt. [redacted]) What other brother?

16

A: (INAUDIBLE) [redacted] He's younger than

that the lawyers and try it at a trial, we can do

17

A: (INAUDIBLE) [redacted] what?

a crazy mother, your mother, probably not easy having

18

A: (INAUDIBLE) [redacted] I know. But how your

A: to (INAUDIBLE). Kid's diaper!

19

Q: (By Sgt. [redacted]) It's the one you've

happens? Now, it's happened to you twice, and

(By Det. [redacted]) You were on there

[redacted]) What's your e-mail

[redacted]) And what about love. At AOL dot com.

[redacted]) You are. (INAUDIBLE).

(End of recording.)

Jeffrey Deskovic, Vanessa Gathers, Byron Halsey, Eddie Lowery, Christopher Ochoa, and Raymond Santana reenact their interrogations, posing as interrogating police officers.

Jeffrey Doskovic

"Did you kill her?"

"Tell me what happend?"

"I asked you whether or not you killed her?"

"Why did you go to the park?"

"What did you do in the park?"

"How did you get there?"

"What do you mean you didn't do it??
The lie detector says that you did!"

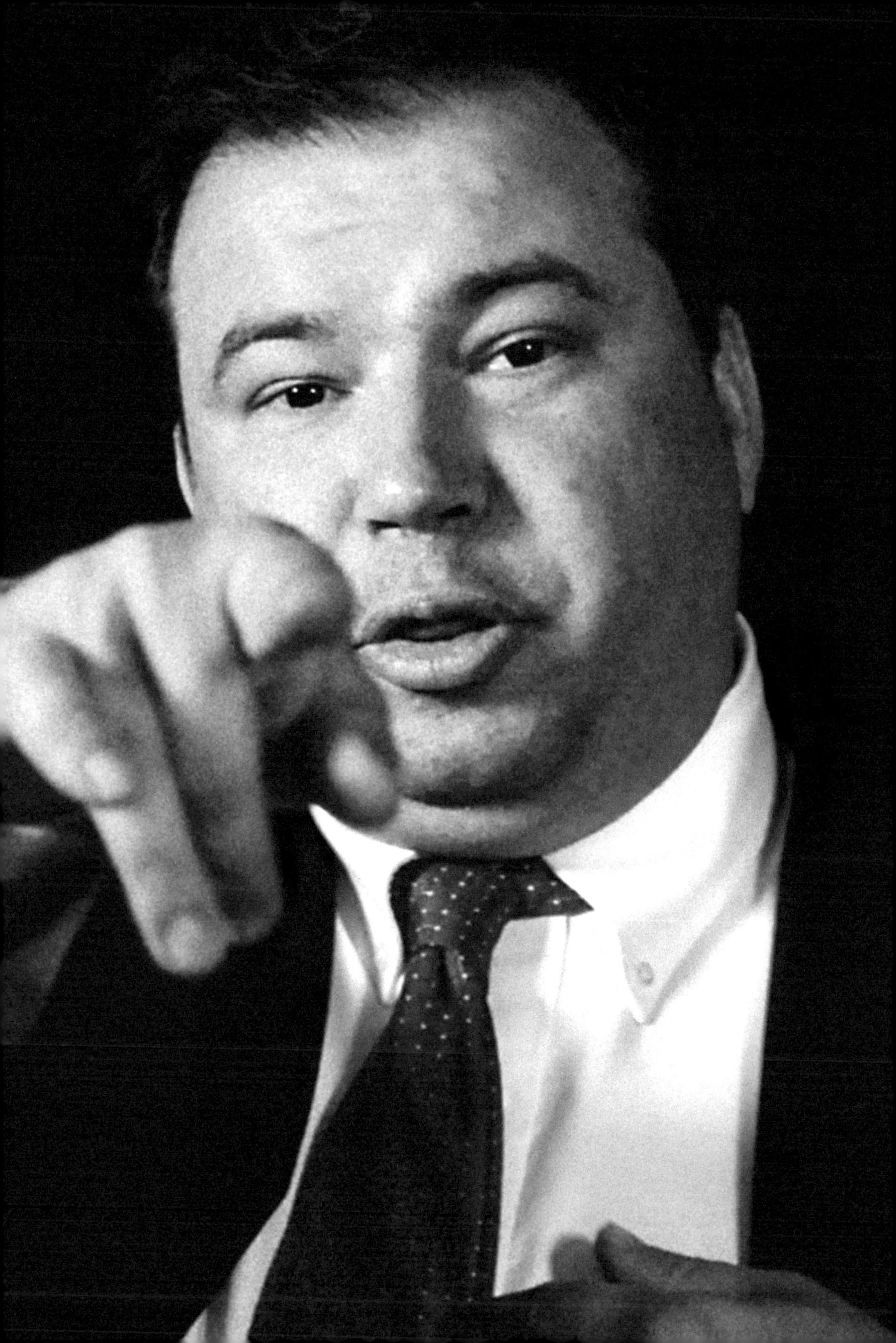

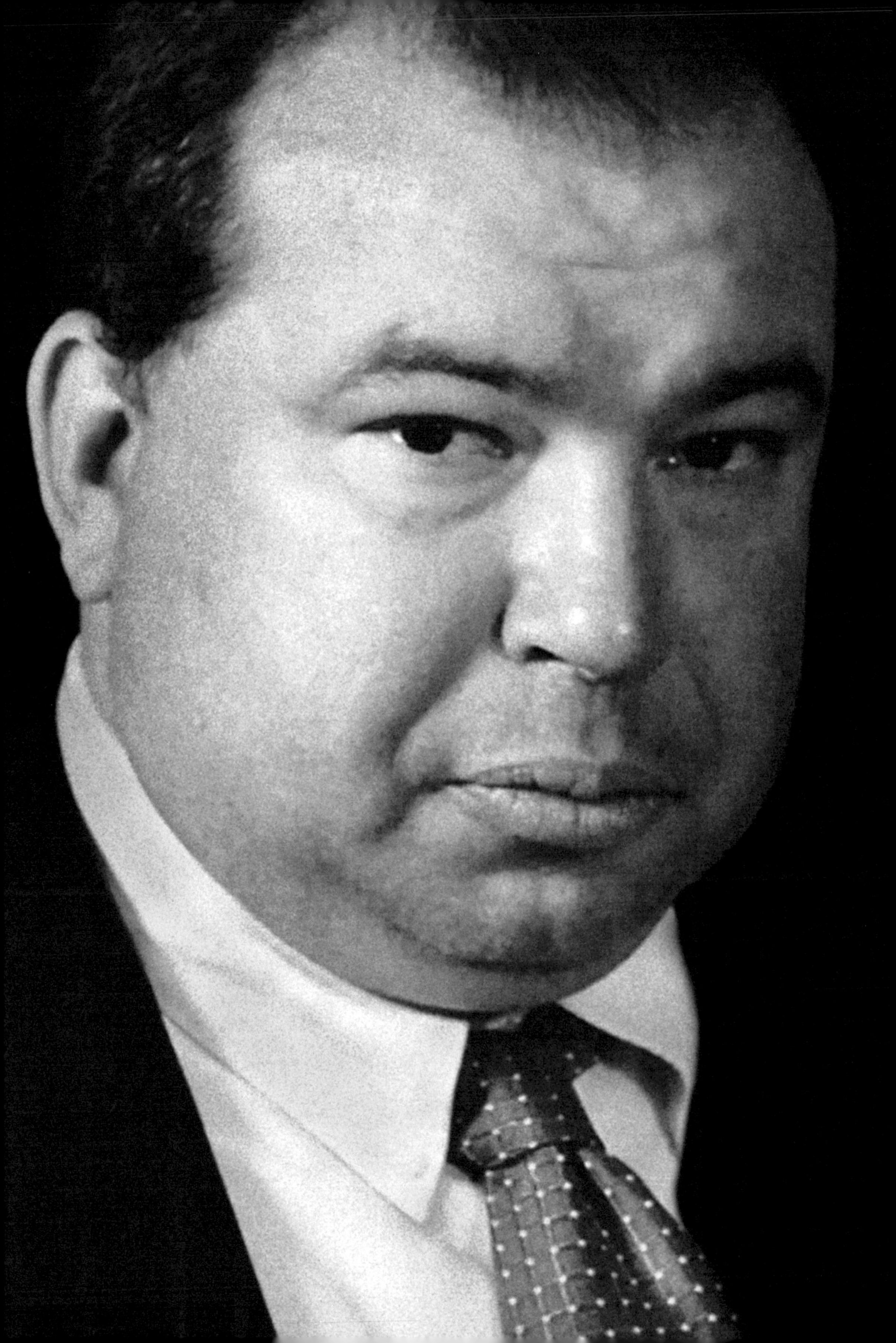

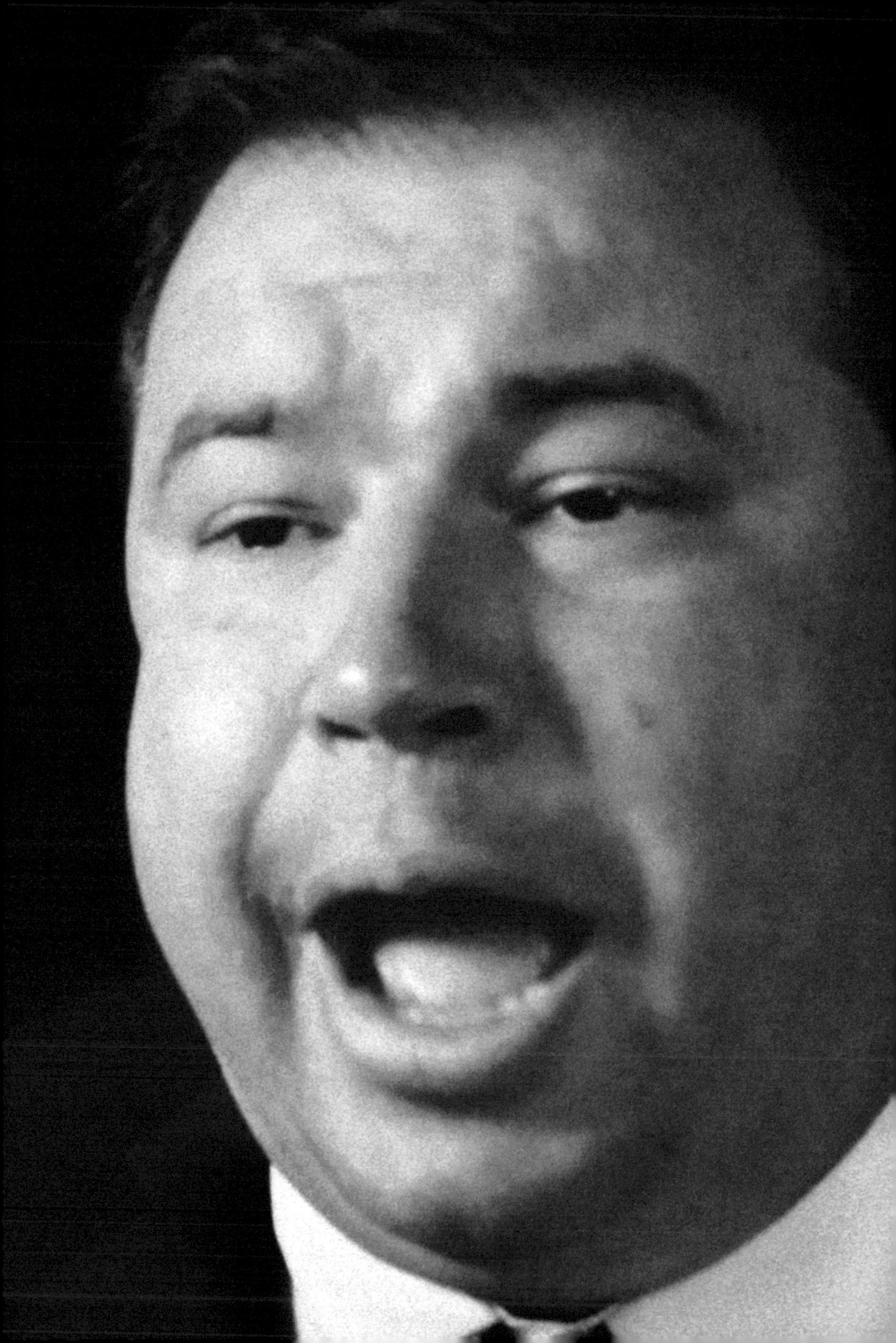

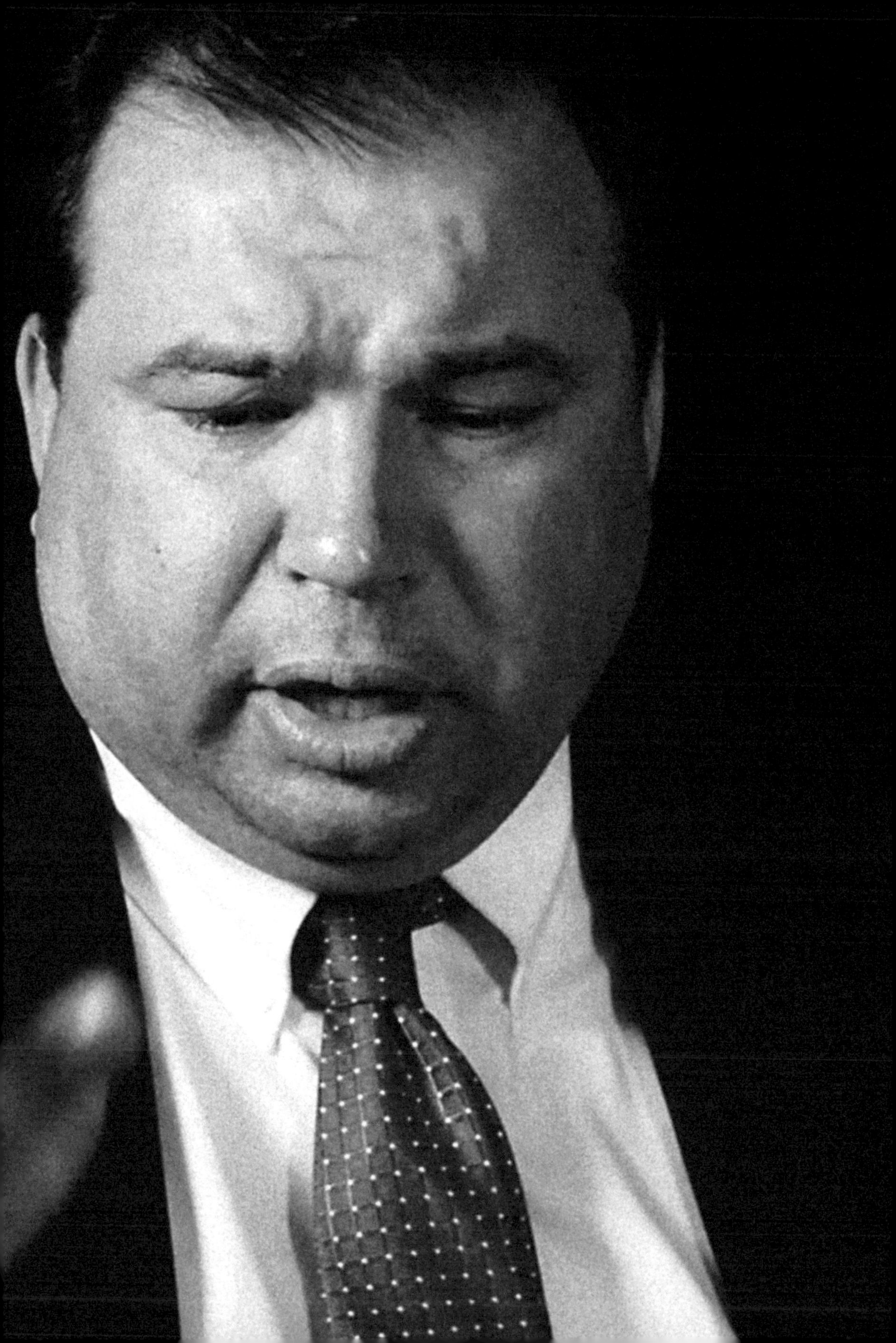

Vanessa Gathers

He was acting fidgety. He got his gun. He took his jacket off and he put his gun on the table between us. He started to play with it. He started to yell. He was screaming. His gun was right there.

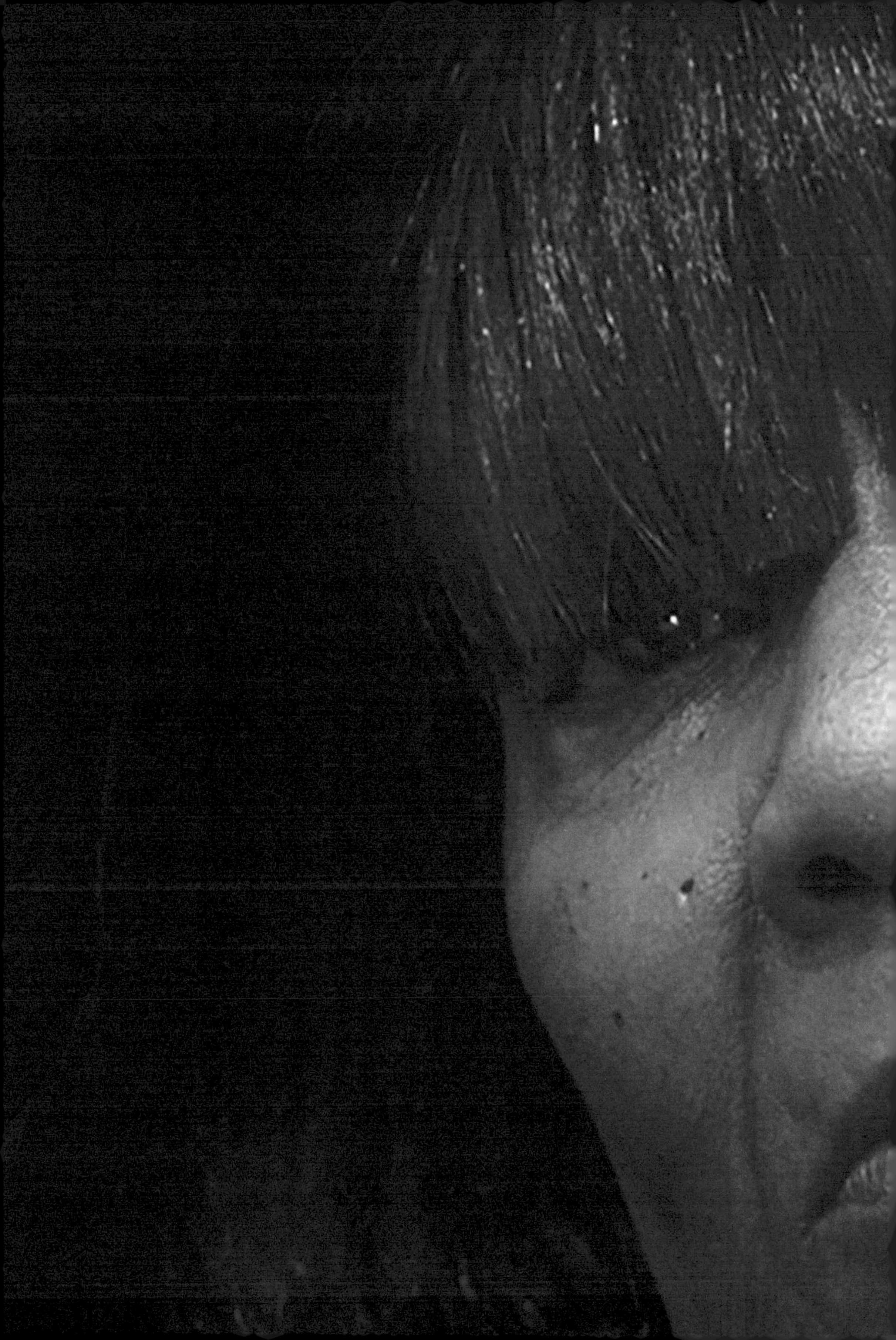

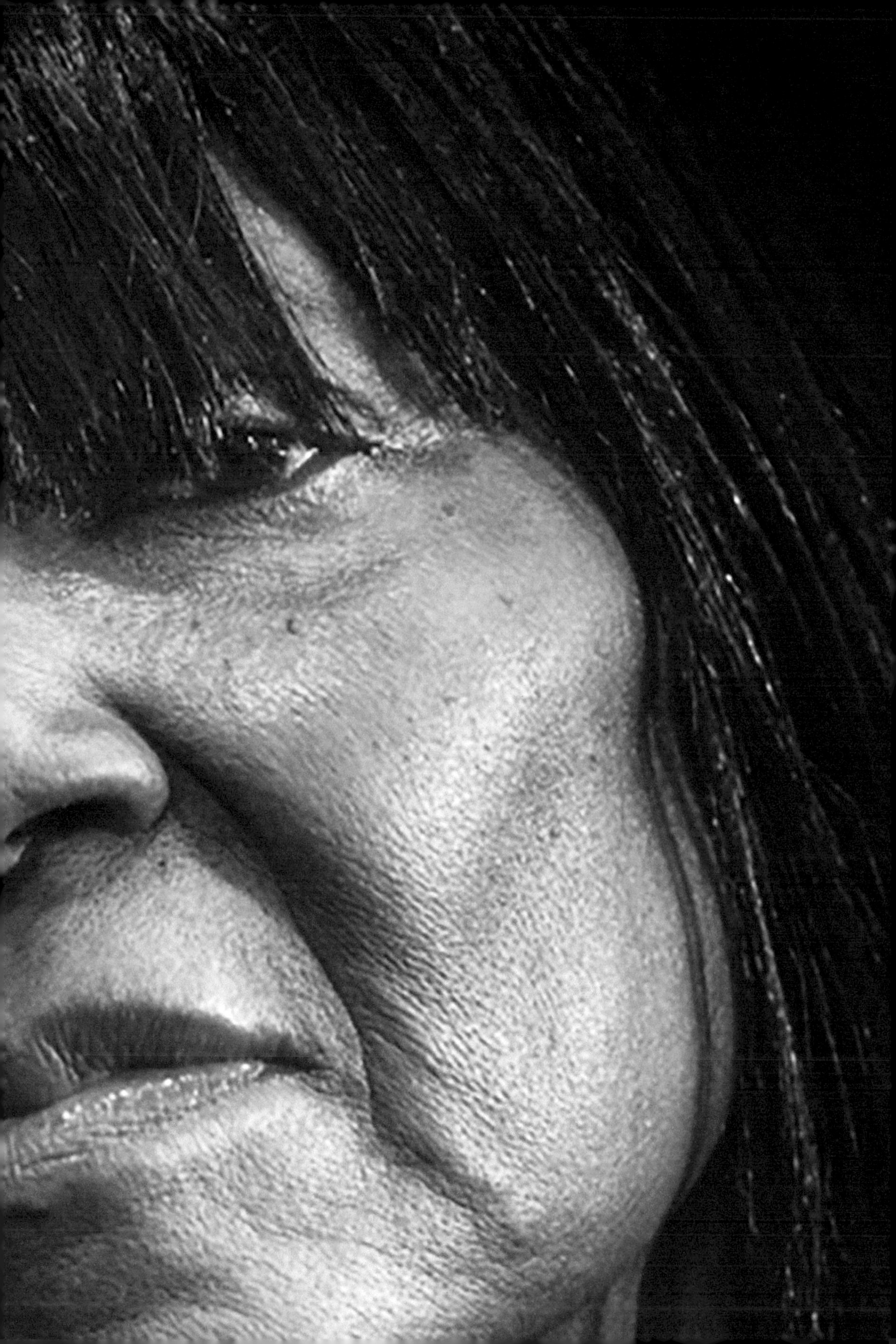

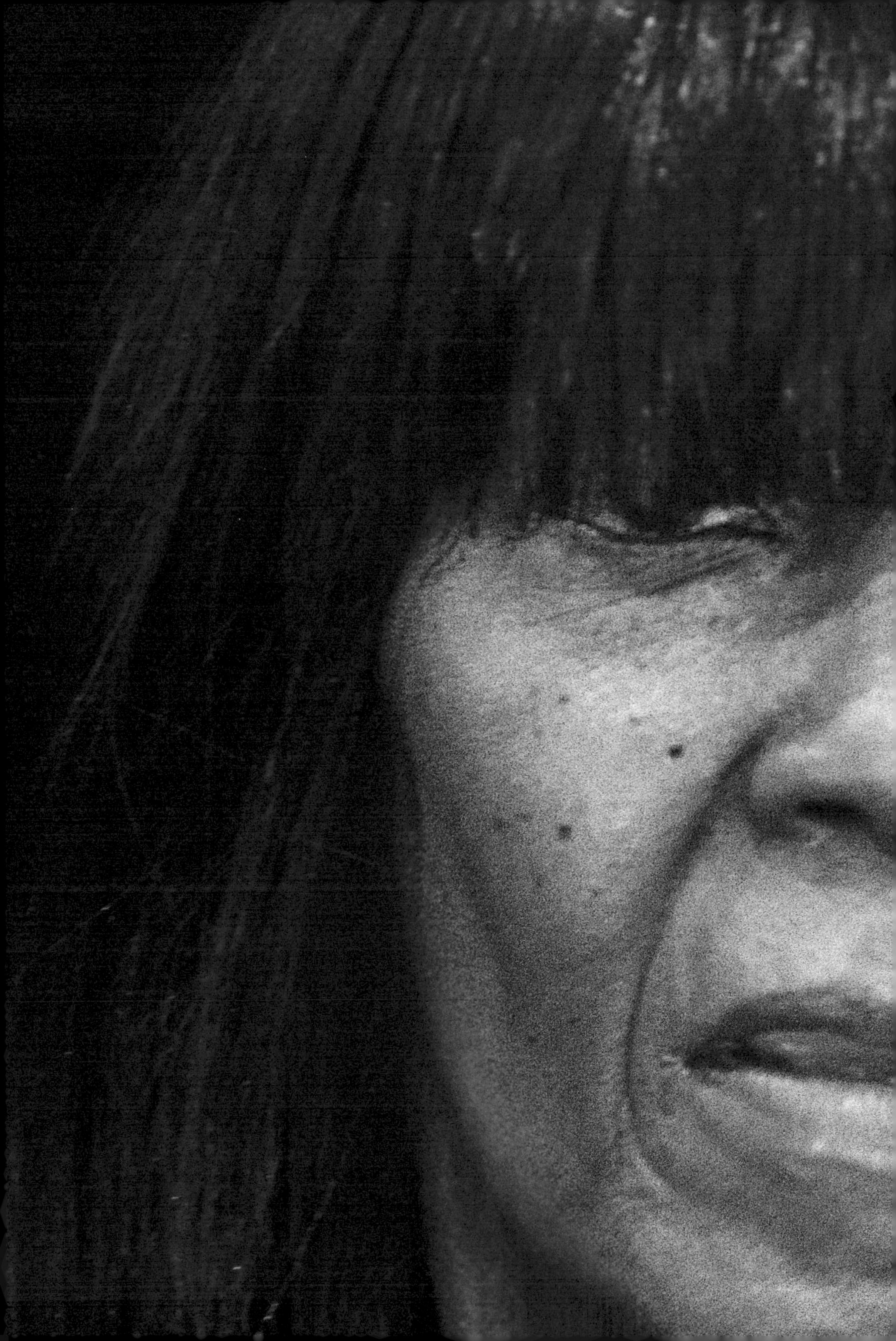

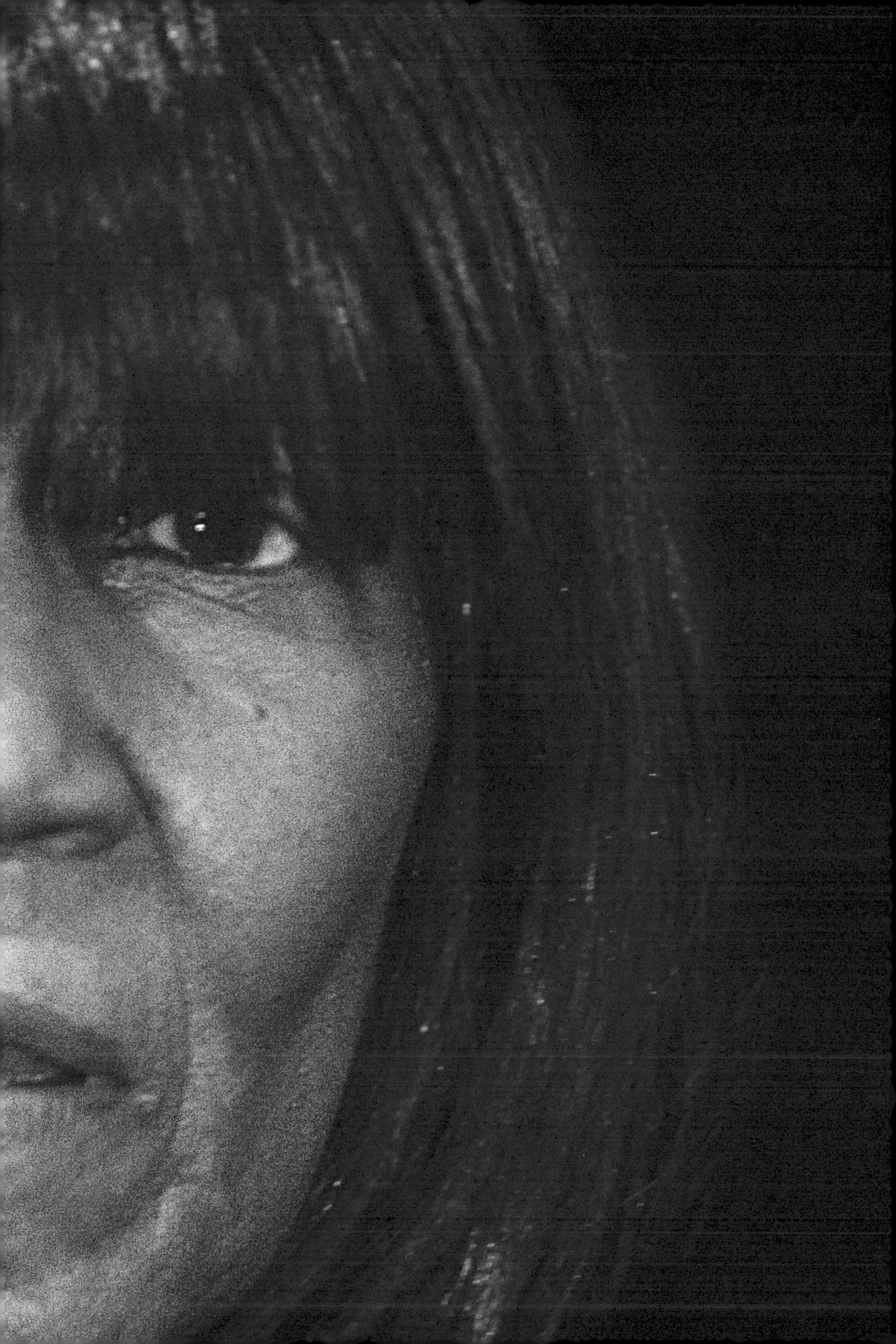

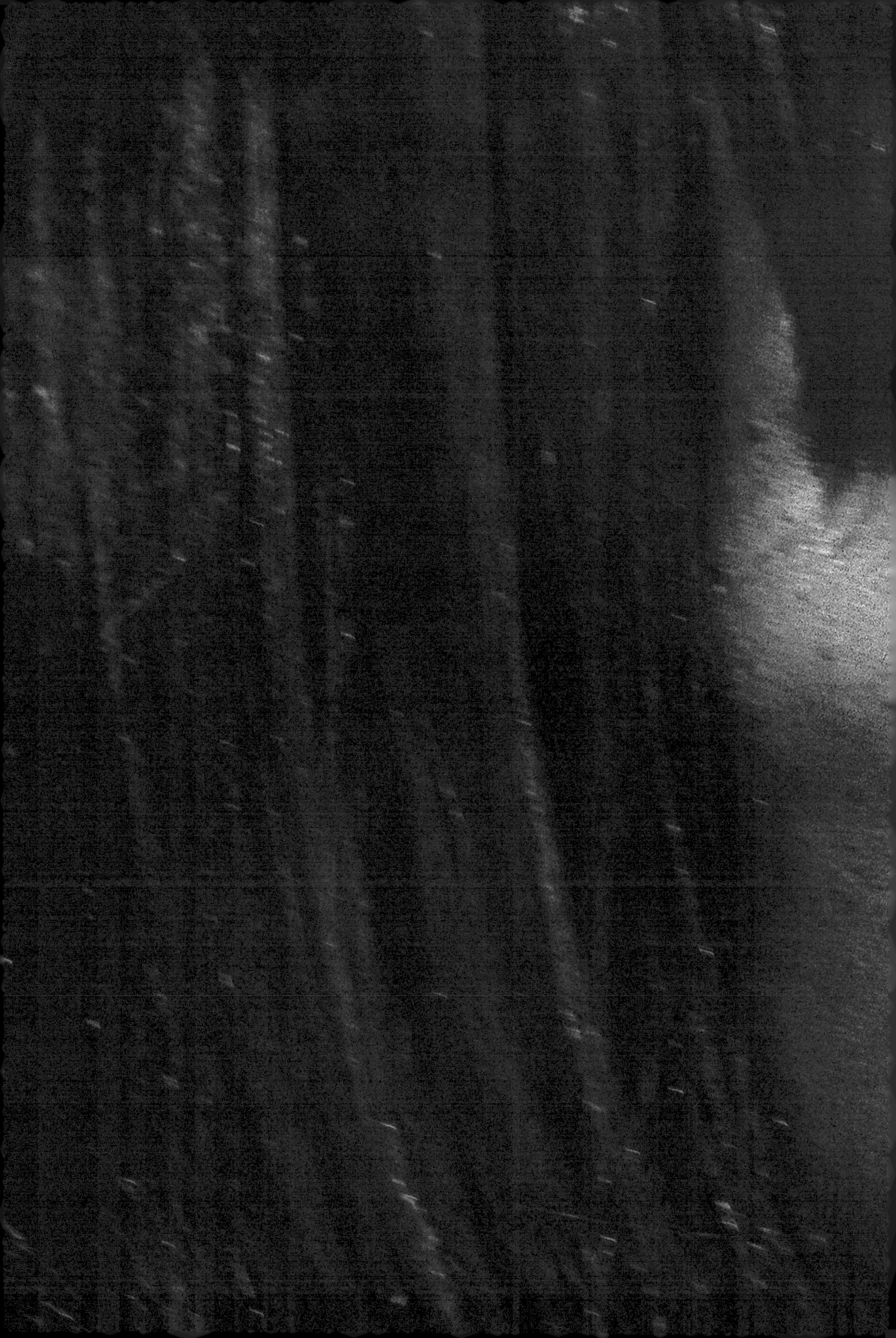

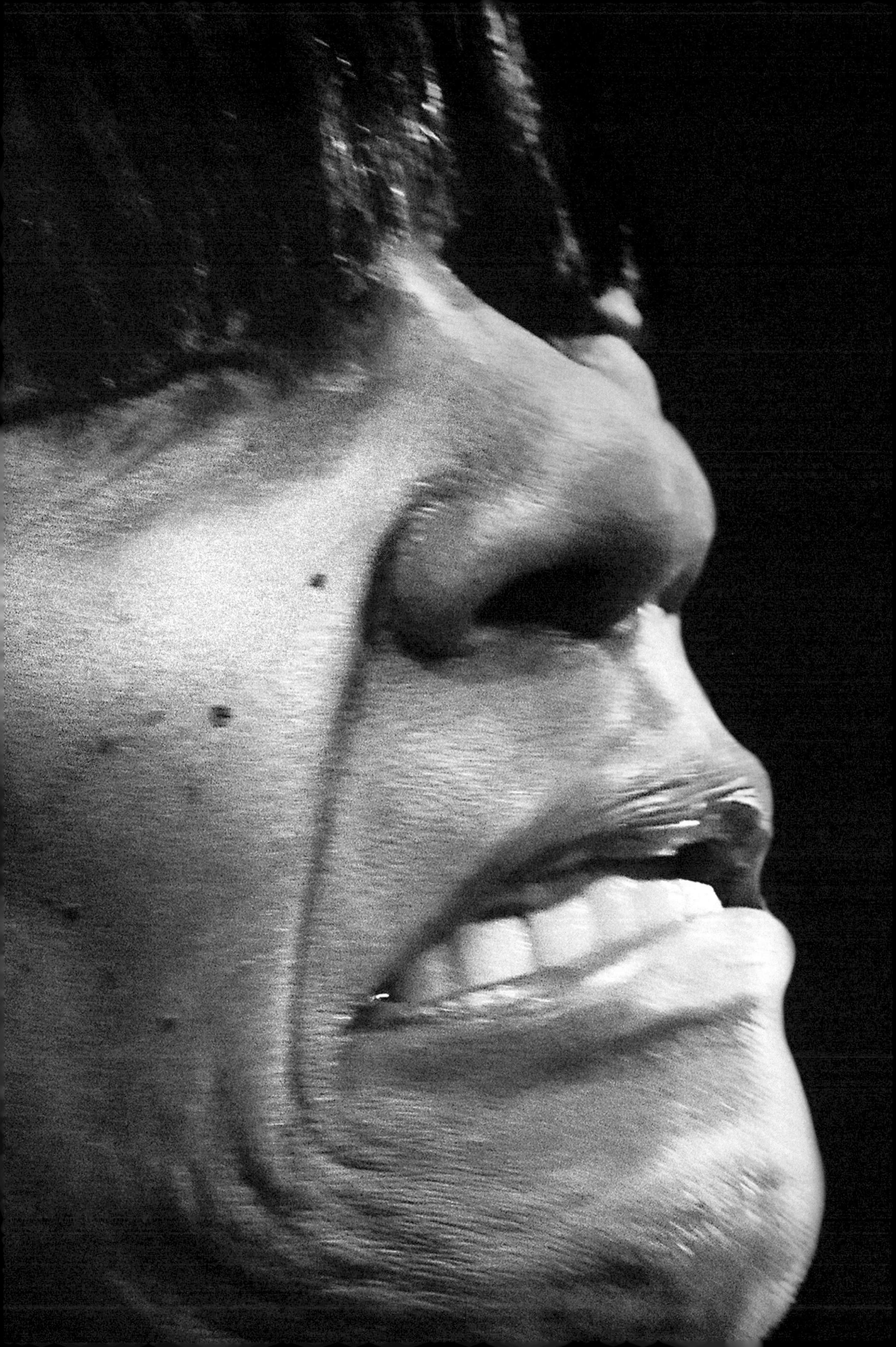

Byron Halsey

It was a small room. It felt like it was
closing in on me. There was no one listening
to me. You could hear loud voices outside.
Oh my God, this is really getting crazy.
I got to get out of here. The voices
outside the room were saying, "He is
lying. You know that he is lying." I am
like, what the fuck is going on here?
I got to get out of here.

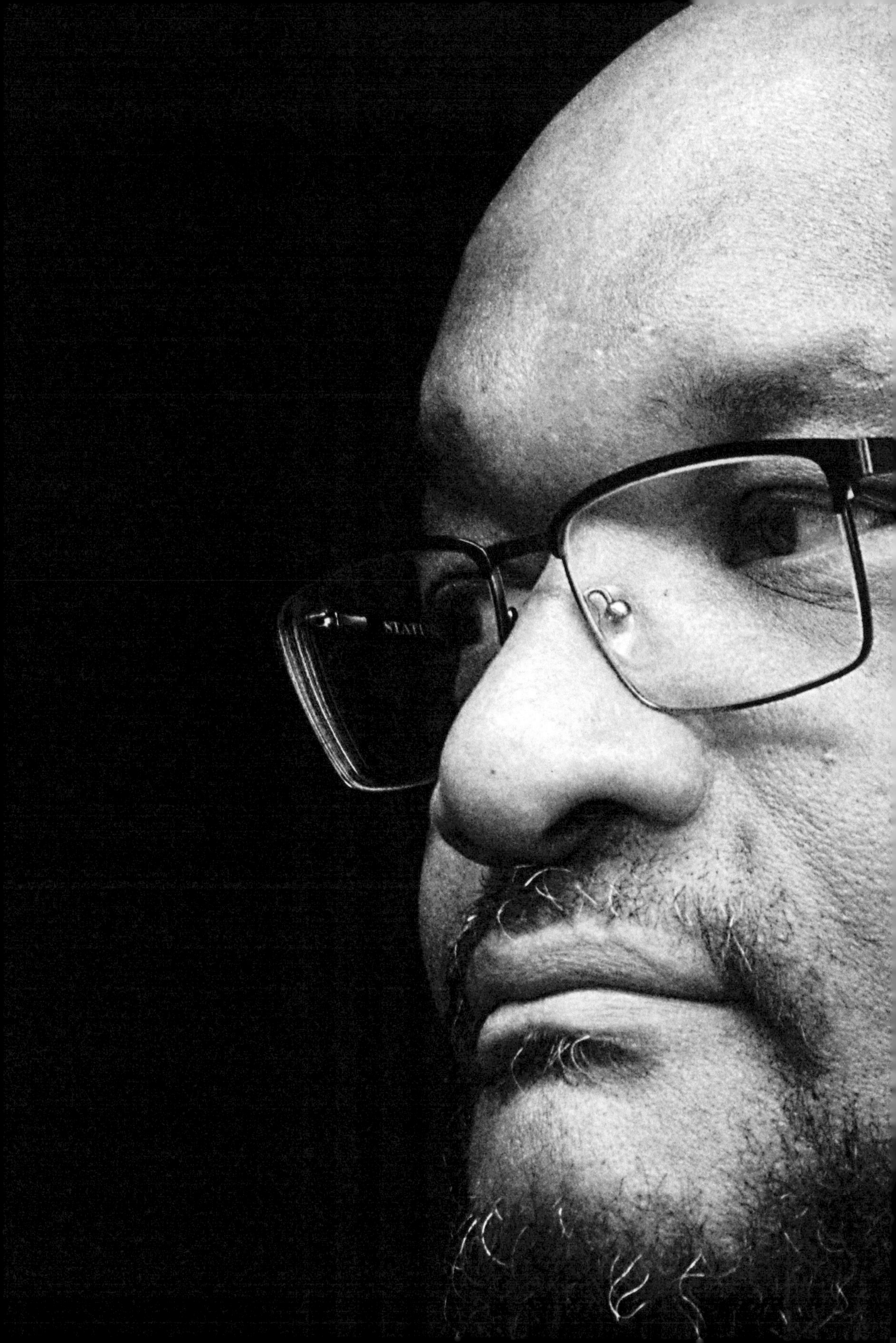

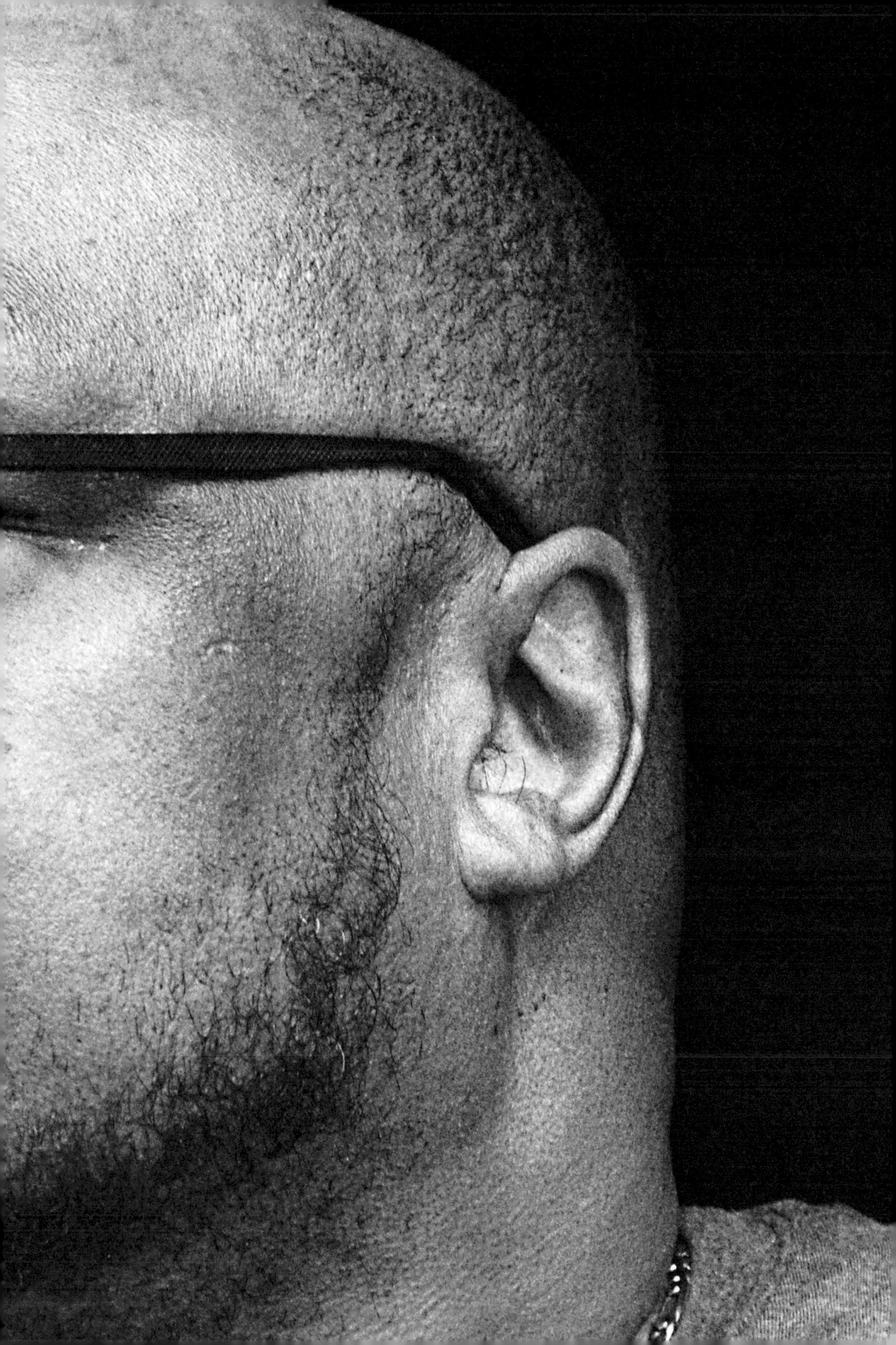

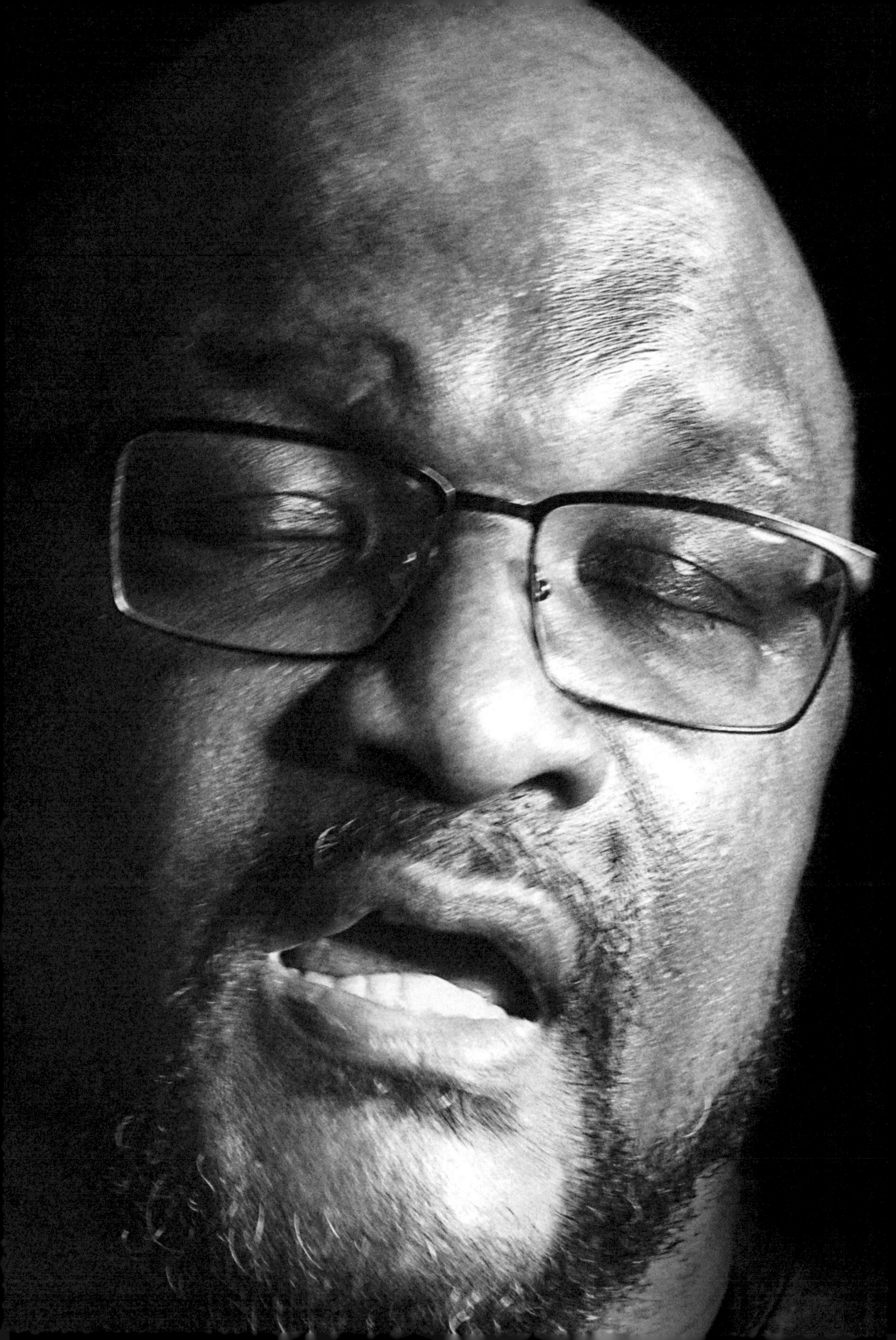

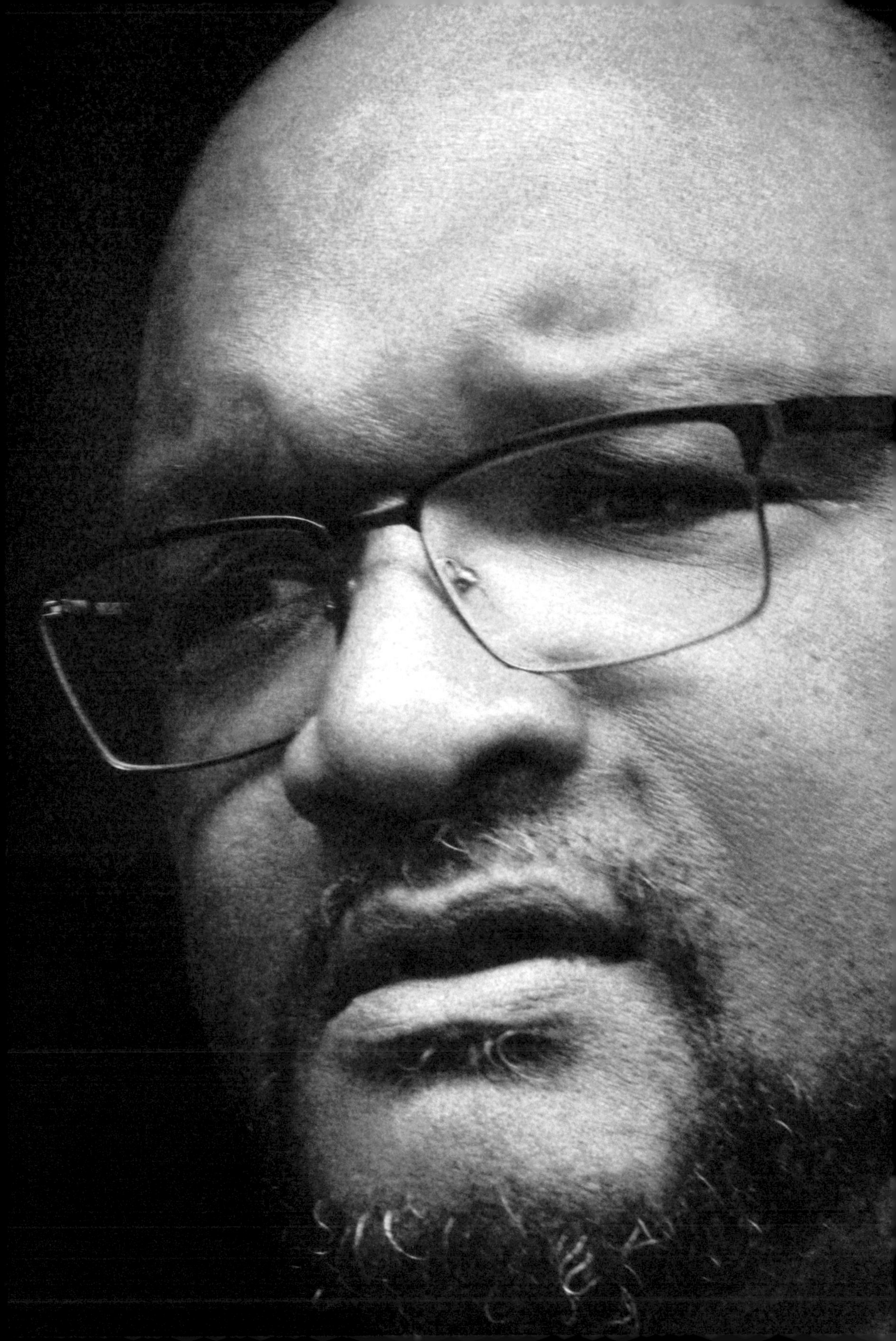

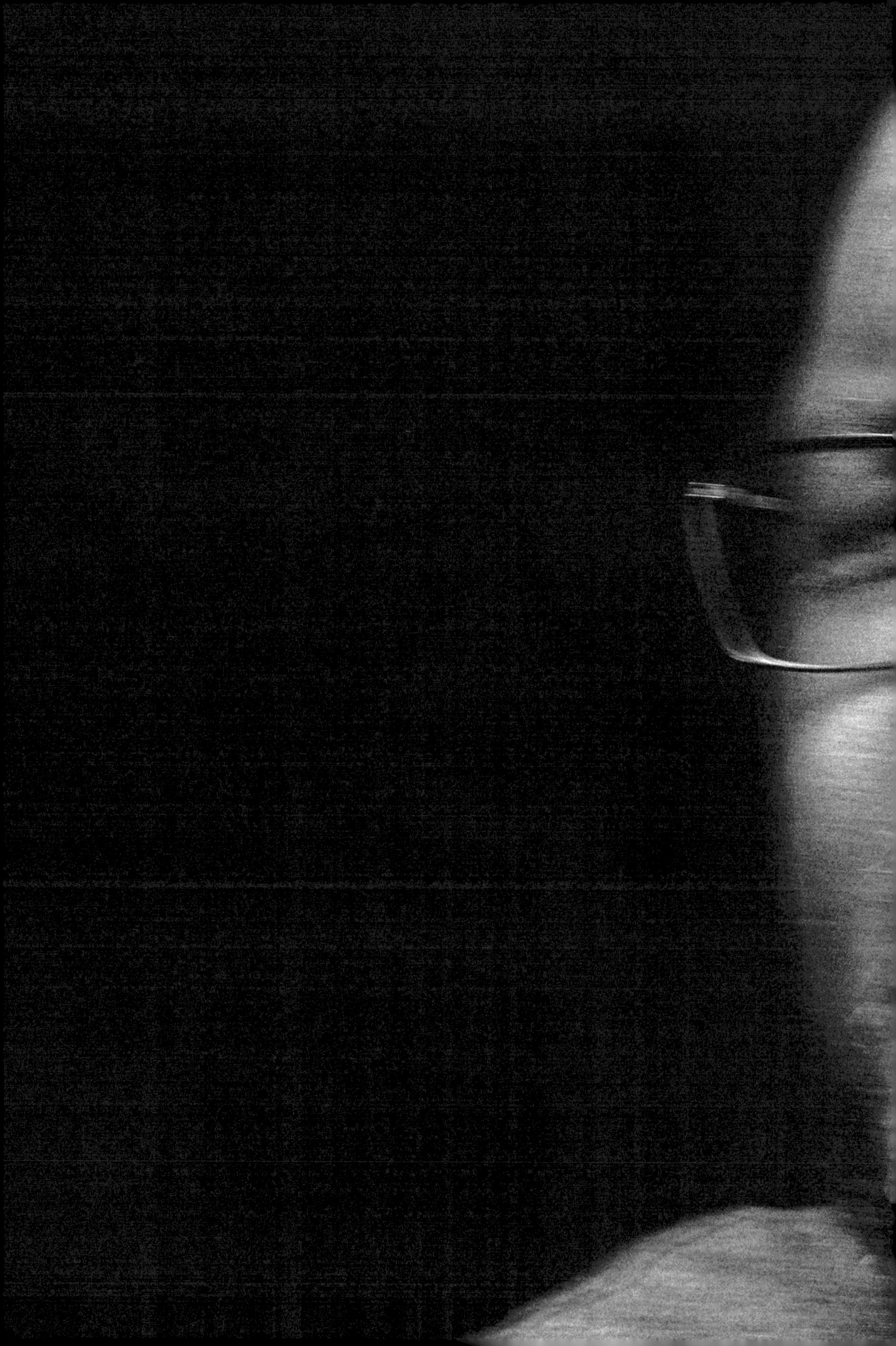

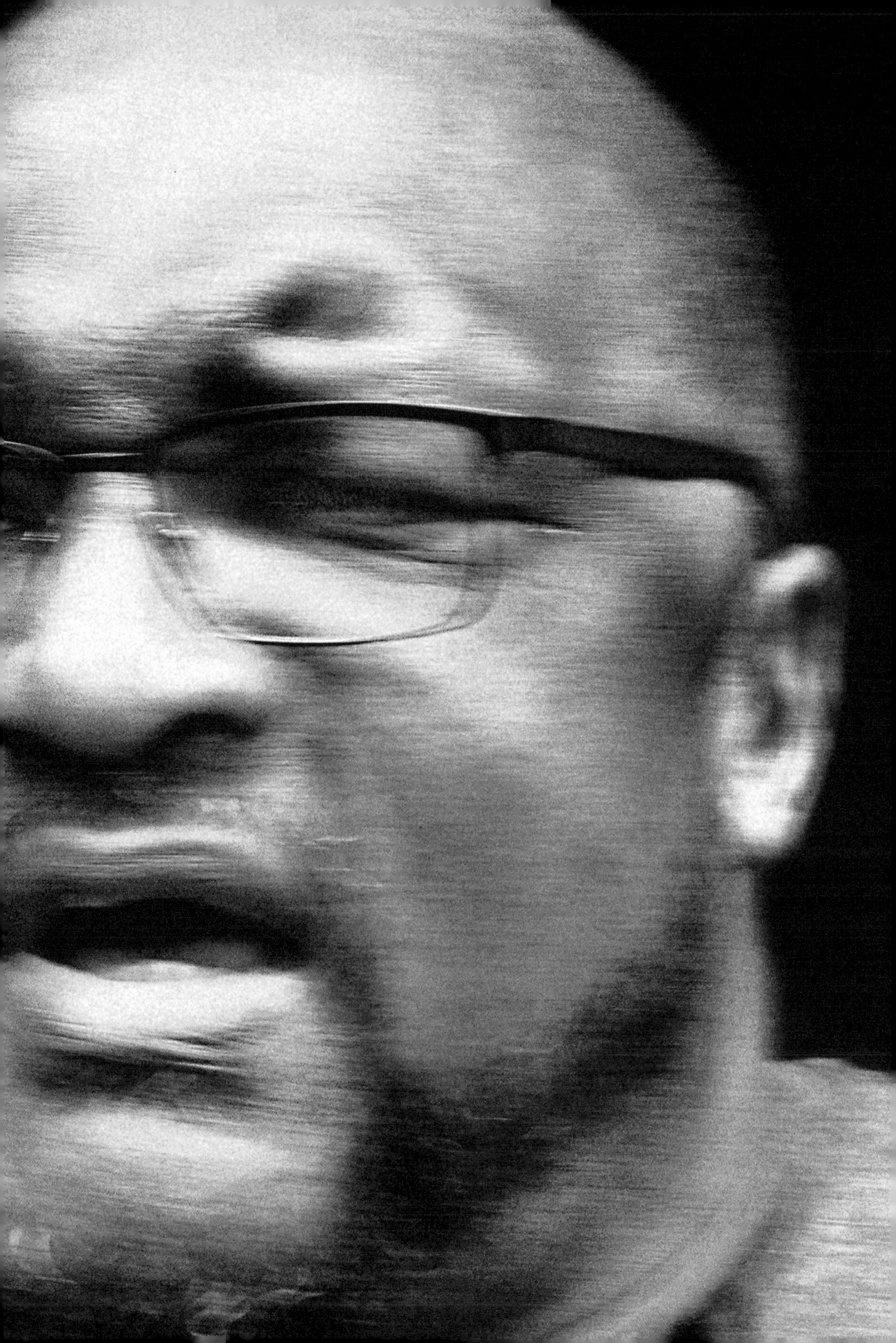

"I know you committed this crime. You had better come clean with me. If you don't, I am going to the judge and I'm going to ask for a life sentence on you."

"YOU NEED TO

COME CLEAN

RIGHT NOW"

Eddie Lowery

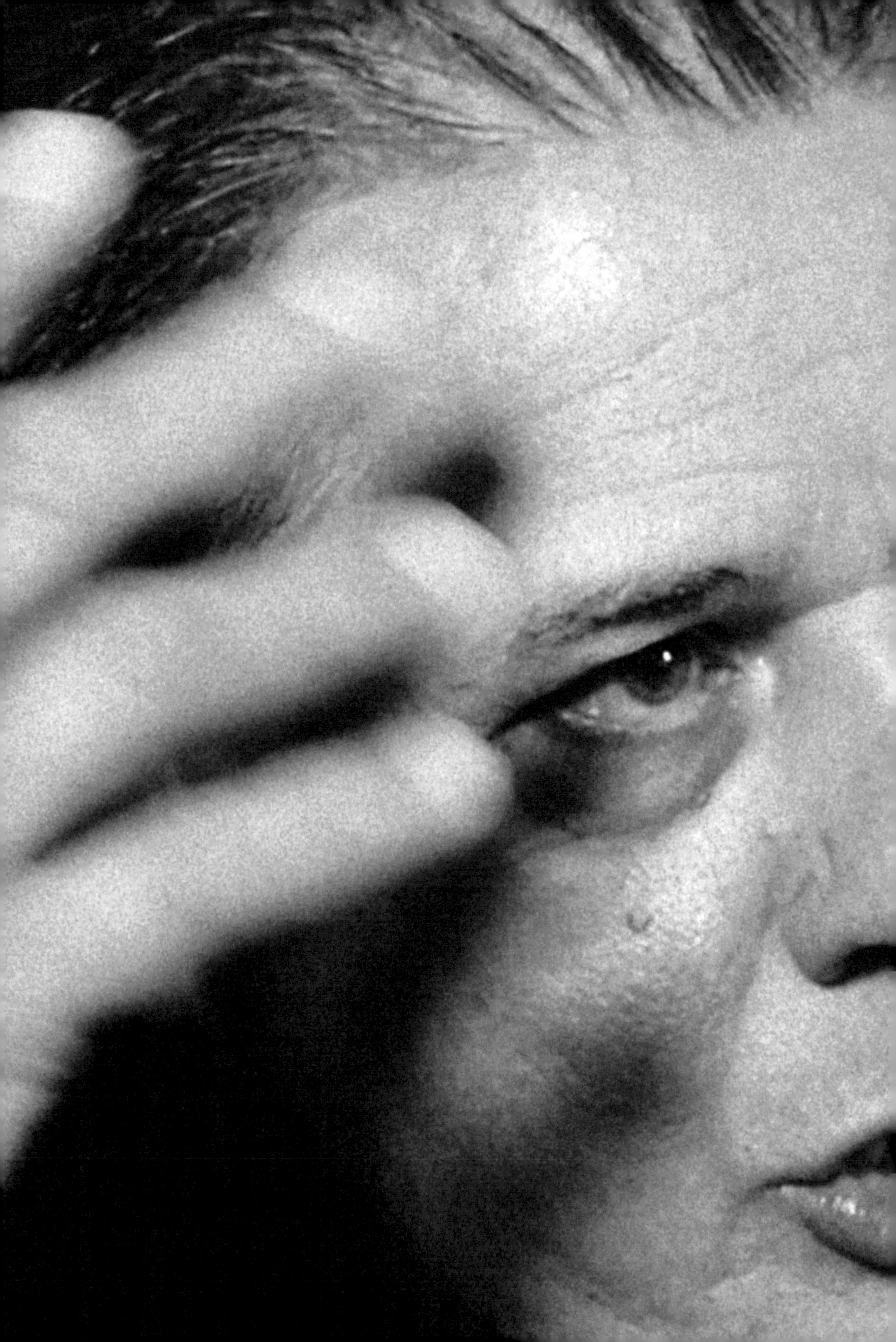

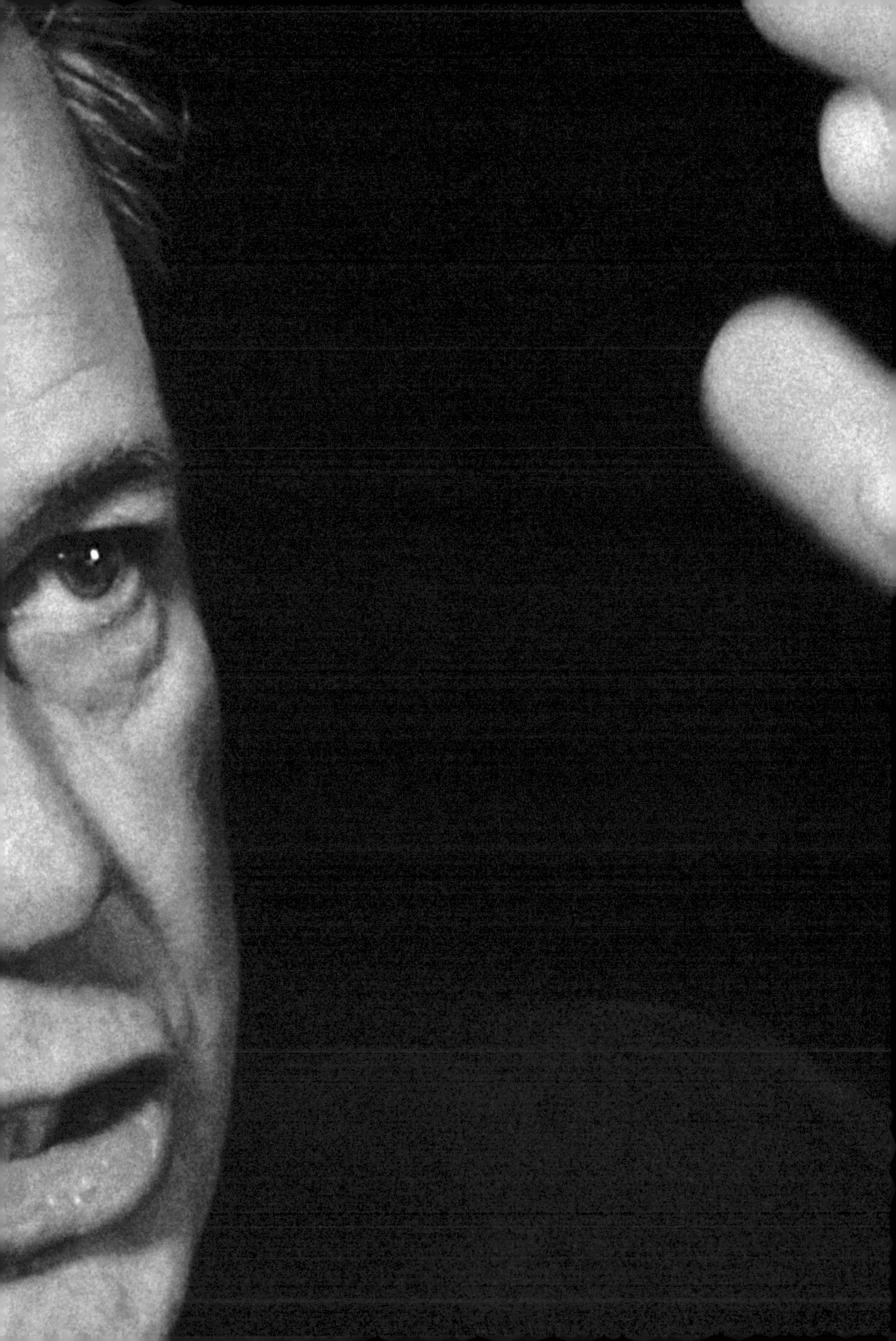

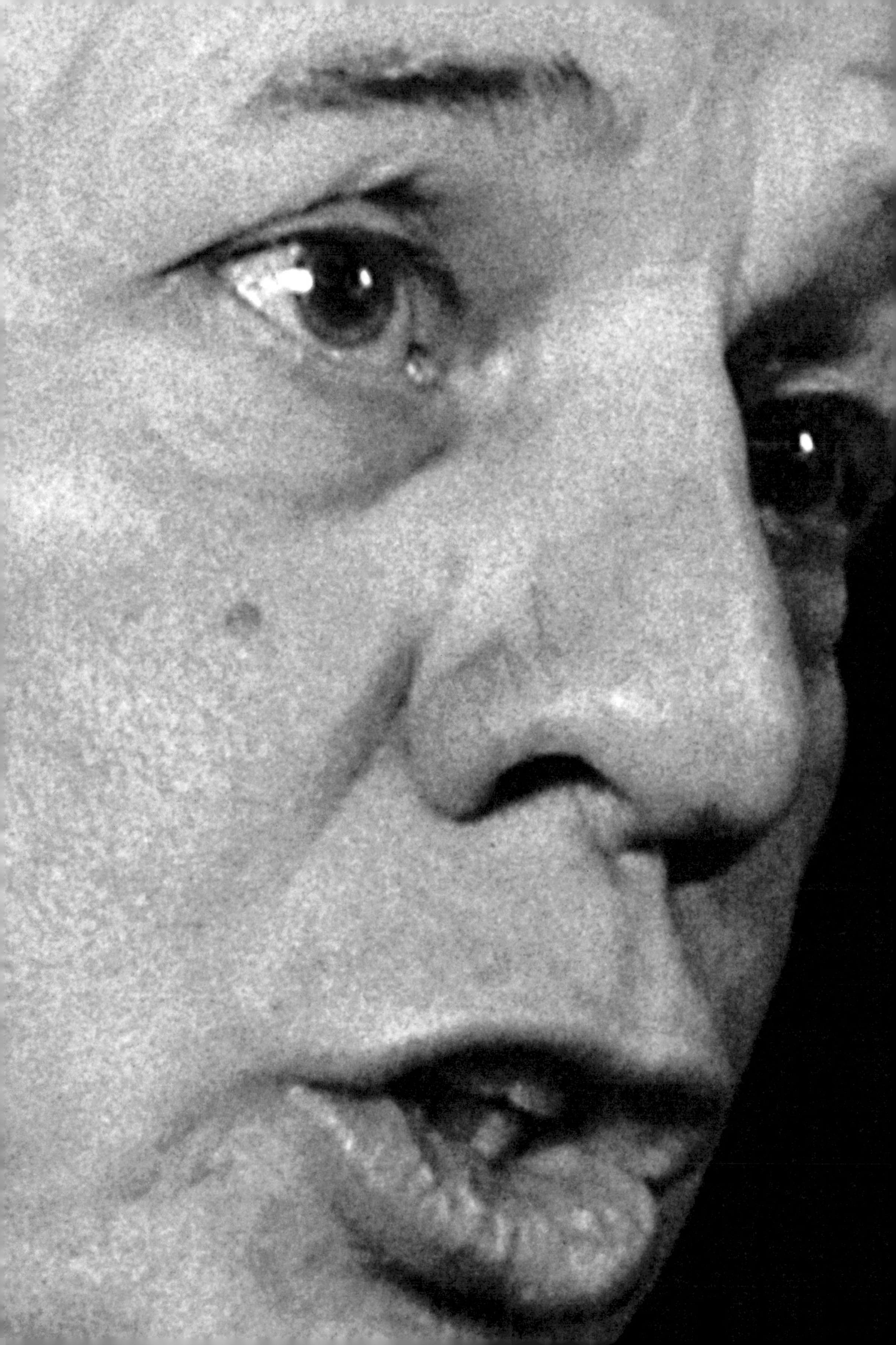

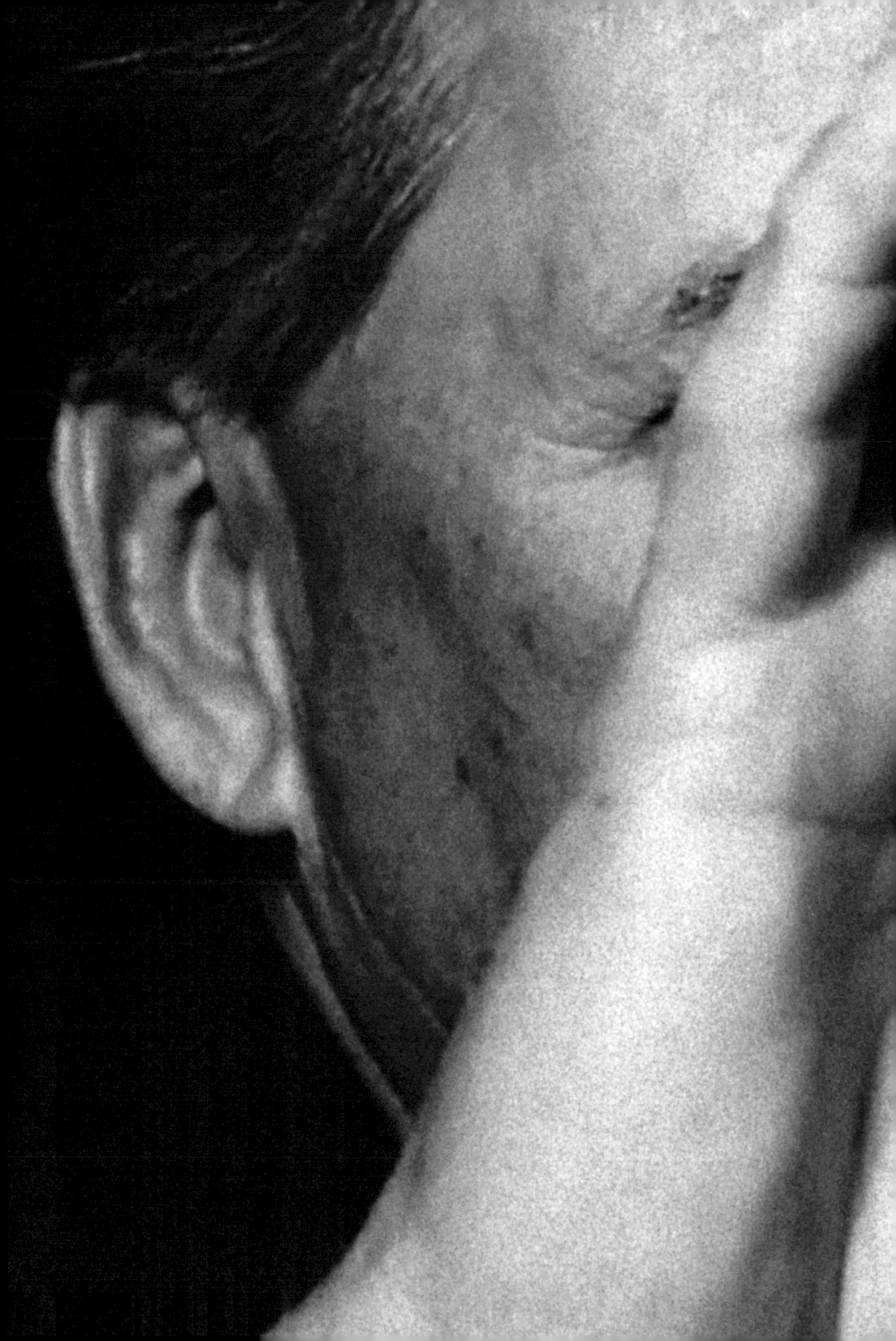

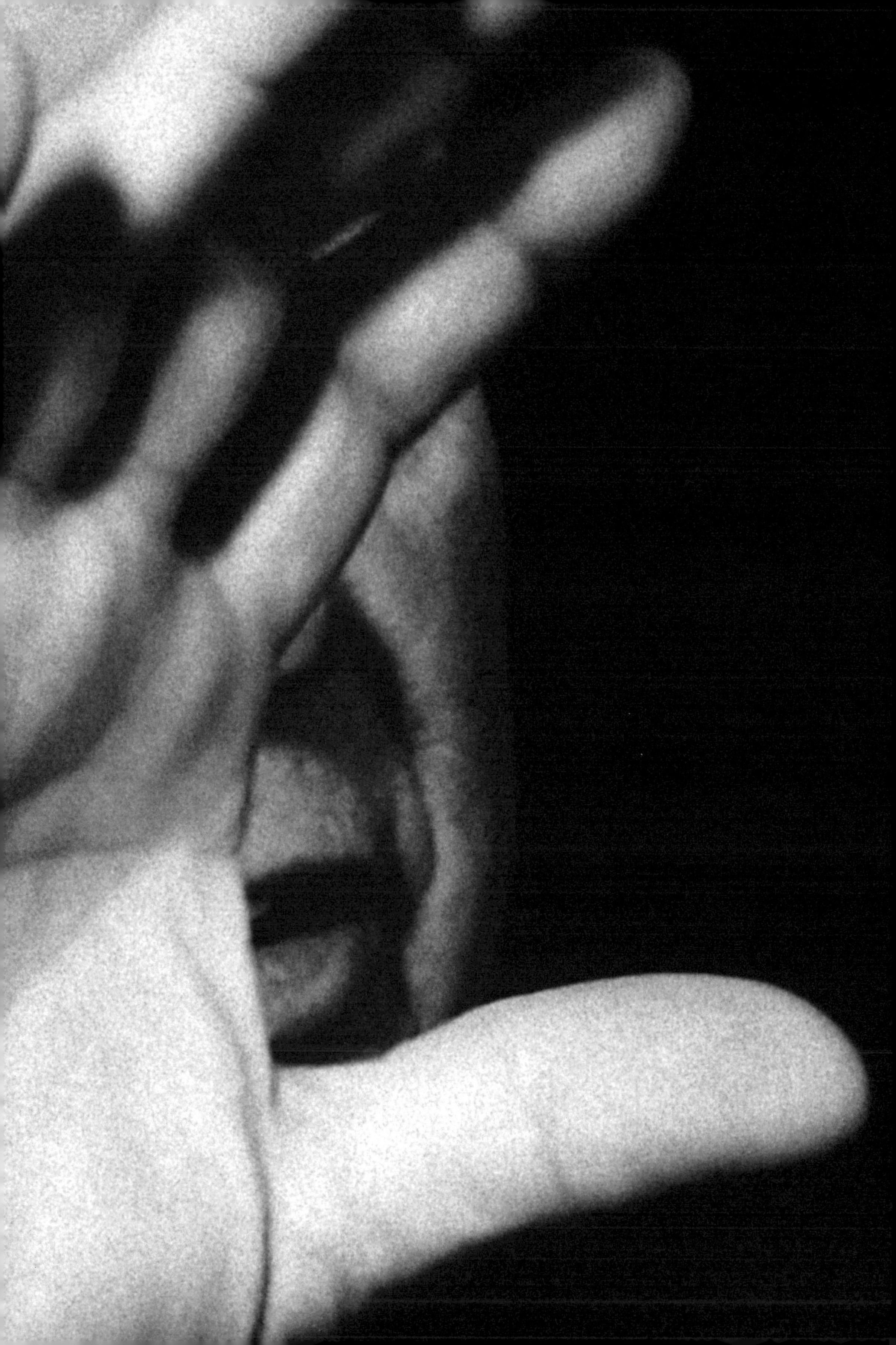

The detective showed me pictures of the autopsy. He was slamming his fist on the table.

"You know something about the crime. If you don't cooperate, you are going to get the death penalty. I am going to put you on death row."

The detective grabbed my arm. "This is where the needle's going to go if you don't cooperate."

He shows me pictures of death row. "This is where you are going to live until you die. You will never be able to hold your family again."

Finally, he says,

"I am tired of your BS. You have never been in jail. You have a clean record. I am going to book you. And you will be fresh meat for those prisoners."

Once I heard that, I thought jailhouse rape.

Christopher Ochoa

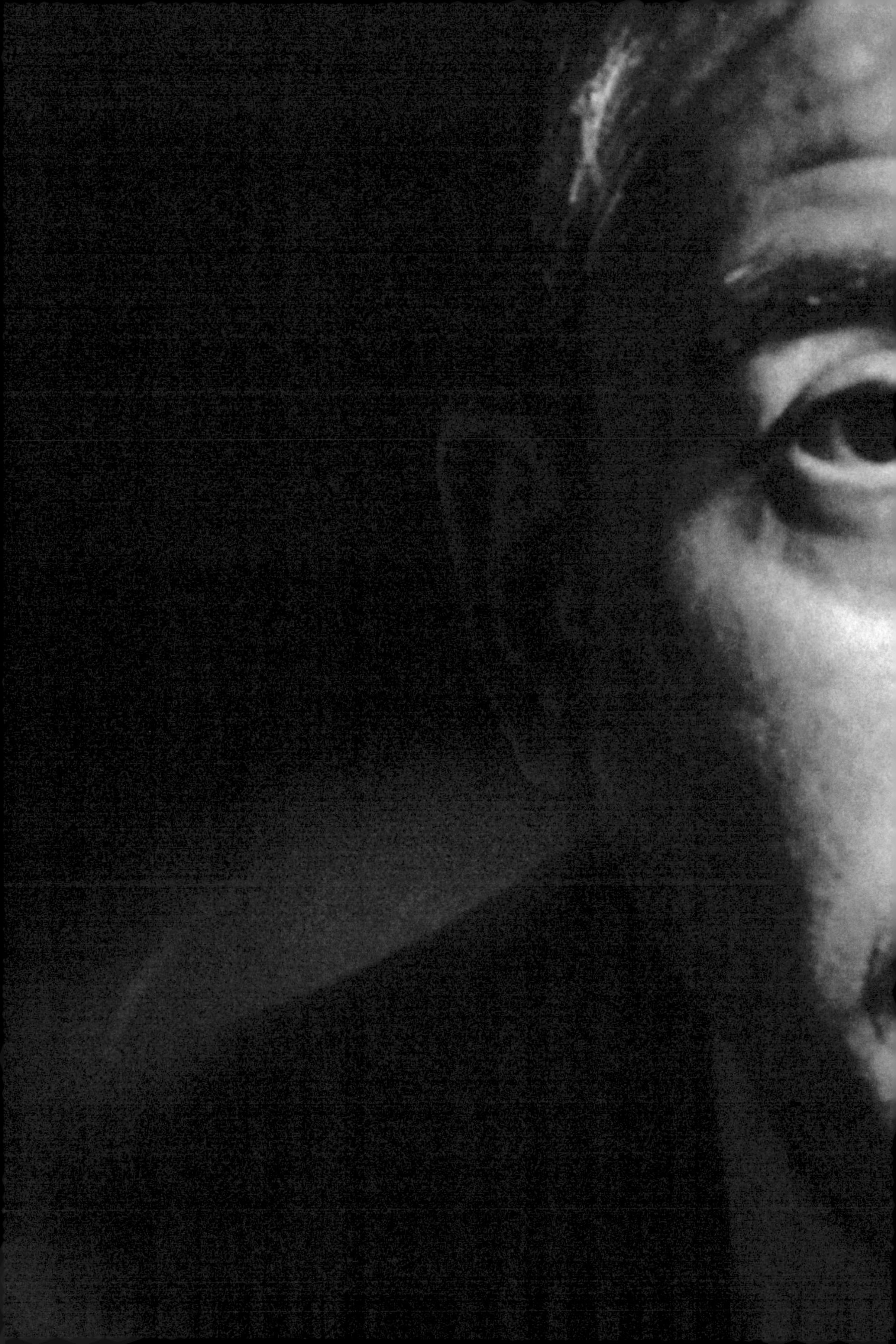

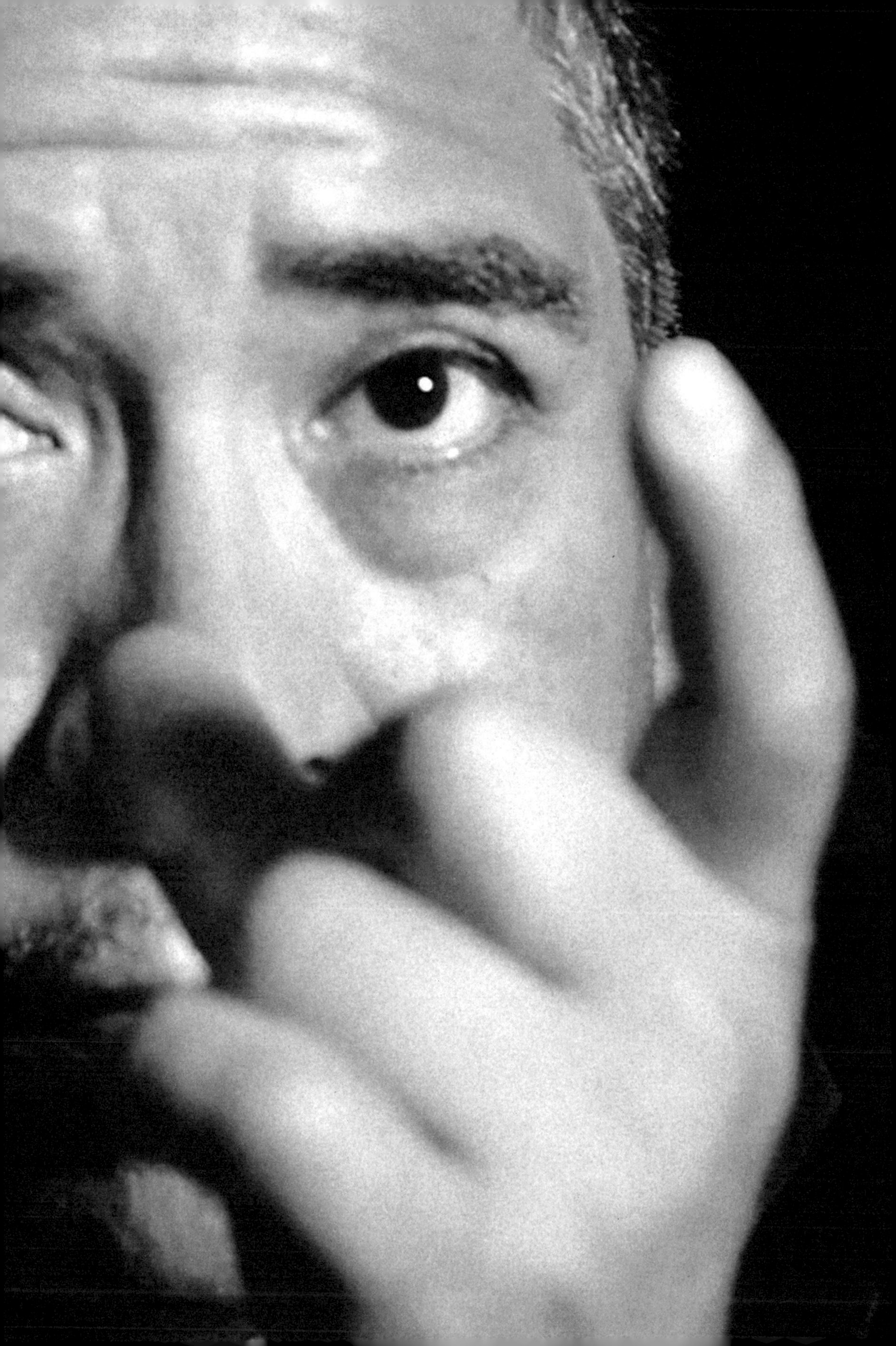

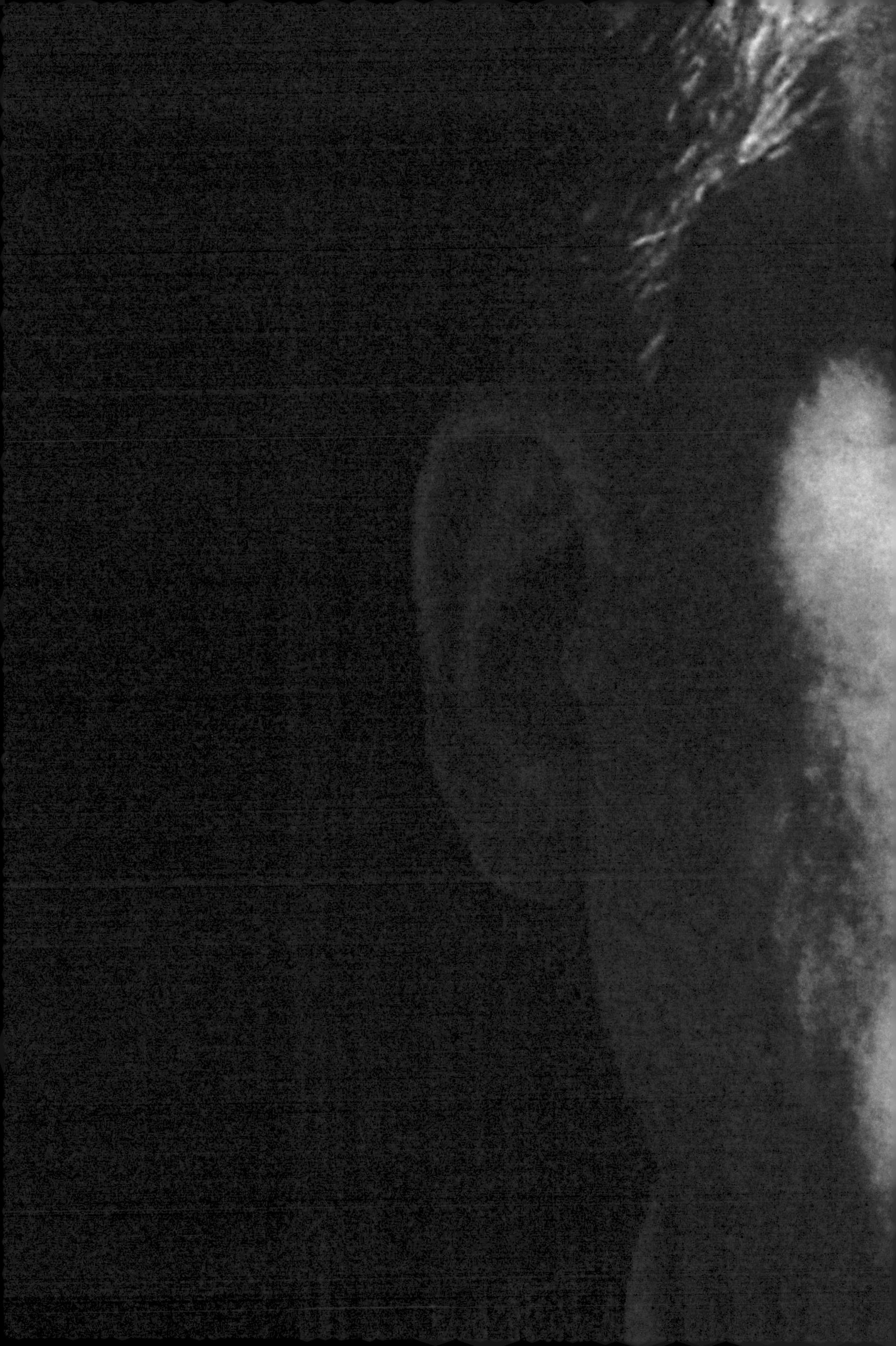

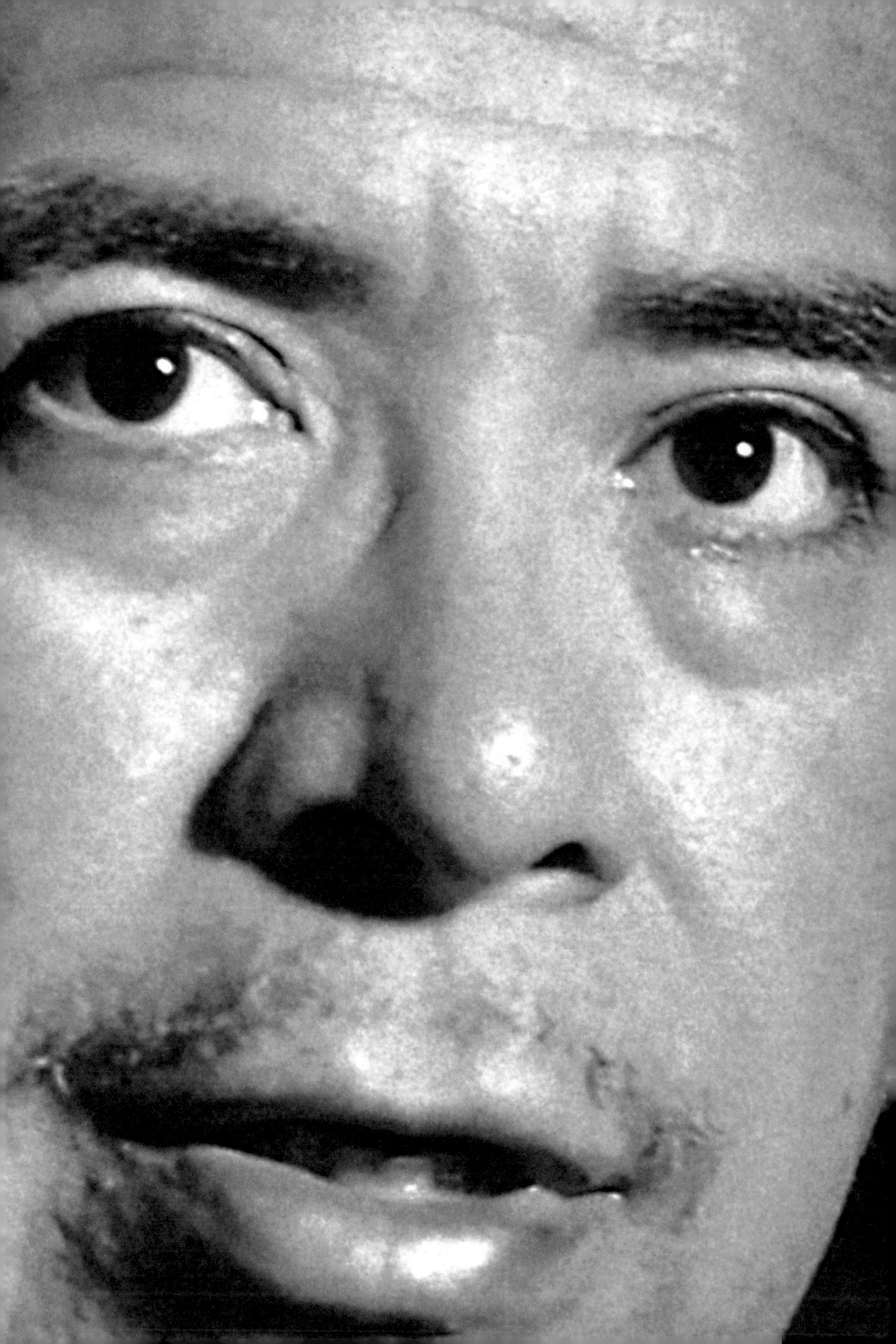

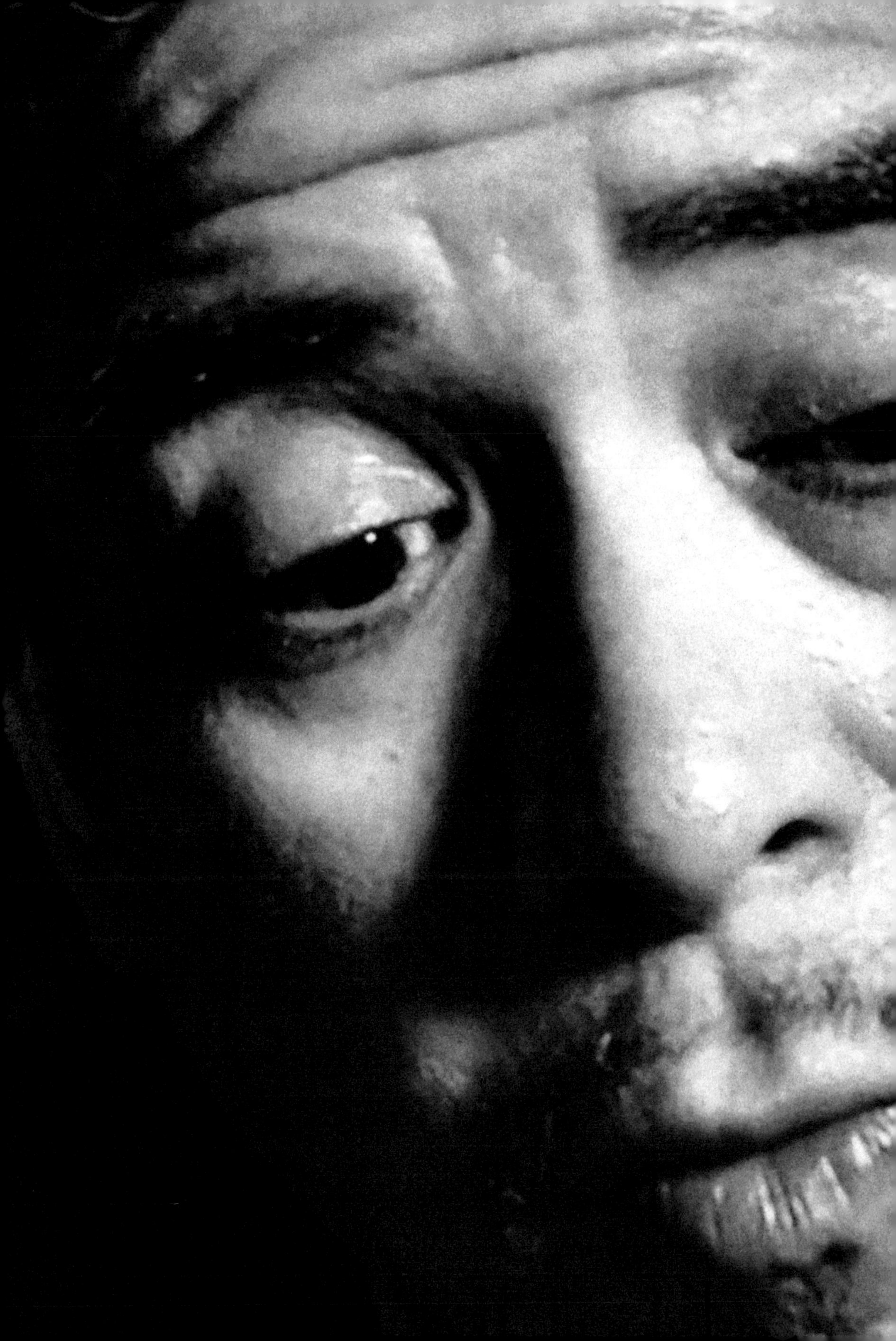

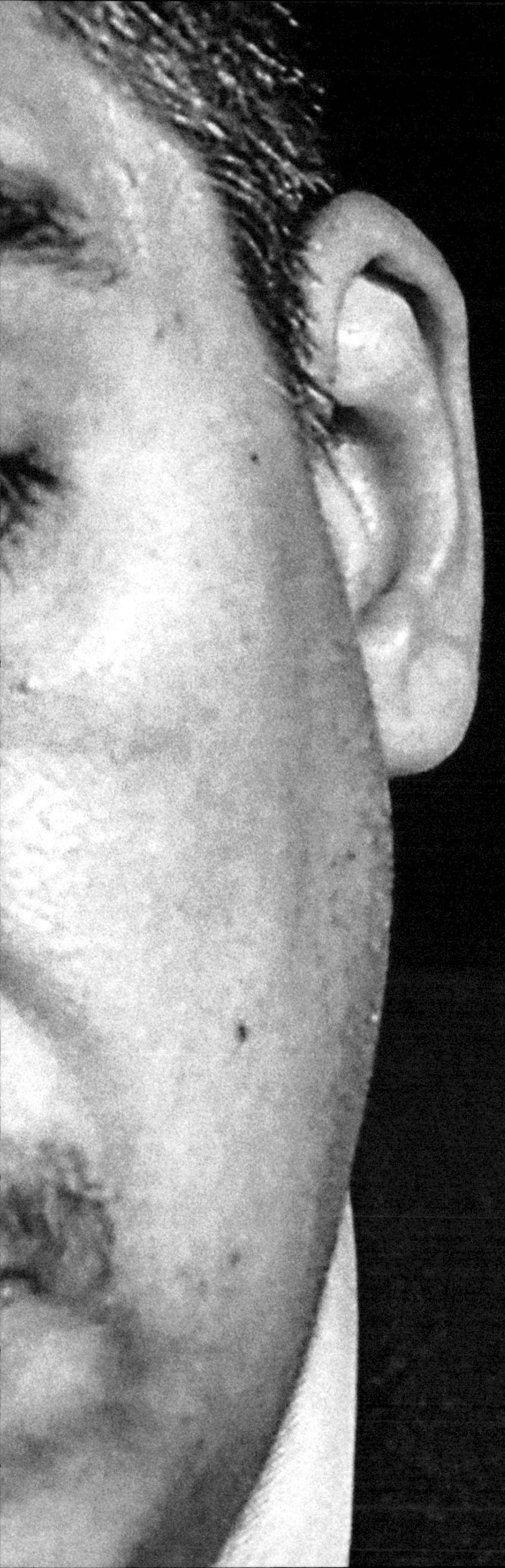

"What the fuck are you looking at?"

"You know that you fucking did it."

"YOU ARE GOING TO JAIL.
YOU ARE GOING
to JAIL FOREVER!

"DON'T FUCKING
LIE TO ME."

Raymond Santana

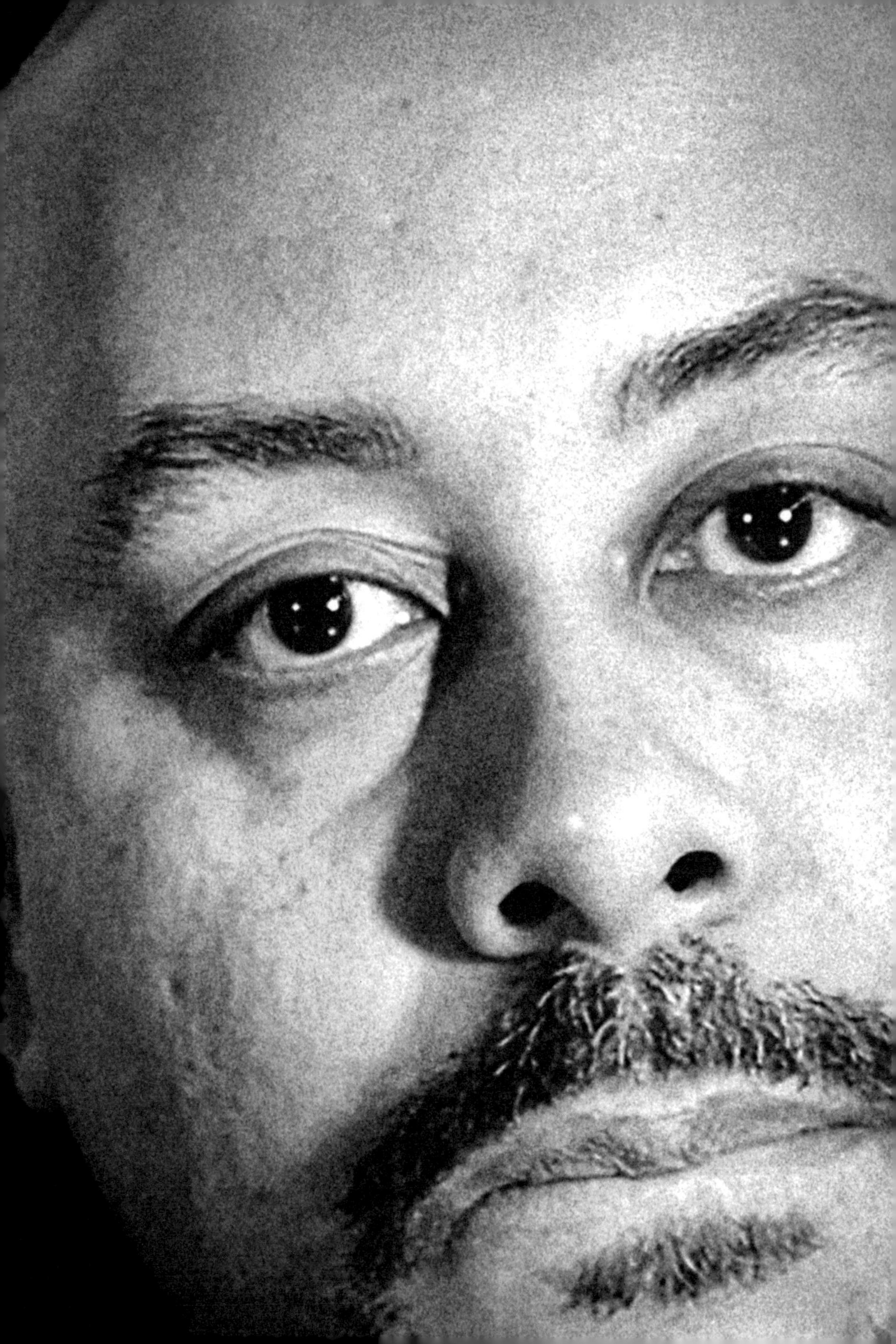

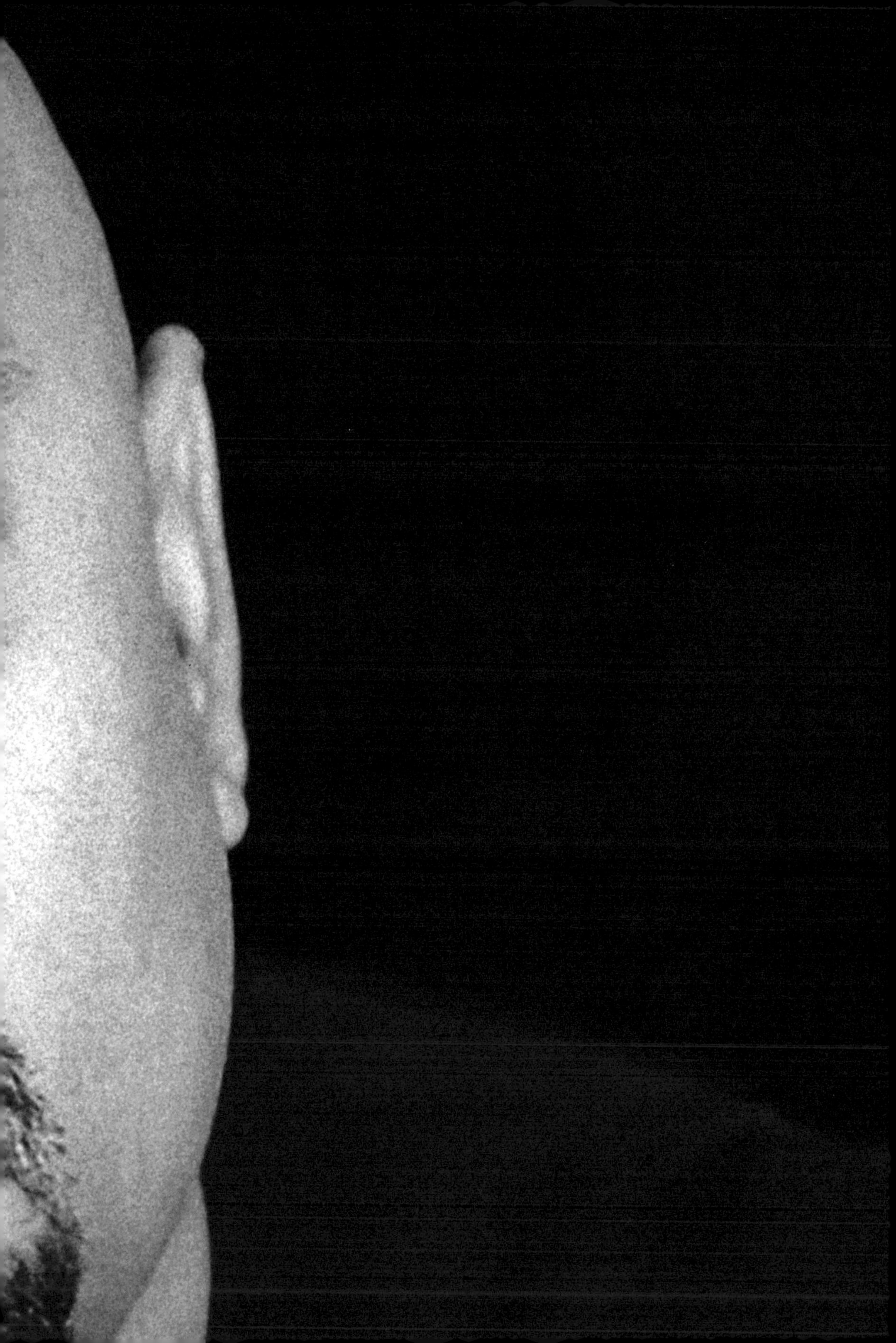

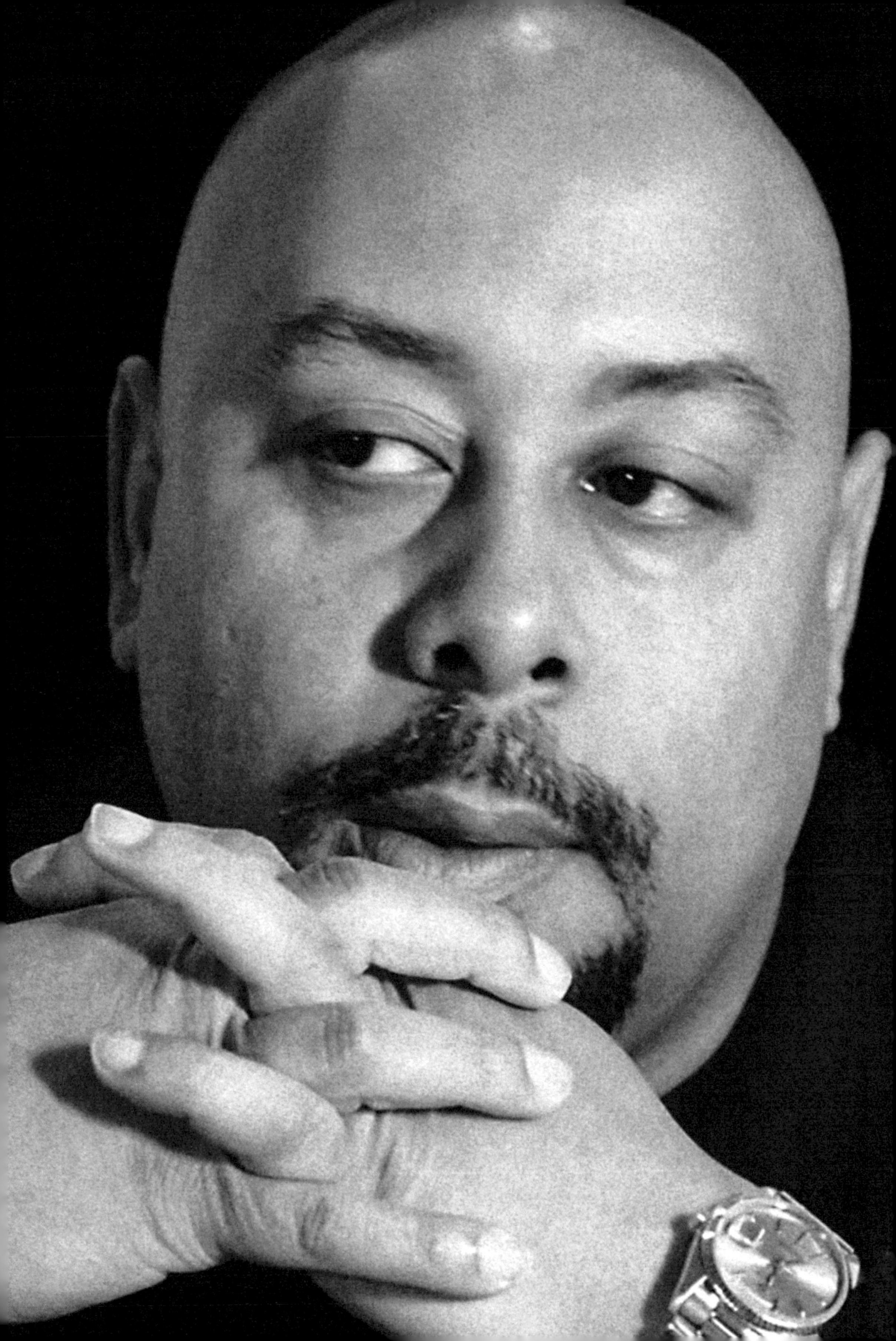

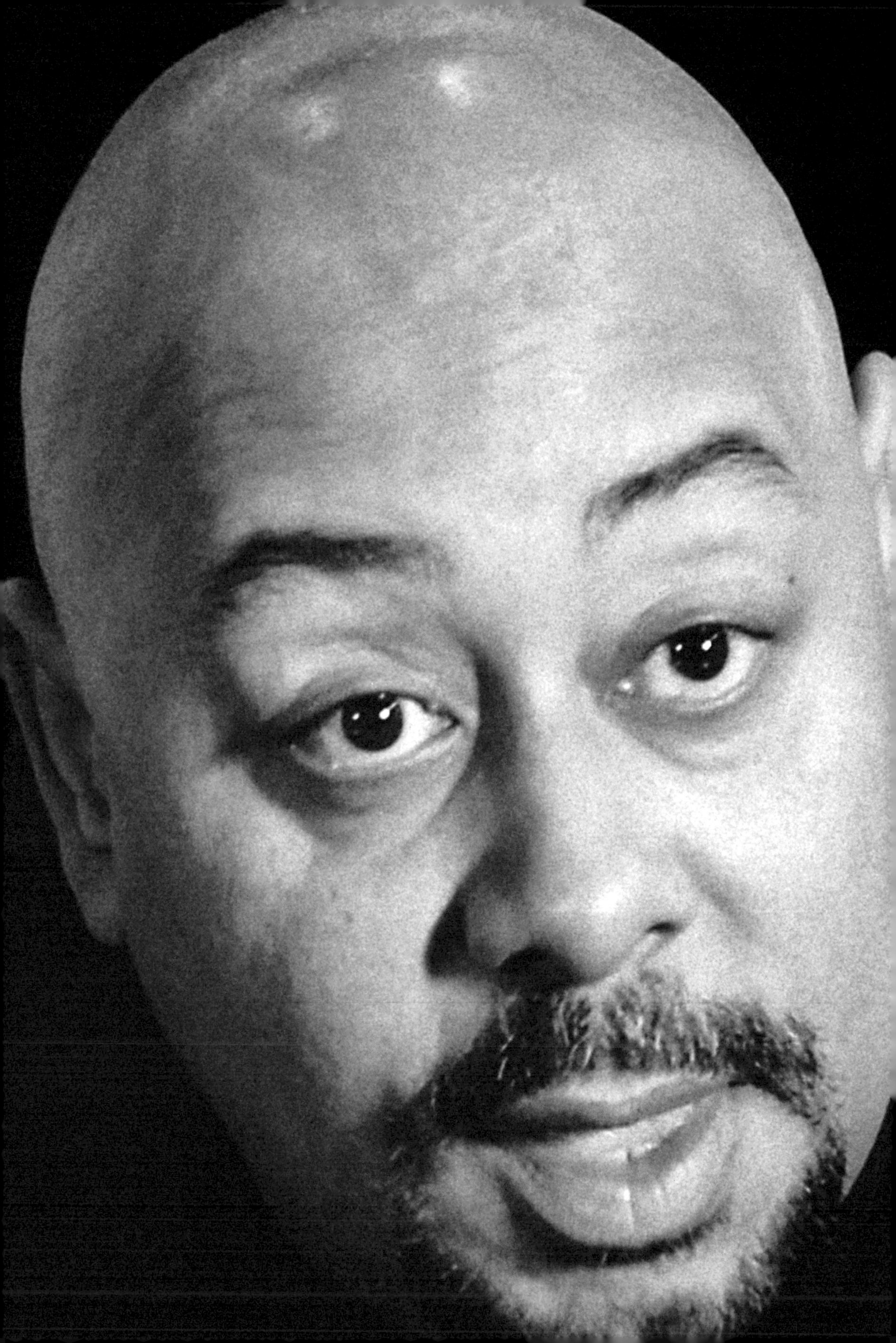

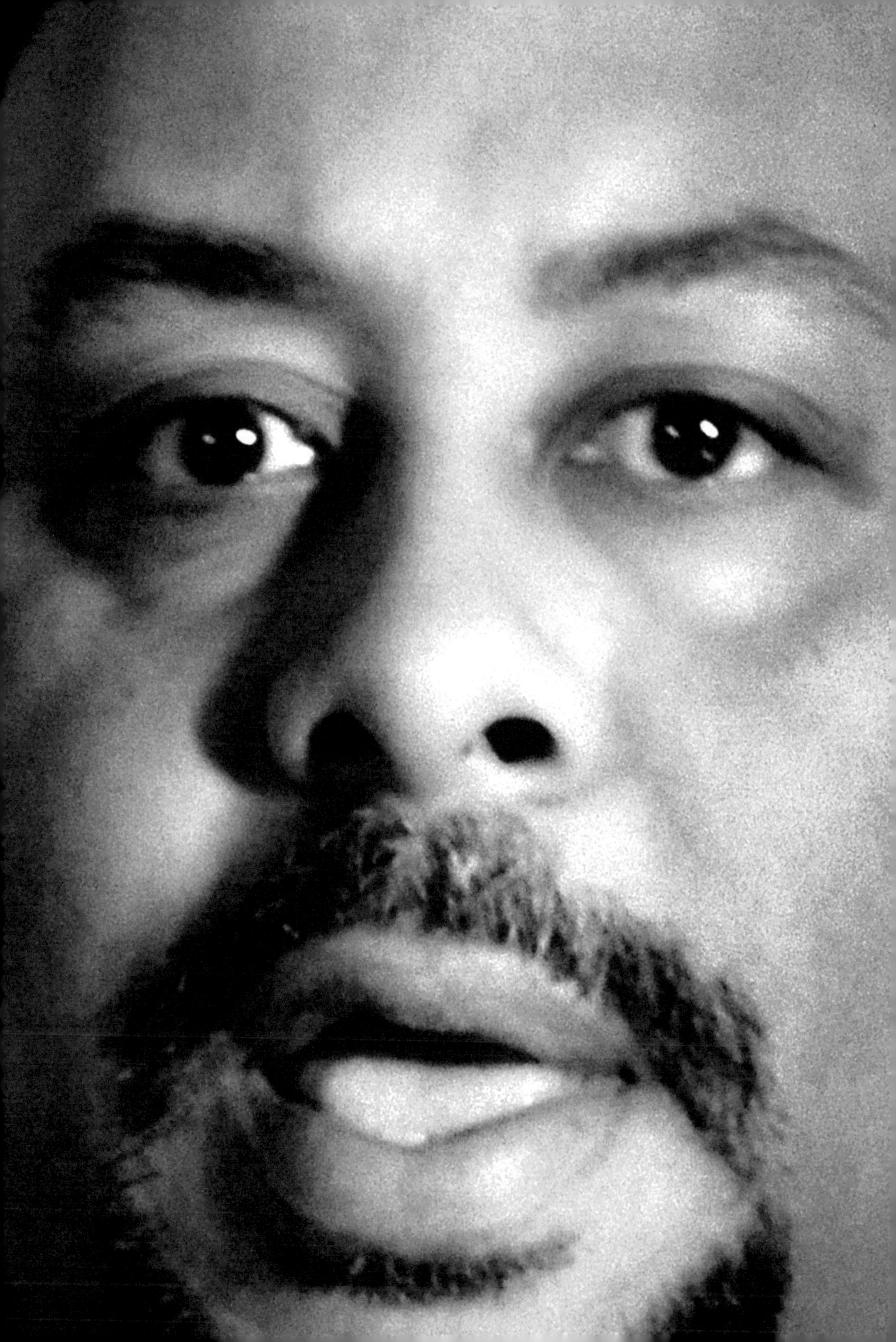

Eddie Lowery

"You ARE SICK"

"You ARE DISGUSTING."

"There is something WRONG
with your head"

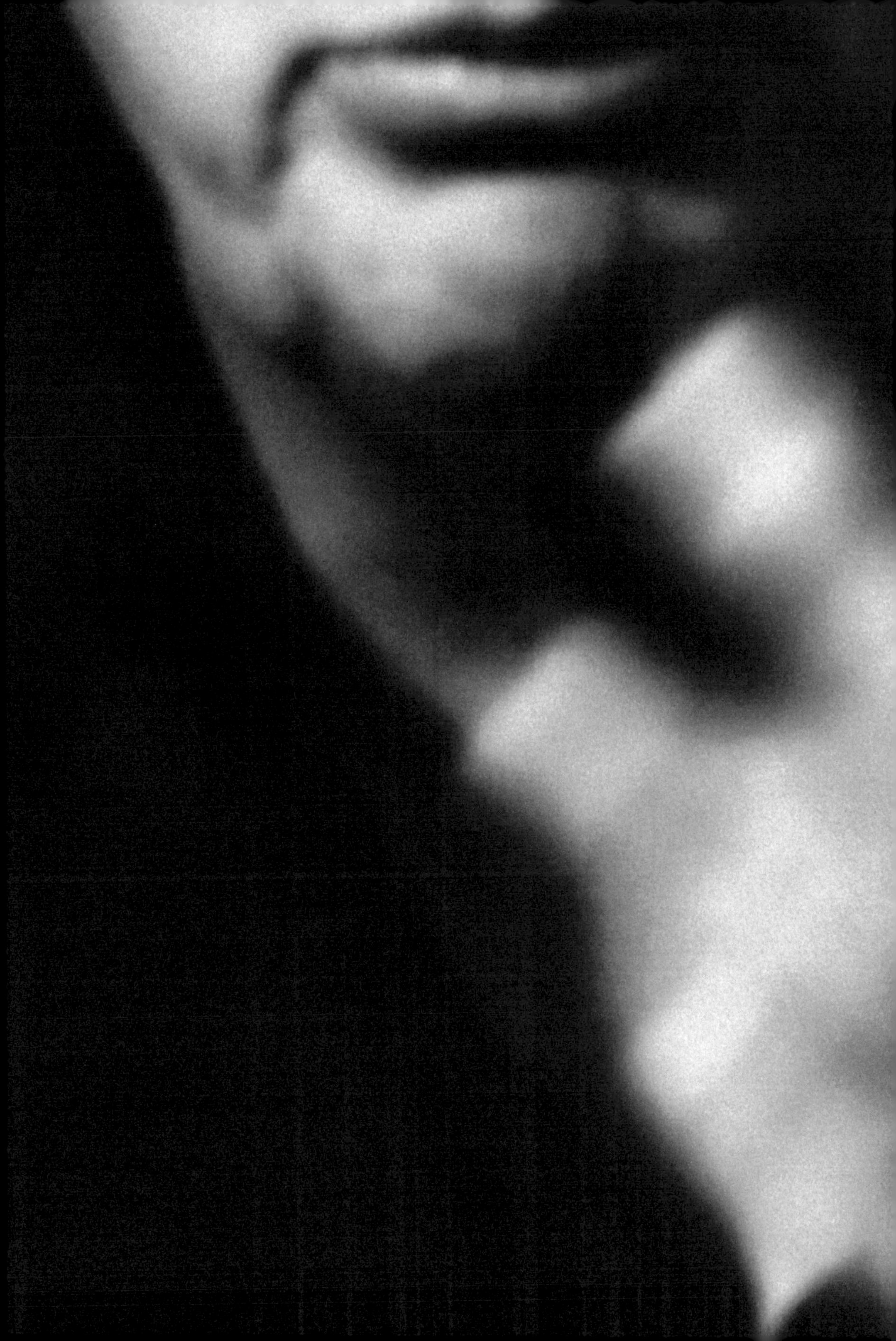

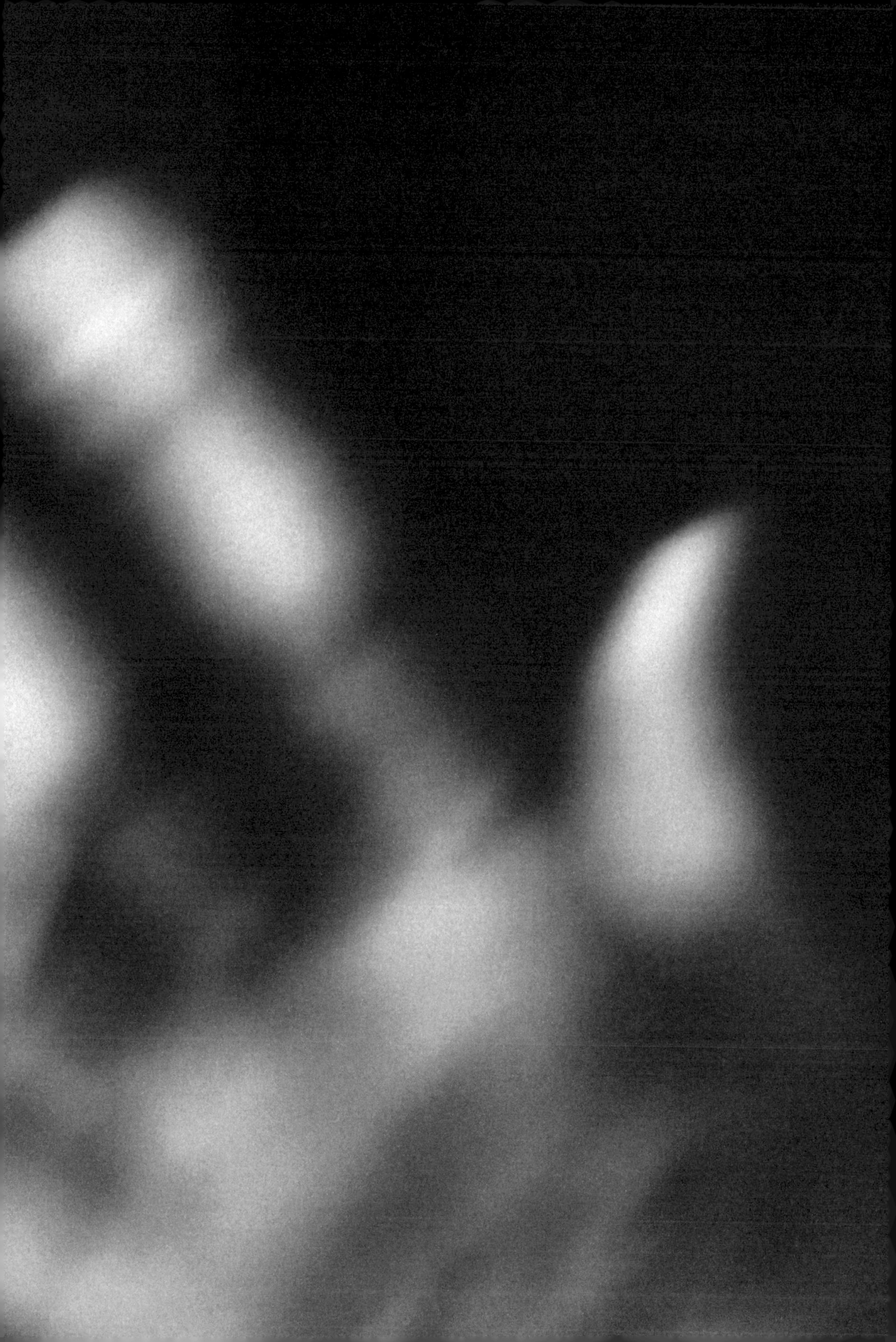

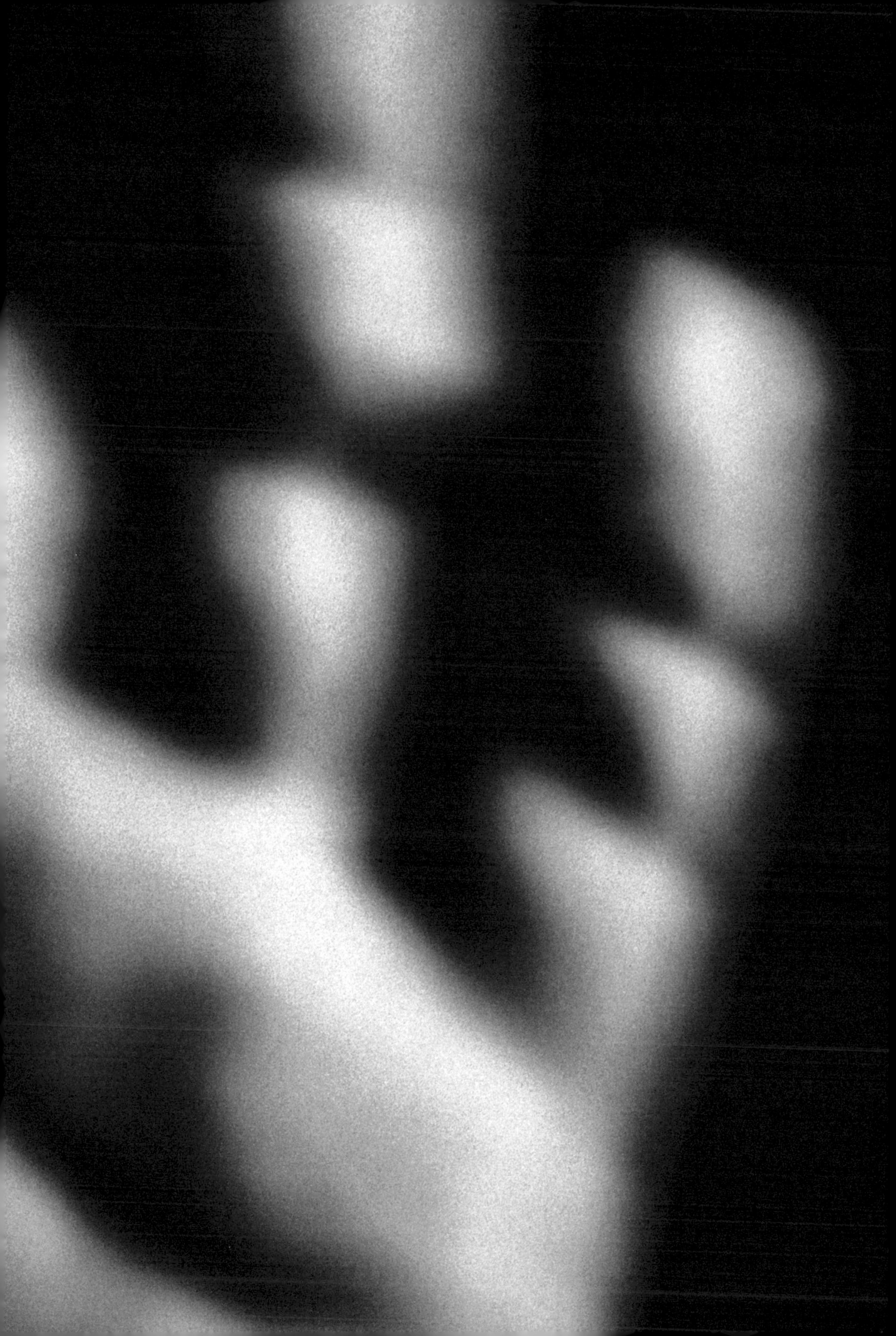

JEFFRY DOSKOVIC

And then another police officer came into the room. He told me that there were other officers in the hallway who wanted to harm me. He was holding them off but he couldn't do so indefinitely.

He advised me to help myself.

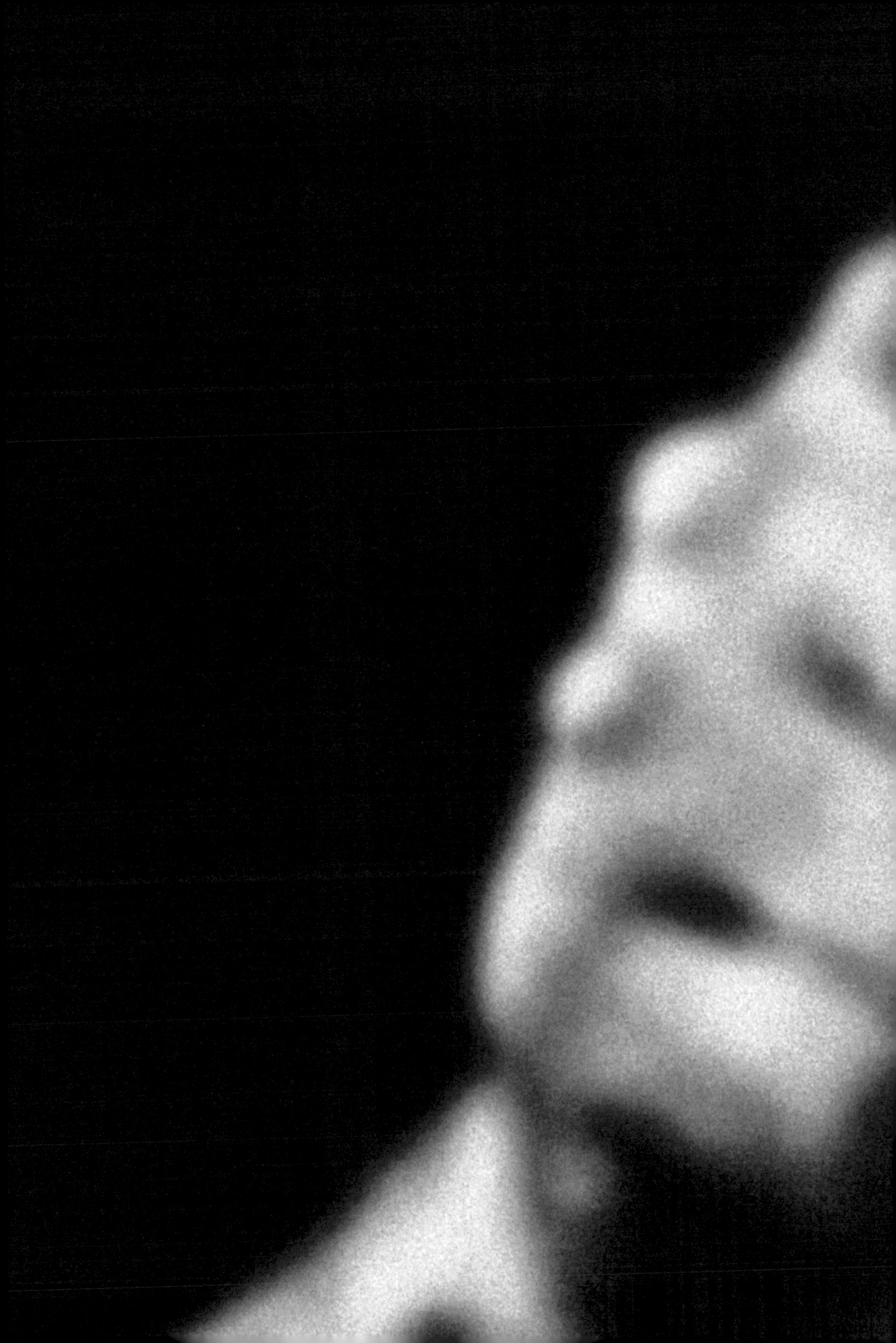

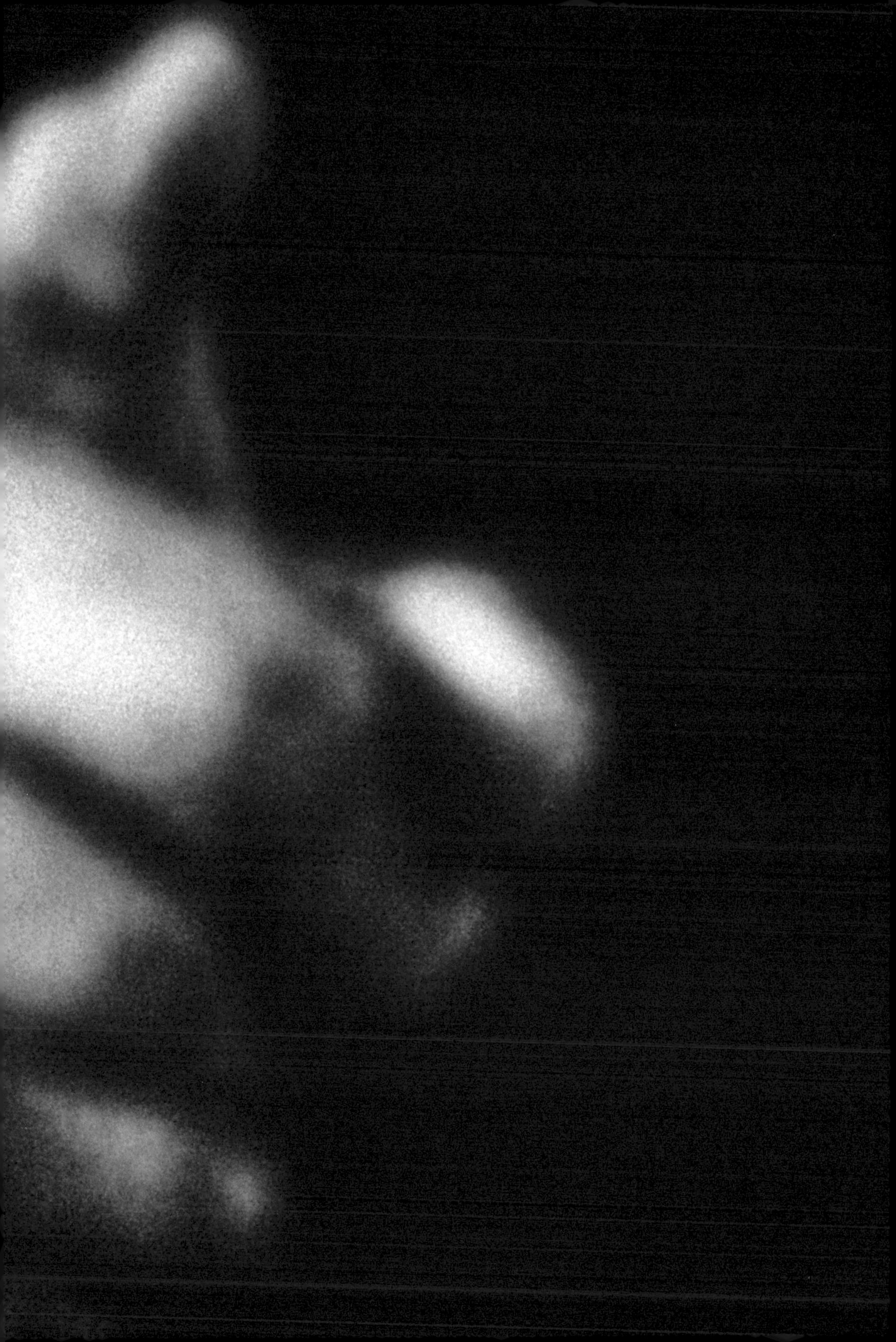

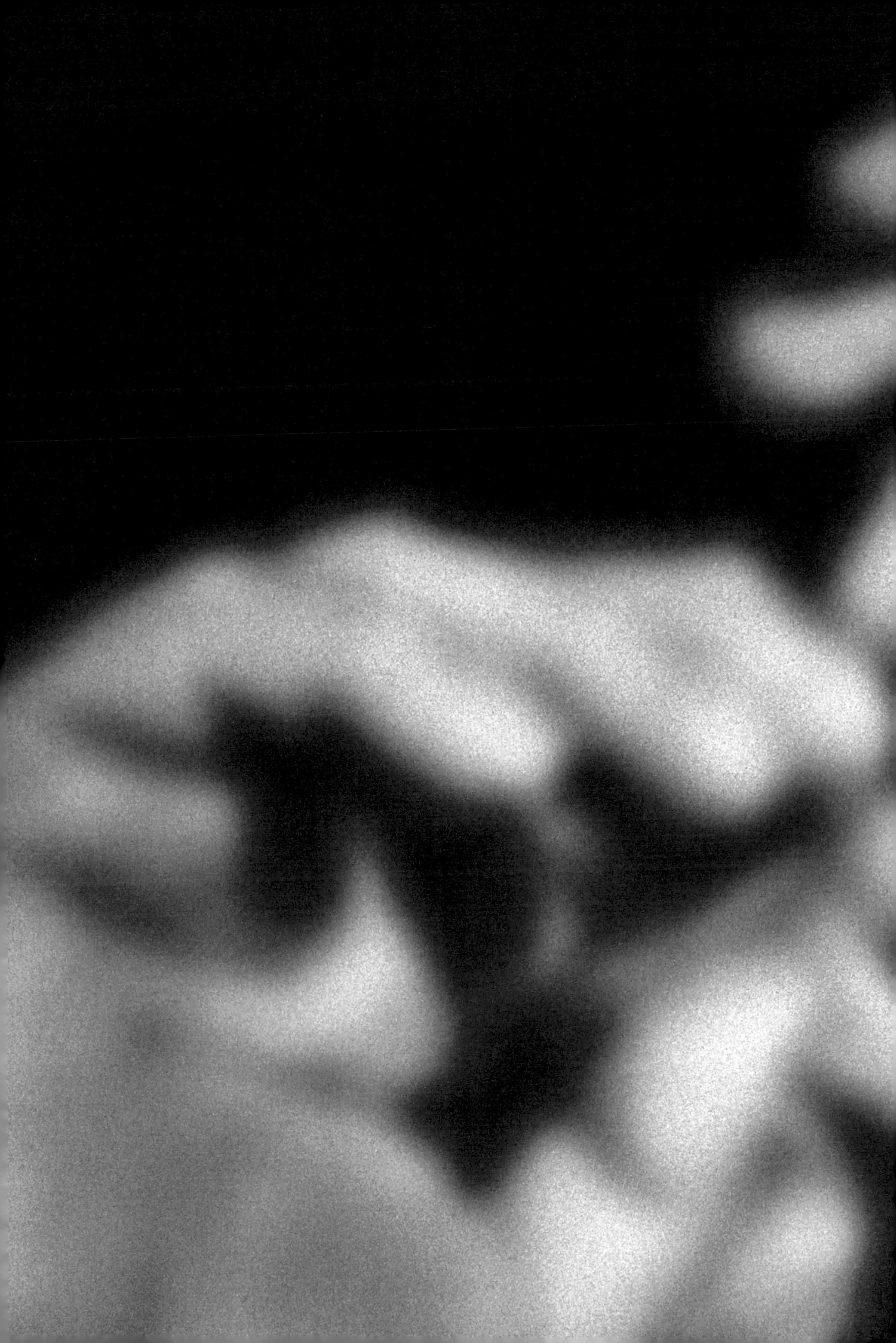

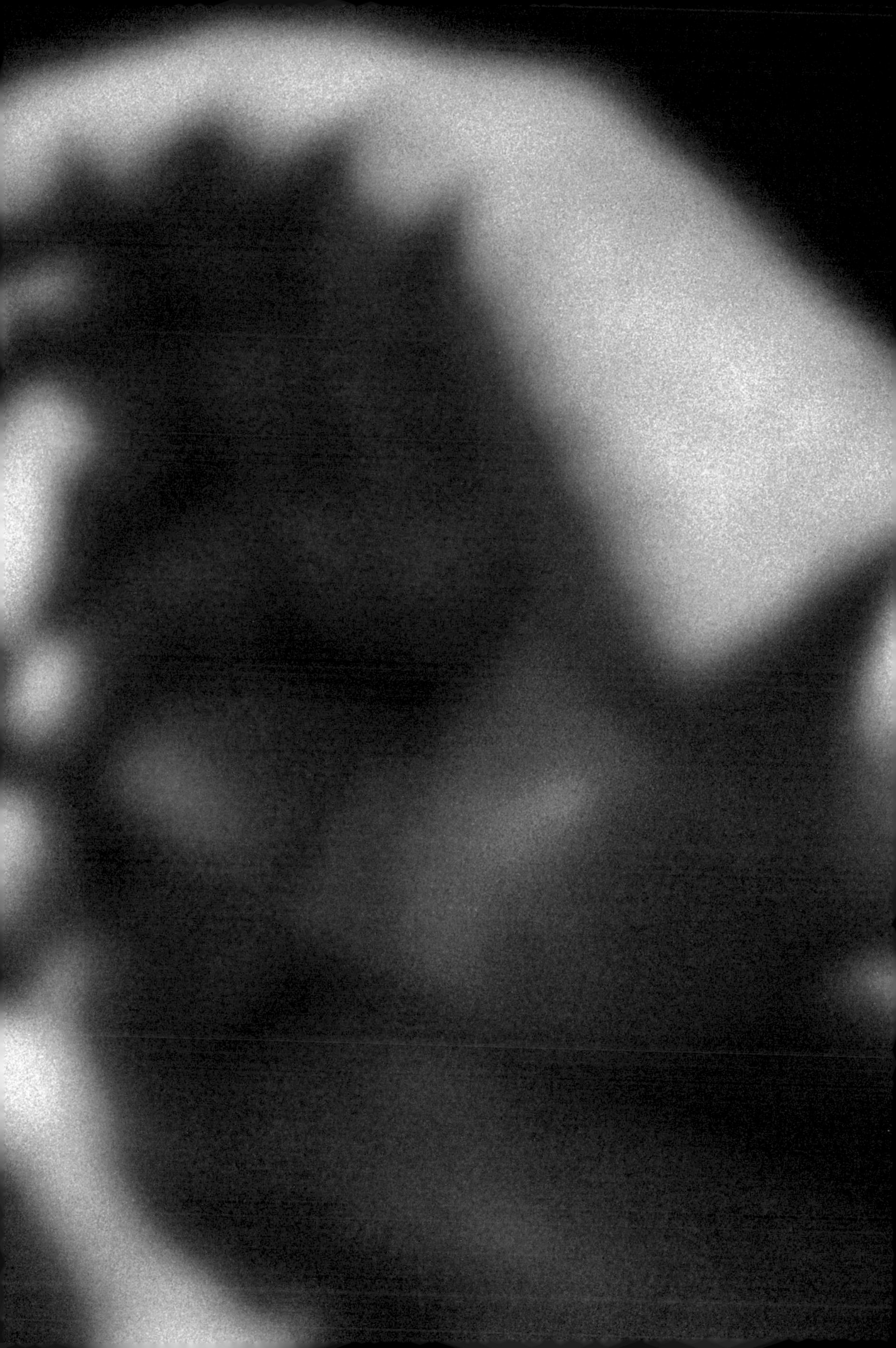

Eddie Lowery

Raymond Santana

Christopher Ochoa

Jeffrey Deskovic

Byron Halsey

Vanessa Gathers

It was just so much pressure.
I didn't know how to handle it.
I was already crying.

I wanted this situation to end.

I did not want the detectives angry.

I was alone and powerless and really frightened.

I feared for my life. They were going to kill me. The cops jump you and there is nothing you can do.

I was scared to death.

Eddie Lowery

Thatls when it came to me.

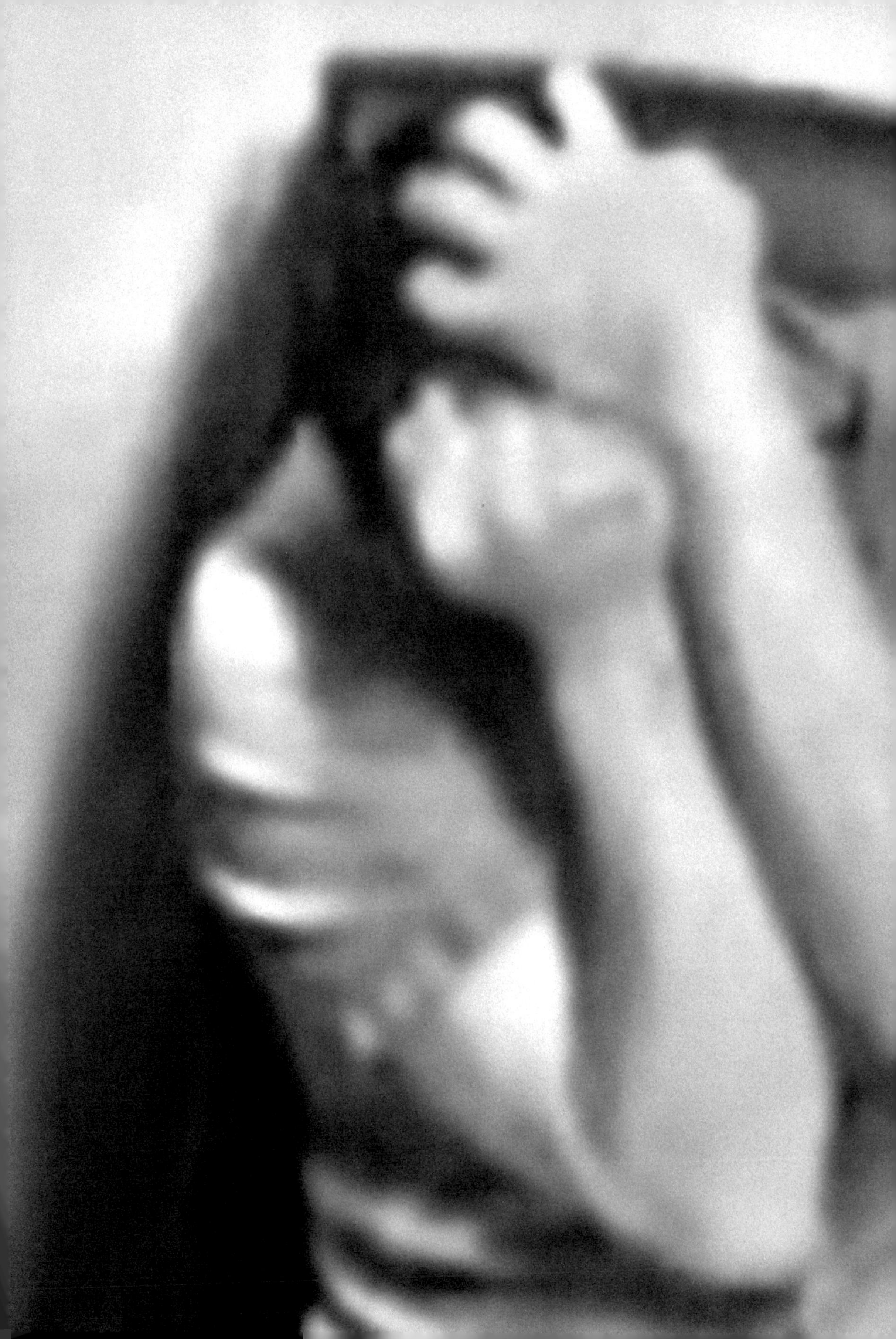

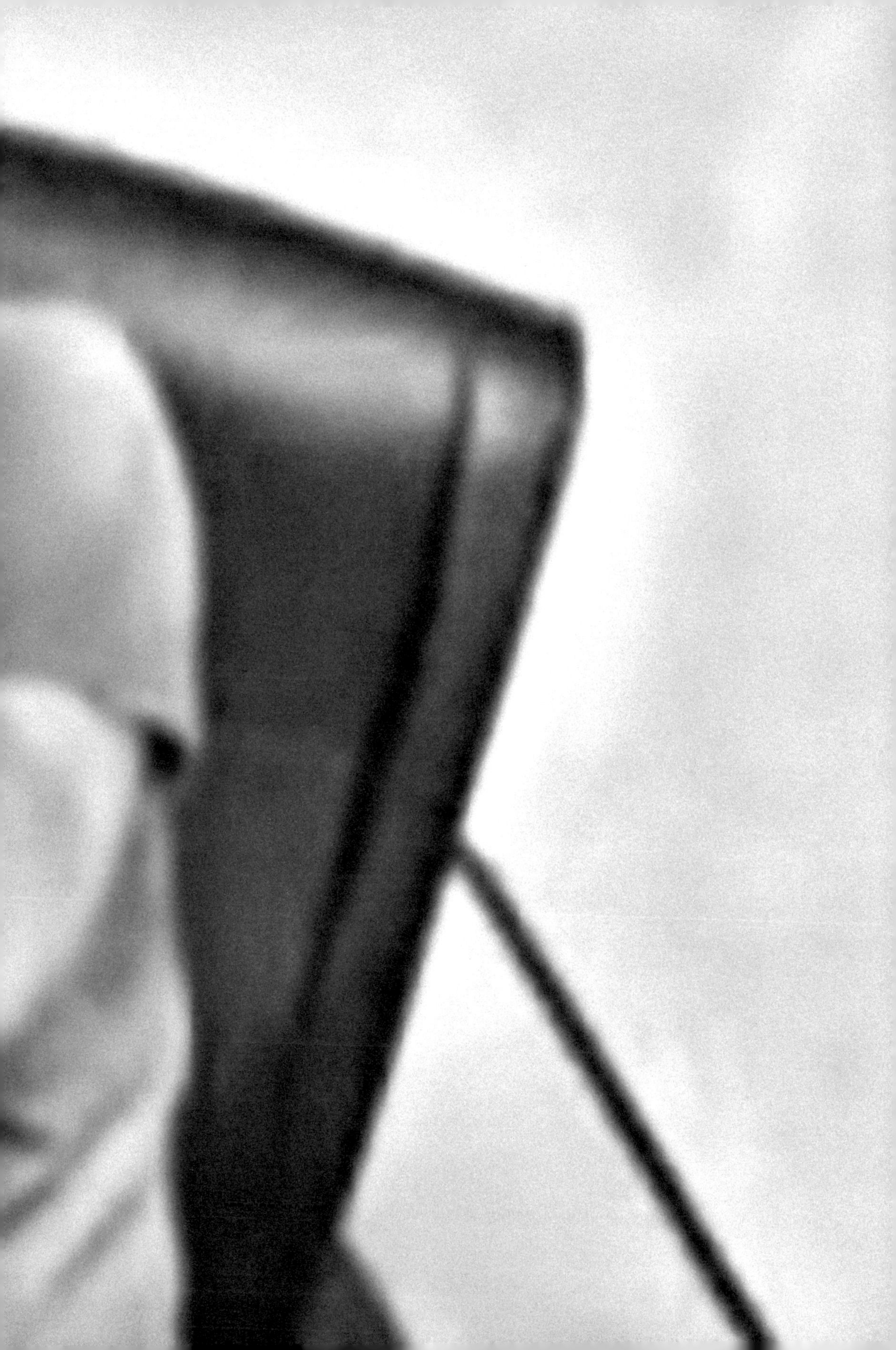

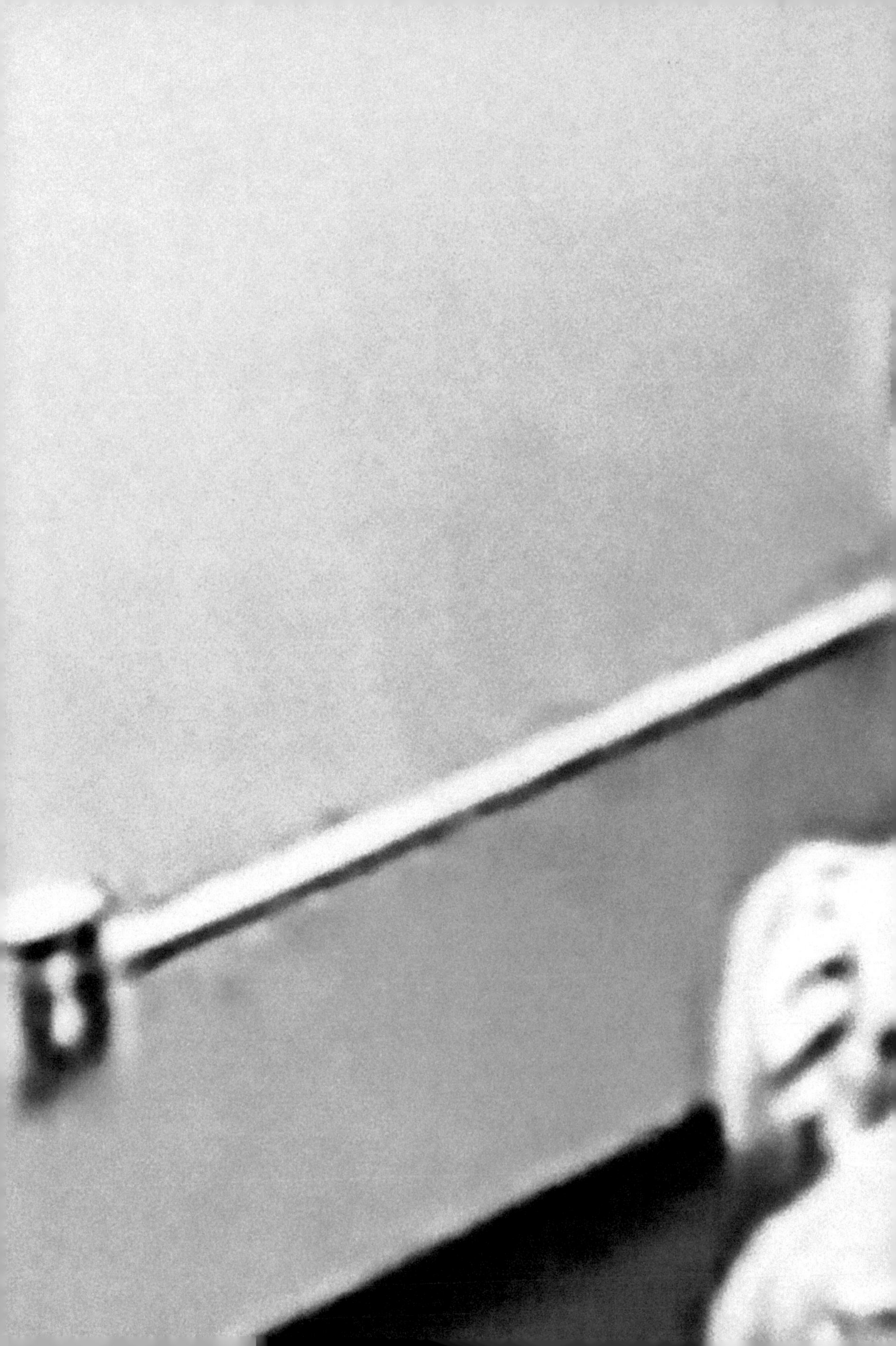

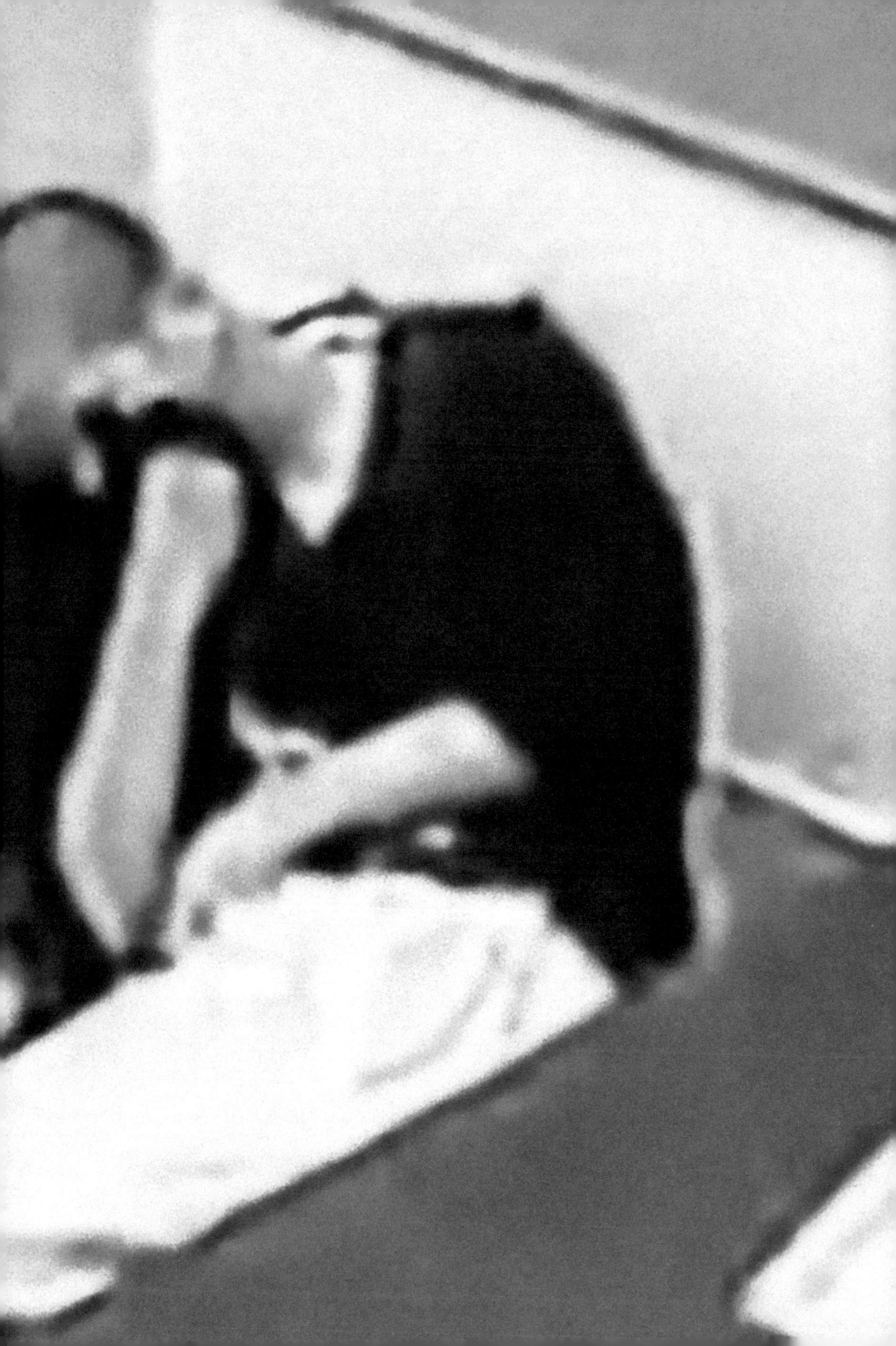

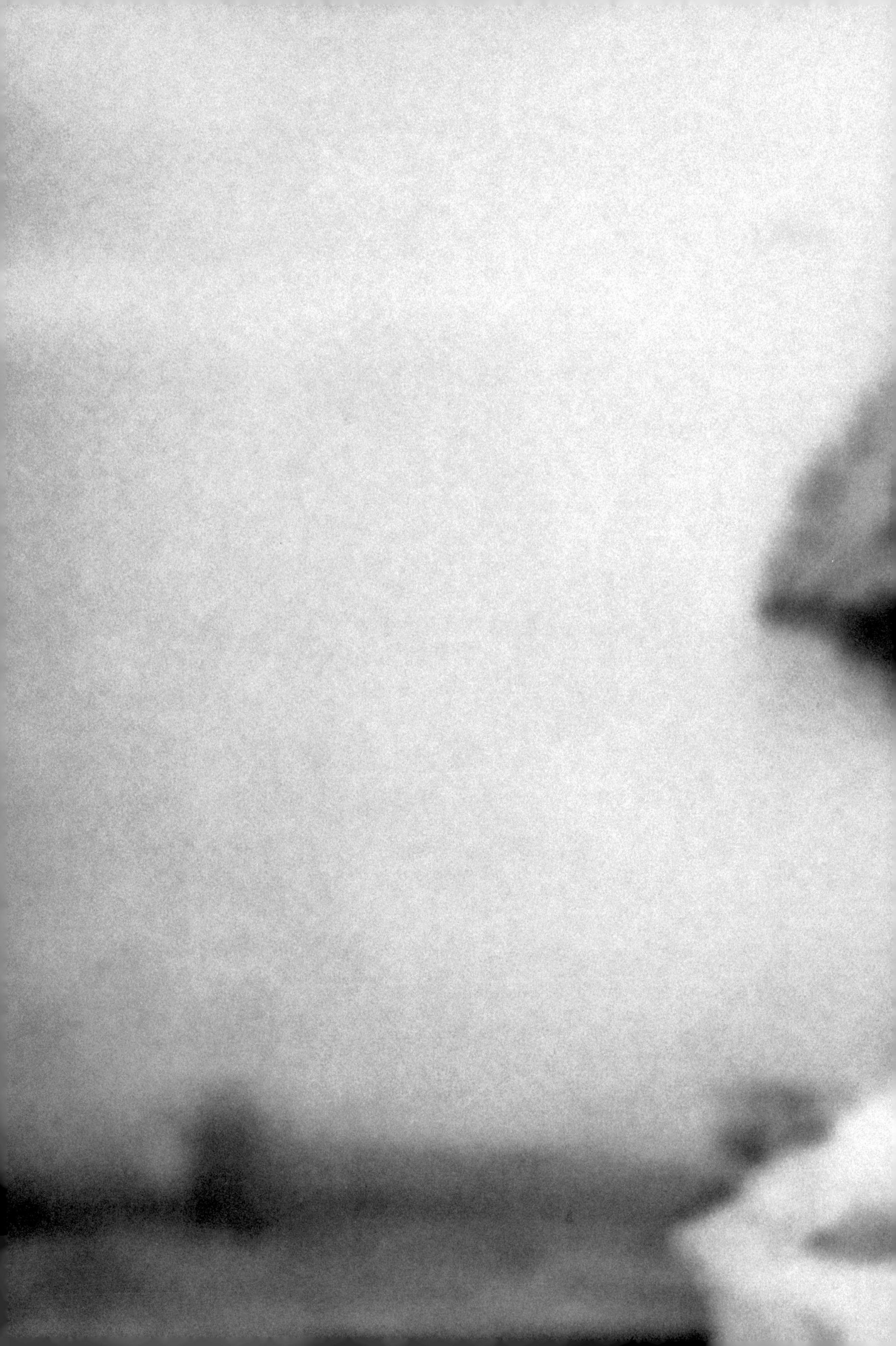

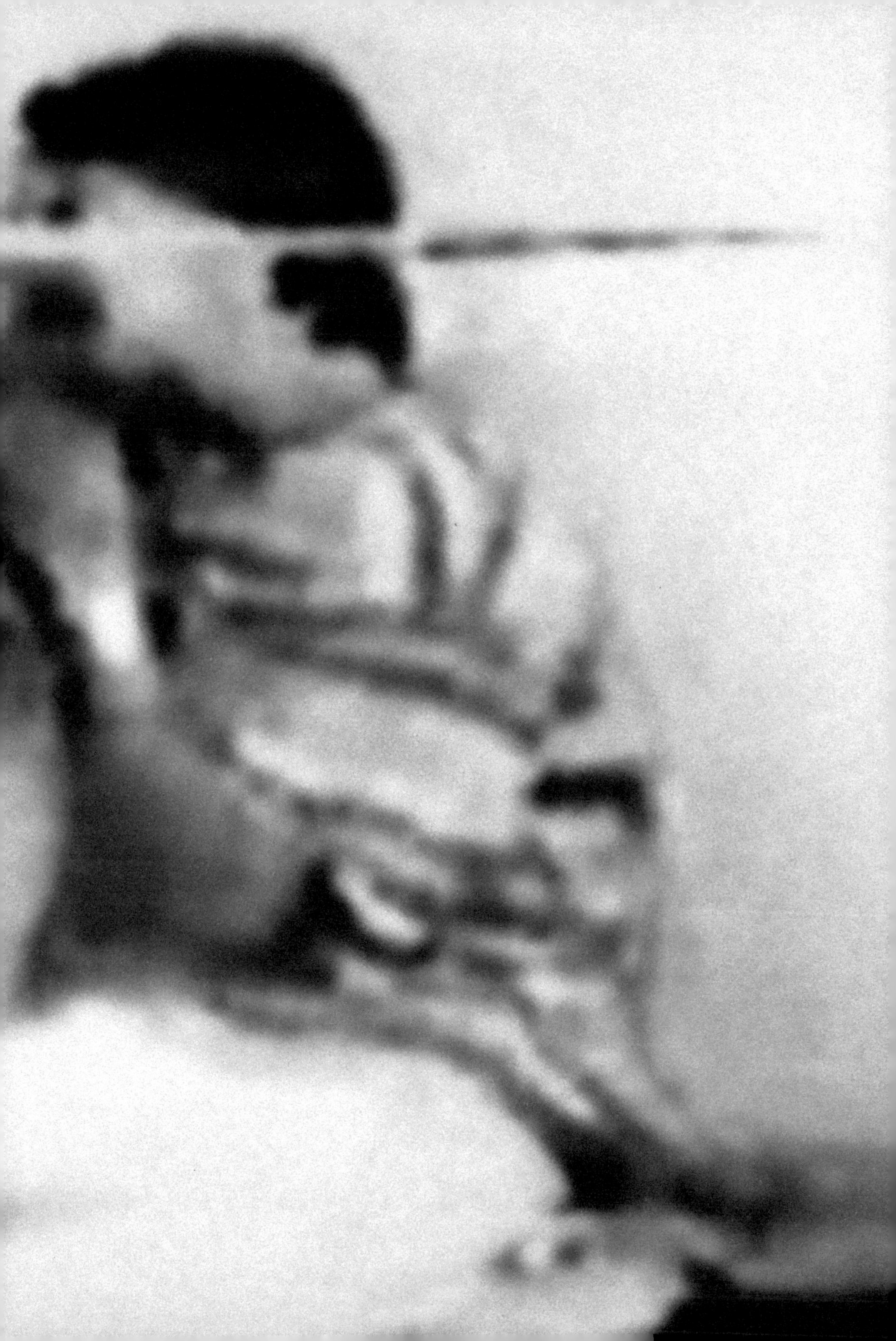

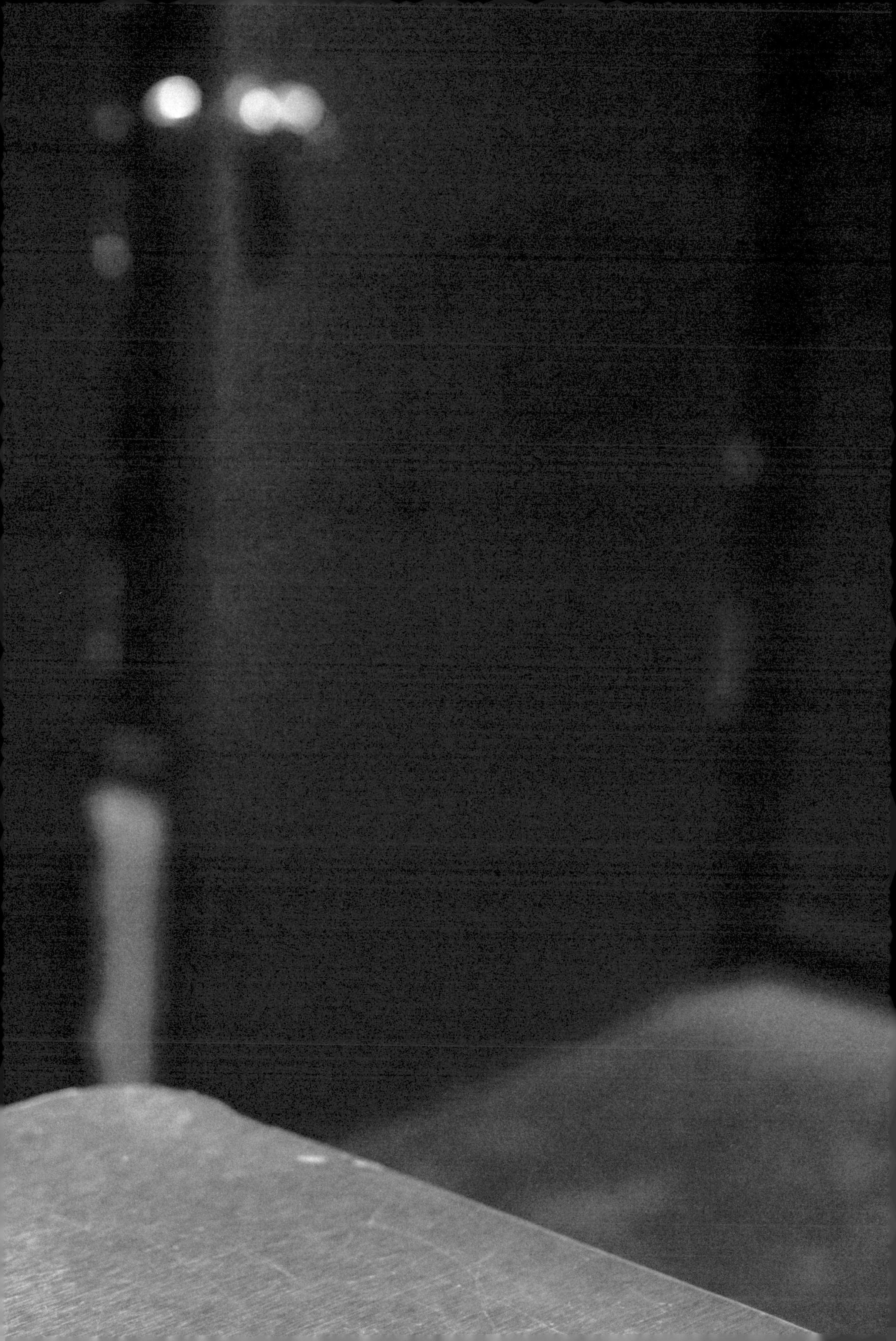

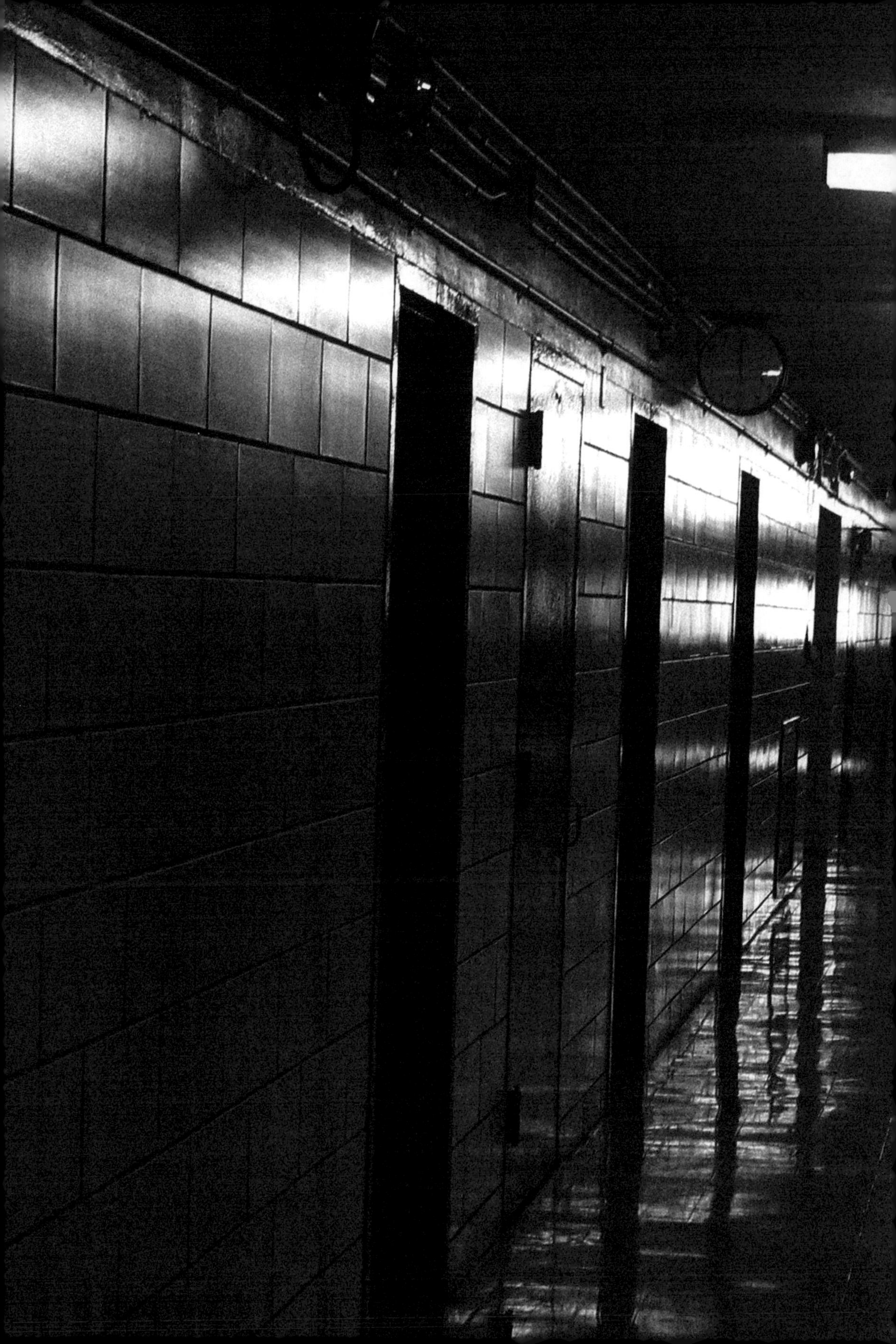

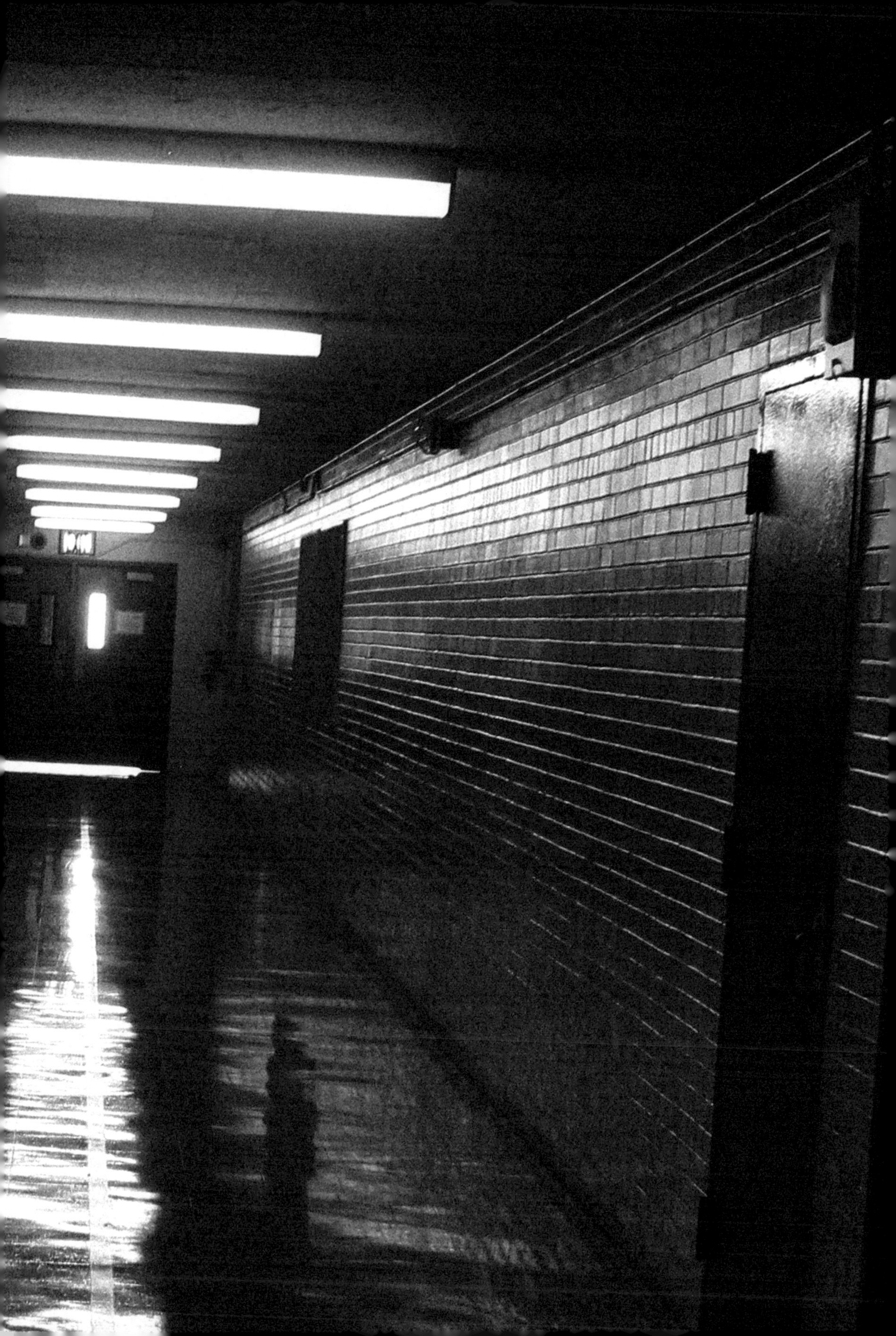

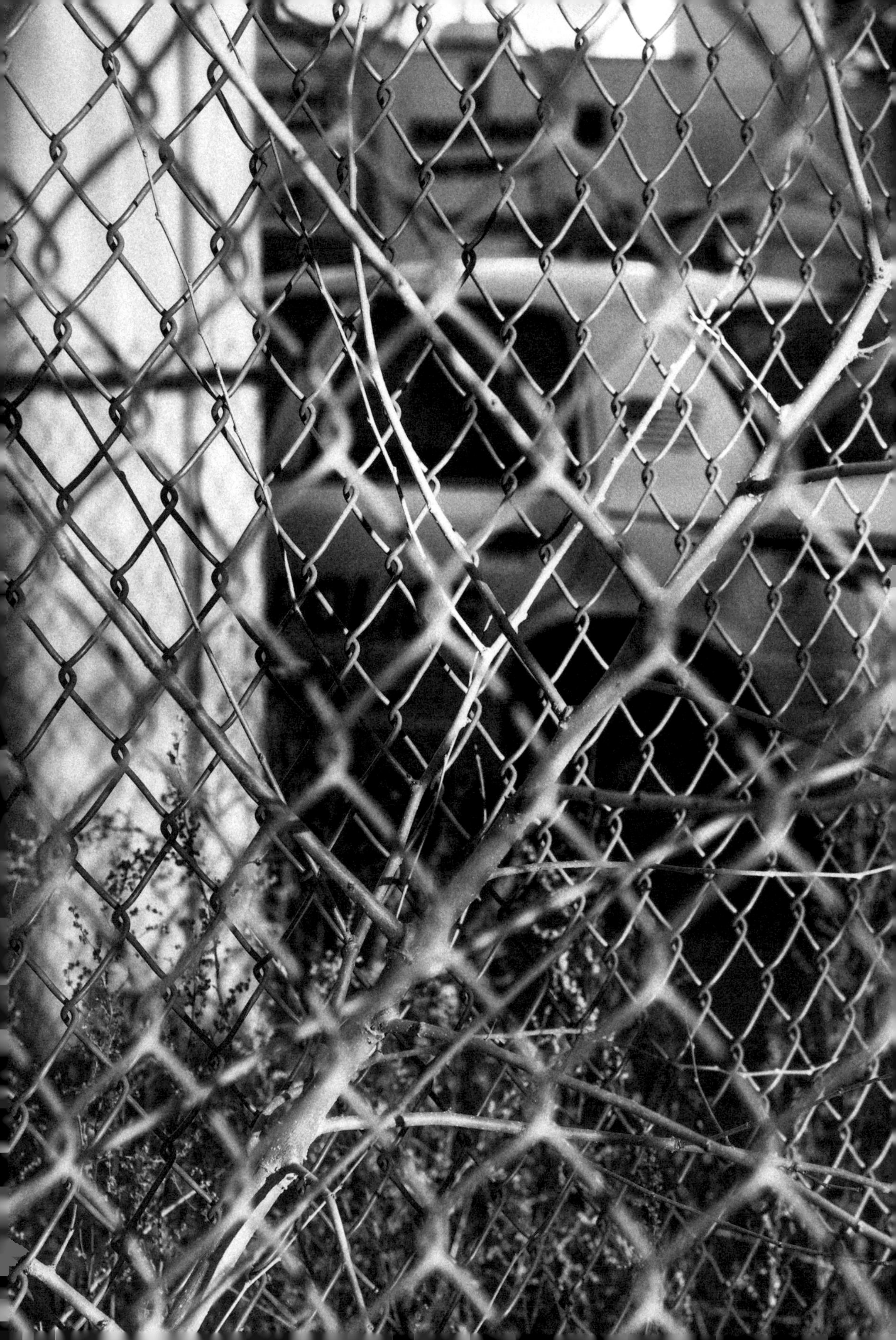

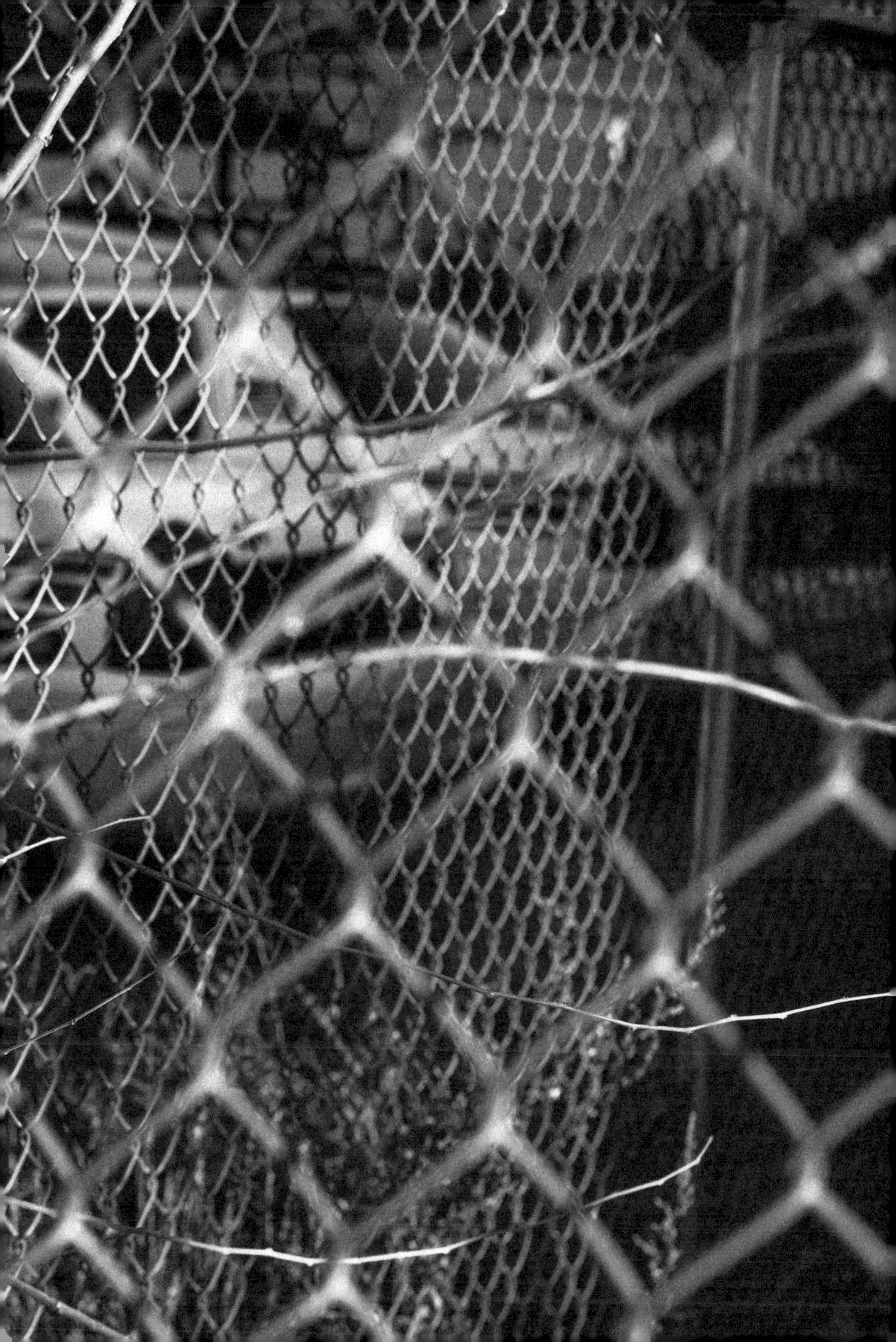

Eddie Lowery

Raymond Santana

I beat myself up a lot about why I confessed. Why did I choose that way? Why wasn't I stronger? But it wasn't my personality to be like that. I had a breaking point.

I kept thinking that somebody would figure out that I had lied. There was no physical evidence linking me to the crime. None.

But that day never came. That day never came.

Christopher Ochoa

Byron Halsey

There are people who tell you that they would never confess, even under the harshest conditions. I tell them, until you are in that situation, you don't know.
You just don't know.

Everybody says that they would never confess. I said the same thing until it happened to me.

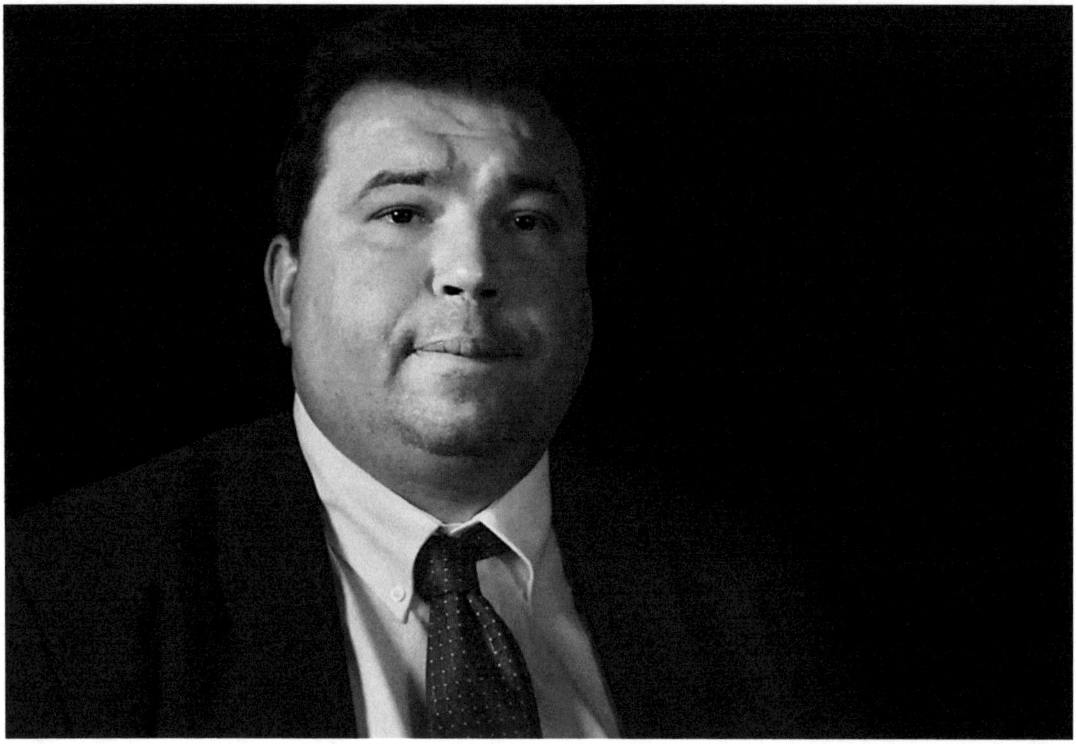

Jeffrey Deskovic **Convicted 1990, Age 16** **Exonerated 2006, Age 32**

In 1989, police in Peekskill, New York, convinced tenth-grader Jeffrey Deskovic that they needed his help to solve the rape and murder of a fifteen-year-old classmate. Over six weeks, officers met with him frequently, feeding him pizza, treating him like a "junior detective," and asking for his theories of the crime. Unbeknownst to Deskovic, the officers had focused on him as their prime suspect—even though DNA from the crime scene did not match his.

At the end of the six weeks, the officers arranged for Deskovic to take a polygraph exam with Daniel Stephens, a polygraphist who boasted he could obtain a confession from anyone. During a six-hour session, Stephens administered three exams, during which he yelled at Deskovic, invaded his personal space, and failed to provide him with food or water. After the third exam, Stephens told Deskovic he had failed all three. He then warned that two officers waiting outside the room intended to harm Deskovic unless he told them what they wanted to hear.

Terrified, overwhelmed, and fearing for his life, Deskovic verbally admitted to the crime. He then collapsed to the floor, curled into a fetal position, and sobbed hysterically. He was later convicted of murder largely based on that confession.

Sixteen years later, Deskovic was exonerated after new DNA testing identified Steven Cunningham as the real perpetrator. Cunningham, already serving a sentence for another murder, confessed when confronted with the DNA results.

WRONGFULLY IMPRISONED | DNA EXONERATES INMATE

Freed after 16 years

Man cleared of killing felt 'day would never come'

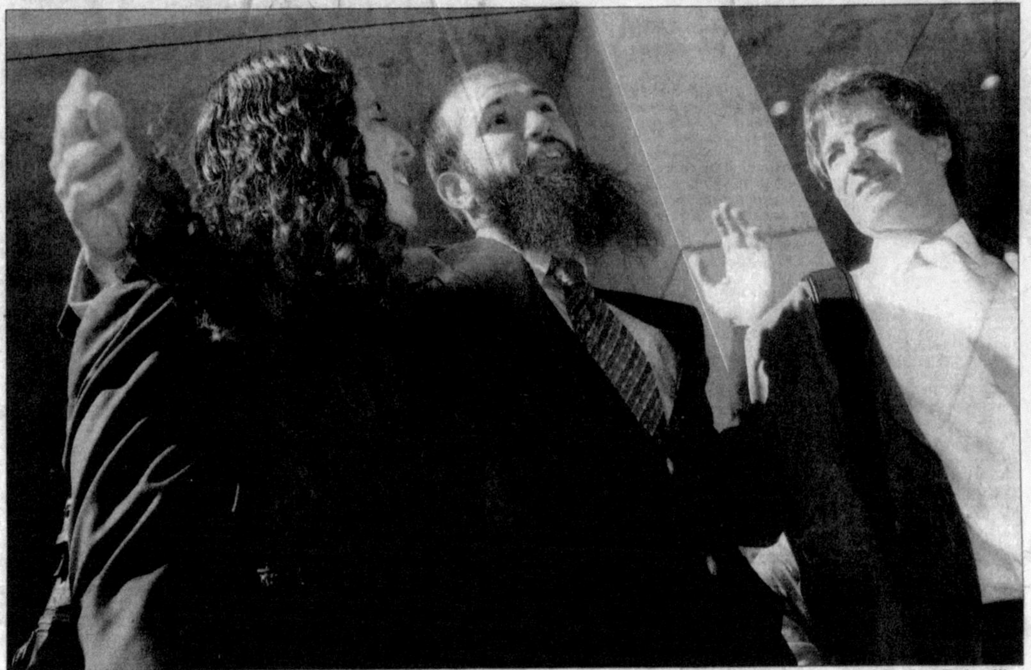

Stuart Bayer/The Journal News

Asking "Is this really happening?" Jeffrey Deskovic left the Westchester County Courthouse in White Plains yesterday, flanked by attorneys Nina Morrison and Barry Scheck after his murder conviction was overturned based on DNA evidence. Deskovic had served almost 16 years in prison for the 1989 slaying of Angela Correa.

Pirro spurned plea to re-examine DNA

Glenn Blain
The Journal News

MINEOLA, N.Y. — Jeanine Pirro was not yet Westchester County's district attorney when Jeffrey Deskovic was convicted of rape and murder, but his exoneration yesterday still proved troublesome for her campaign for state attorney general.

During her tenure as county prosecutor, Deskovic said, Pirro rudely rejected a desperate request he made in 1997 for her to re-examine the case, especially the DNA evidence that ultimately led to his exoneration.

Deskovic said he had been hopeful that Pirro would respond positively to his request because she had spoken previously about the ability of DNA evidence to reverse wrongful convictions, but he received a "very rude letter, the gist of which is, 'Mr. Deskovic, the DNA issue that you raise was considered by the jury which convicted you. ... There will be no prison interview.' "

Pirro, during a public appearance yesterday on Long Island, stressed that Deskovic's case was handled by her predecessor, Carl Vergari, and that the legal group that worked on Deskovic's behalf,

Please see PIRRO, 8A

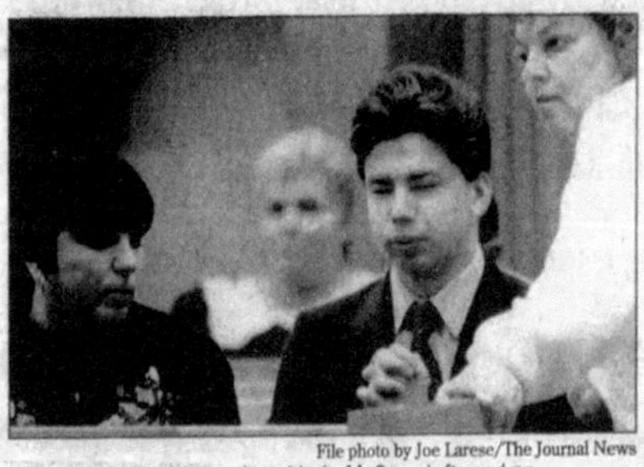

File photo by Joe Larese/The Journal News

Jeffrey Deskovic, his mother, Linda McGarr, left, and an unidentified aunt listen as the judge announces the jury has reached a verdict on Dec. 7, 1990.

Inside

- For a stepfather, DNA results bring back Peekskill tragedy, **4A**
- Judge in case says verdict was 'a travesty of justice', **4A**
- Editorial, **6B**

On the Web

Visit our Web site, LoHud.com, and click on this story for links to the DNA report, motions to vacate the sentence and Jeffrey Deskovic's statements filed in 1991.

Jonathan Bandler
The Journal News

WHITE PLAINS — Jeffrey Deskovic walked free for the first time in nearly 16 years yesterday after his conviction was thrown out in the rape and murder of a Peekskill High School classmate.

The 32-year-old was cleared in the death of Angela Correa because another man confessed to the crime after more sophisticated DNA testing linked him to the girl's death. Authorities would not identify the suspect but said he is serving a life sentence for his conviction in an unrelated Westchester County homicide.

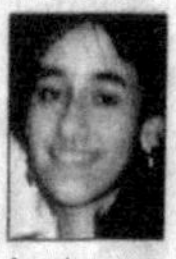

Angela Correa

"There was a long time that I felt this day would never come," Deskovic said after leaving the Westchester County Courthouse. "It hasn't hit me yet. I'm still waiting to wake up."

Deskovic's conviction and 15-year-to-life prison sentence were vacated in a brief court hearing by acting state Supreme Court Justice Richard Molea at the request of lawyers from the Innocence Project, a legal clinic of Benjamin N. Cardozo Law School that has now exonerated 184 inmates through DNA testing.

"We are here today to correct, as best we can, a terrible injustice that was done to Jeffrey Deskovic 17 years ago," said one of the lawyers, Nina Morrison. "We are humbled by what Mr. Deskovic has gone through."

Please see VERDICT, 4A

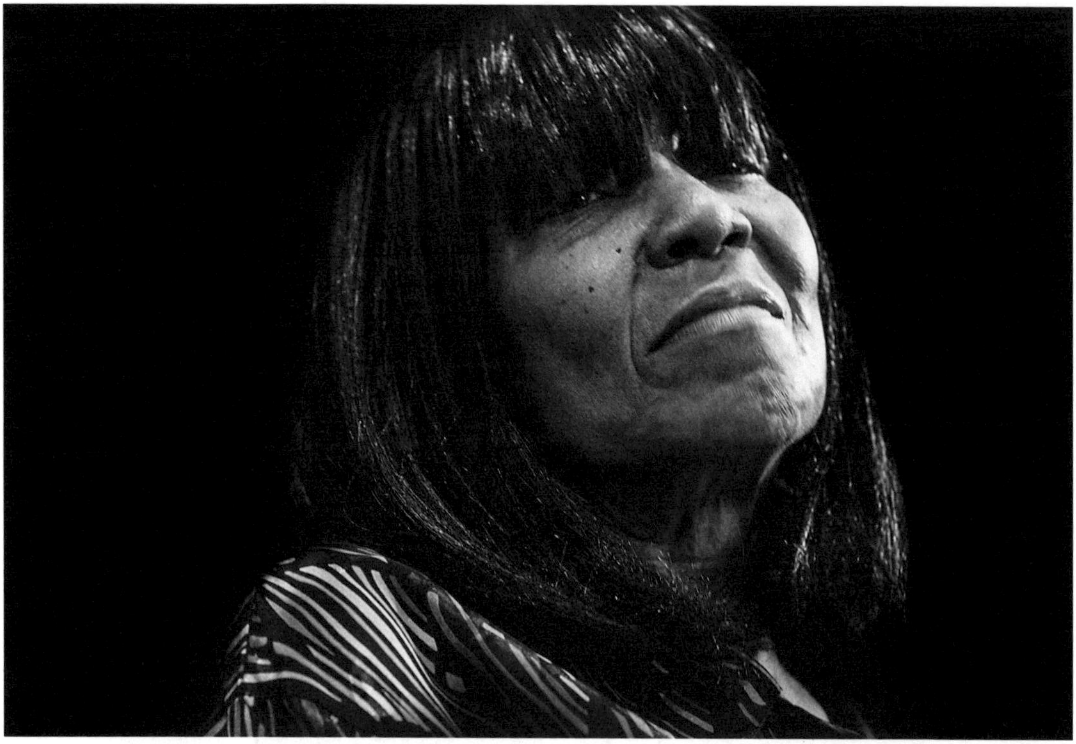

Vanessa Gathers **Convicted 1998, Age 39** **Exonerated 2016, Age 58**

In 1997, Detective Louis Scarcella of the New York City Police Department was reassigned from one of Brooklyn's homicide divisions to its 77th Precinct to work on unsolved cases. One of the first cases he revisited was the 1991 beating of a seventy-one-year-old man who later died of his injuries.

As part of the renewed investigation, Scarcella re-interrogated Vanessa Gathers. He had first questioned her in 1992, shortly after the victim's death. She lived in the neighborhood and regularly walked her dog by the victim's apartment building.

At the start of the second interrogation, Scarcella removed his gun from his jacket and placed it on the table in front of Gathers. When she insisted she was innocent, he grew angry and aggressive, handling the gun in a menacing way. He refused to let her call her family, told her she did not need a lawyer, and insisted that if she wanted to go home, she had to admit to being present at the crime.

After three hours, Gathers—worn down, terrified, and fearing for her safety—agreed. She recanted almost immediately, but her statement became the centerpiece of the prosecution's case. No physical or eyewitness evidence linked her to the crime. She was convicted of manslaughter and served ten years of a five-to-fifteen-year sentence before being paroled in 2007.

In 2016, the Brooklyn District Attorney vacated her conviction after concluding that her confession was false and that Scarcella had engaged in coercive and unethical conduct. As of 2024, Scarcella had been implicated in at least twenty wrongful conviction cases.

Woman Exonerated After Serving 10 Years for Manslaughter Conviction

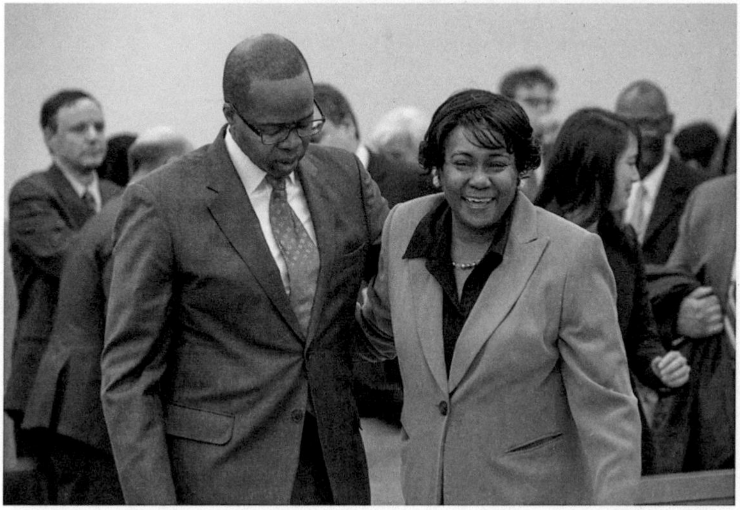

Vanessa Gathers, 58, with Ken Thompson, the Brooklyn district attorney, after her manslaughter conviction was vacated on Tuesday. Andrew Kelly for The New York Times

By Sarah Maslin Nir
Feb. 23, 2016

In a gray suit, her short hair neatly curled, Vanessa Gathers sat in State Supreme Court in Brooklyn on Tuesday, beaming as the judge spoke words she had waited nearly two decades to hear: The manslaughter conviction for which she had spent 10 years in prison was vacated, the judge said, after an investigation revealed that her confession to the crime was false.

In an instant, Ms. Gathers was no longer a convicted criminal. The judge, Justice Matthew J. D'Emic, smiled back. "Good luck!" he said.

Ms. Gathers, 58, is the first woman to have been exonerated by the Conviction Review Unit, a special unit created by the Brooklyn district attorney to look into scores of cases linked to Louis Scarcella, a retired detective whose tactics led to the wrongful convictions of more than a dozen people, according to the district attorney's office. The unit is examining 100 cases, many of them involving Mr. Scarcella.

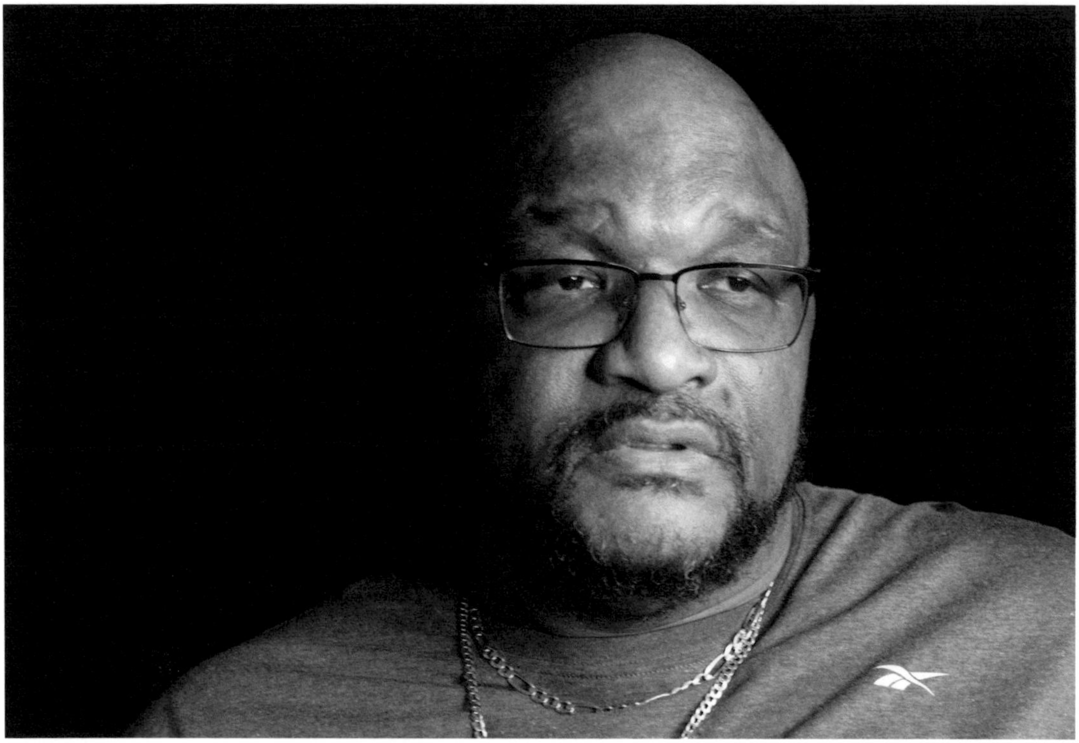

Byron Halsey **Convicted in 1988, Age 28** **Exonerated in 2007, Age 46**

In 1985, twenty-four-year-old Byron Halsey was living in a Plainfield, New Jersey, apartment with his girlfriend and her two young children. One night, when both Halsey and his girlfriend were out, the children disappeared. The next morning, they were found dead in the building's basement. They had been sexually assaulted and murdered. Plainfield police officers immediately focused on Halsey.

During a forty-hour period, officers interrogated Halsey for more than thirty hours. They badgered him, refused to listen to him, physically intimidated him, falsely told him that he had failed a polygraph test, and fabricated evidence against him. Halsey, who had a sixth-grade education and significant learning disabilities, eventually broke down. Exhausted and distraught, he signed a blank sheet of paper upon which officers wrote a confession.

At trial three years later, Halsey was convicted of murder and sentenced to two consecutive life terms. With no direct evidence tying him to the crime, the case relied largely on his alleged confession and the testimony of the interrogating officers.

In 2007, Halsey was exonerated after new DNA testing implicated his former next-door neighbor, Clifton Hall, in the murders. Hall was already serving sentences for three separate sex crimes committed in 1991. He died in prison before he could be tried for the children's murders.

Before his exoneration, Halsey spent twenty-two years in prison—three awaiting trial and nineteen after conviction. He estimates that more than half of that time was spent in solitary confinement.

EXONERATED BY DNA: 205 people nationally; five in New Jersey

BYRON HALSEY: Can be compensated $20G for every year behind bars

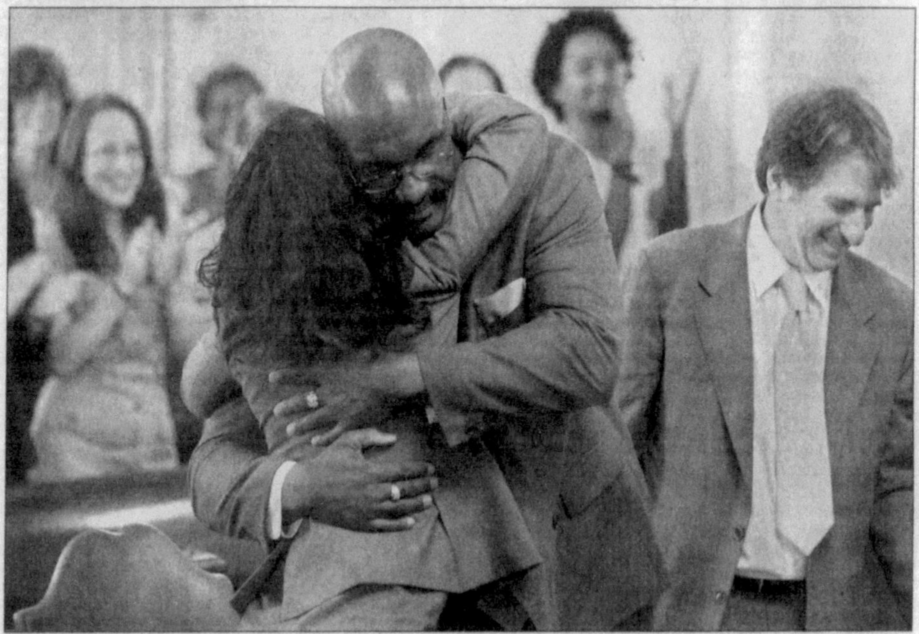

Byron Halsey (center) hugs one of his attorneys, Vanessa Potkin, as his other attorney, Barry Scheck (right), smiles after all charges against Halsey were dropped Monday at the Union County Courthouse in Elizabeth. (AP PHOTO)

All charges are dropped

22 years served for rape, murder of 2 kids; DNA links another man to crime

THE ASSOCIATED PRESS

ELIZABETH — All charges against a man who served 22 years in prison for the murder and rape of two children were dropped on Monday after prosecutors cited new DNA testing they said links another man to the crime.

In a prepared statement released before a court hearing Monday, Union County Prosecutor Theodore J. Romankow said he decided not to pursue the charges following "careful re-evaluation of the case" against Byron Halsey.

Halsey, 46, was released from prison on May 15 after a judge threw out his convictions. New DNA testing, not available when he was convicted, linked a neighbor to the crime.

However, until Monday, Halsey could have been retried on charges of aggravated sexual assault, aggravated manslaughter, felony murder, child abuse and possession of a weapon for an unlawful purpose.

Instead, on prosecutors' recommendation, Superior Court Judge Stuart L. Peim dropped all charges in a hearing that lasted about two minutes.

Halsey, dressed in a gray suit and flanked between his lawyers, stood up and asked the judge, "Can I have your autograph please?"

Outside the courtroom, Halsey thanked prosecutors for "acknowledging the truth." He also thanked his grandmother, standing behind him in a crowd of supporters, and God.

"I want to thank my Lord savior for carrying me through the years," he said.

Halsey said he is trying to absorb his new freedom, which began Monday with the removal of an electronic ankle bracelet that monitored his whereabouts.

> **"I want to thank my Lord savior for carrying me through the years."**
>
> *— Byron Halsey, after serving 22 years in prison for the rape and murder of two children*

Though he said he is still angry, he doesn't have immediate plans to sue the state.

Halsey was convicted in 1988 of murdering and sexually assaulting Tyrone and Tina Urquhart, the children of his girlfriend, with whom he lived at a Plainfield rooming house.

The bodies of Tyrone, 8, and Tina, 7, were found in the home's basement in November 1985.

The new DNA test showed that a neighbor in the rooming house, Clifton Hall, was the source of semen recovered at the scene and may have been responsible for the crimes, said Eric Ferrero, a spokesman for the Innocence Project, which is affiliated with the Cardozo School of Law at Yeshiva University and is representing Halsey.

Halsey had made a confession before trial, but Innocence Project co-director Barry Scheck said the statement followed 30 hours of interrogation over a 40-hour period.

Scheck said the next step would likely be applying for compensation and filing a civil lawsuit. Vanessa Potkin, a lawyer with the Innocence Project, said he could be compensated $20,000 per year of imprisonment.

Halsey is the 205th person nationwide exonerated and the fifth in New Jersey through DNA evidence, Ferrero said.

Hall, 49, has now been charged with two counts of murder and one count of aggravated sexual assault, authorities said. He is being held at a prison for sex offenders because of three sex crimes convictions in the 1990s.

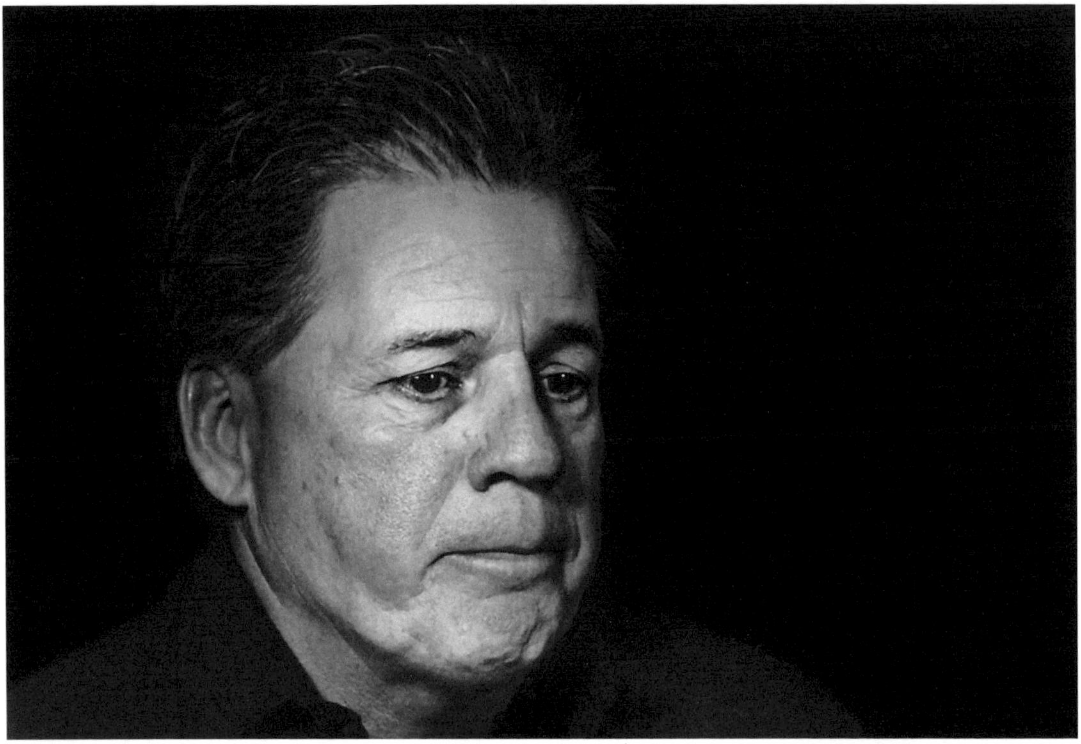

Eddie Lowery **Convicted 1982, Age 22** **Exonerated 2003, Age 43**

In 1981, twenty-two-year-old Army soldier Eddie Lowery, stationed at Fort Riley, Kansas, became a suspect in the rape of a seventy-four-year-old woman. Riley County detectives brought him in for questioning after learning that he had had a car accident on the same street where the crime took place at around the same time.

During an eleven-hour interrogation over two days, officers yelled at Lowery, invaded his personal space, physically intimidated him, deprived him of food and water, and denied his requests to speak with a lawyer or his company commander. They falsely told him he had failed a polygraph test and used his siblings' struggles against him. Exhausted and overwhelmed, Lowery confessed, believing he could clear him name once the interrogation was over.

Although he recanted his confession almost immediately, prosecutors introduced it at trial. Lowery's first trial resulted in a mistrial, but he was convicted at a second and sentenced to eleven years to life in prison. After serving nine years, he was paroled but forced to register as a sex offender.

Lowery spent the next decade fighting to overturn his conviction. In 2002, DNA testing of crime scene evidence identified serial rapist Daniel Brewer as the true perpetrator. In 2011, Brewer pled guilty to the rape for which Lowery had been wrongfully convicted.

An innocent man

Imprisoned for a rape he did not commit, Eddie Lowery is cleared Thursday

Scott Daugherty
Staff Writer

Twenty-one years after a Riley County jury wrongfully convicted him of the rape of a 74-year-old Ogden woman, Eddie James Lowery was cleared of all charges Thursday afternoon.

"I thank God for answering my prayers," Lowery said, extending thanks to various court officials and to his attorney Barry Clark. "I am excited and very happy that justice is being served."

The reversal finally came about after a clerk found DNA evidence that proved him innocent in a manila folder that had been in the basement vault of the courthouse since his 1982 conviction. Procedures to test the material did not exist at the time of his trial.

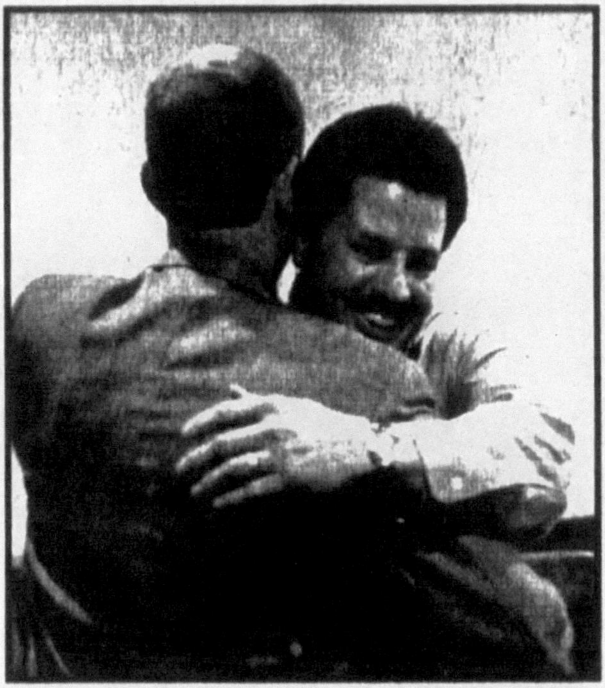

Staff photo by Rod Mikinski

Edie Lowery (facing camera) hugs Barry Clark.

"Nothing that I say or do today will give back to you the years you spent in prison or the years you spent registering as a sex offender," said Riley County District Court Judge Meryl Wilson. "I can today, by signing this order, restore to you your reputation and perhaps your dignity."

Lowery's reputation and dignity are precisely what he wanted to salvage by clearing his name. Every June he was required to go to the Liberty, Mo., courthouse to register as a sex offender.

"Going to the courthouse, to the sheriff's office, and having to register — that was very hard for me," Lowery said. "I was emotionally torn up every time I had to go

SEE No. 4, BACK PAGE

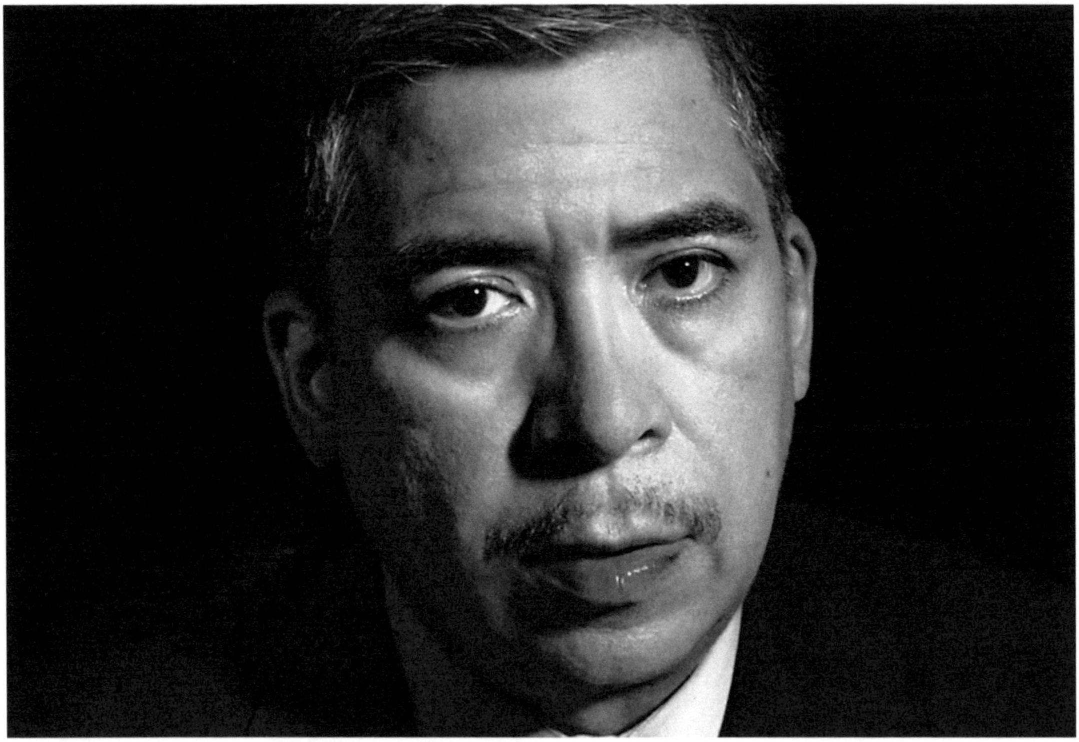

Christopher Ochoa **Convicted 1989, Age 22** **Exonerated 2002, Age 34**

In 1988, twenty-two-year-old Christopher Ochoa was living in Austin, Texas, and working at a pizza restaurant when a manager at another location was raped and murdered. A few weeks later, Ochoa and his roommate visited the crime scene to pay their respects. Although there was no evidence tying either man to the crime, police detectives found this suspicious and brought both in for questioning.

Over twenty-four hours across two days, officers interrogated Ochoa, screaming at him, slamming doors and fists on a table, throwing a chair at his head, and invading his personal space. They denied him access to a lawyer, falsely told him he had failed a polygraph, and showed him graphic autopsy photos. They threatened him with the death penalty, jabbing his arm to demonstrate where a lethal injection needle would go, and warned he would never see his family again. At the end of the second day, they threatened him with jailhouse rape.

Terrified and unable to think clearly, Ochoa confessed. He pled guilty, was sentenced to life in prison, and spent twelve years behind bars before the real perpetrator, Achim Marino, confessed. DNA testing on forensic evidence from the crime scene confirmed Marino's guilt, exonerating Ochoa.

'It was very difficult not to give up. Keep fighting because there are people that care.'

Chris Ochoa

Wrongly convicted in 1988 slaying, urging other innocent inmates not to abandon hope

His name cleared, Ochoa marks independence day

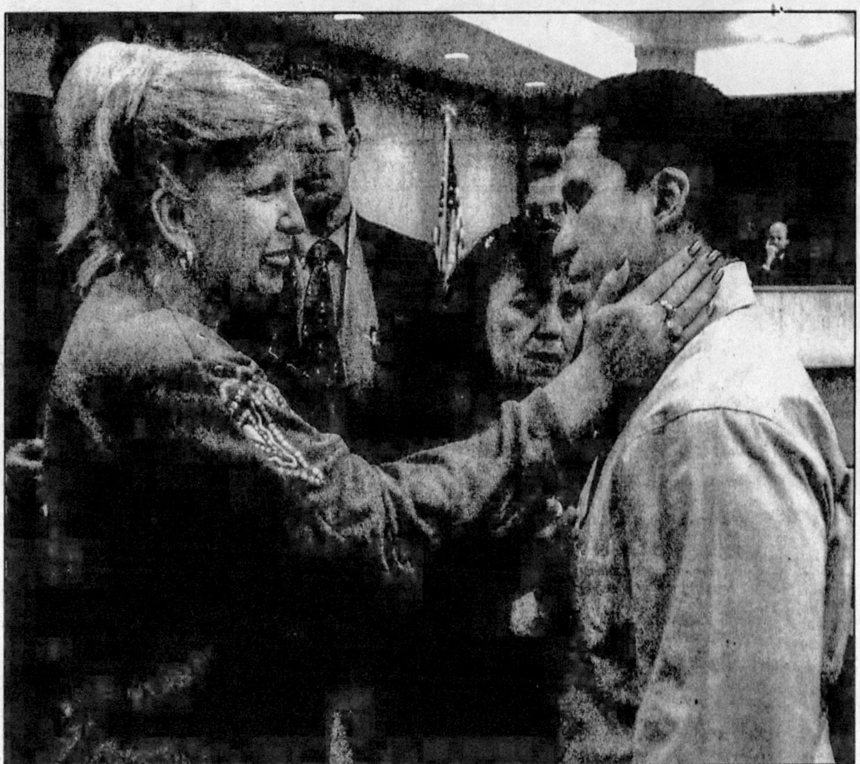

Rodolfo Gonzalez/AA-S photos

Jeannette Popp embraces Chris Ochoa, who was exonerated in the 1988 rape and slaying of her daughter Nancy DePriest. Popp and Ochoa's mother, Dora Ochoa, center, had waited together for his freedom. Below, mother and son embrace in the court of state District Judge Bob Perkins, background, who once sentenced Ochoa to life in prison and Tuesday ordered his release.

Focus turns to system that wrongly jailed him for slaying

By David Hafetz
American-Statesman Staff

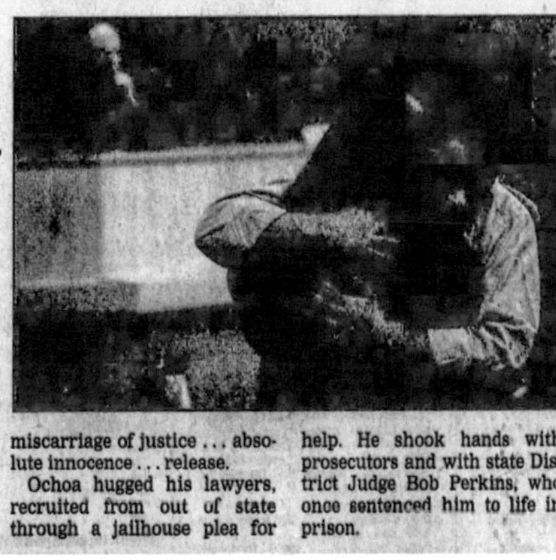

The two mothers sat in the courtroom's first row, one waiting to reclaim her wrongly imprisoned son, the other still grieving for a daughter killed 12 years ago.

That slaying once placed the women on opposing ends of the justice system. Dora Ochoa's son confessed — repeatedly and, it turns out, falsely — to killing Jeannette Popp's 20-year-old daughter, Nancy DePriest.

But as Chris Ochoa sat at the defendant's table Tuesday morning, the mothers sat side by side, joined in wishing for his freedom.

Chris Ochoa, 34, listened silently as the longed-for words left the judge's mouth: miscarriage of justice . . . absolute innocence . . . release.

Ochoa hugged his lawyers, recruited from out of state through a jailhouse plea for help. He shook hands with prosecutors and with state District Judge Bob Perkins, who once sentenced him to life in prison.

Everyone made way for a crying Dora Ochoa, who said she still couldn't believe this day had arrived. Then her son hugged Popp.

"Freedom has not set in yet. I mean, I had a decent sandwich," Ochoa said later at a news conference at the Capitol. Flanked by other wrongly imprisoned Texans, Ochoa and his lawyers appealed for reforming the justice system to prevent future cases like his.

Lawyer Barry Scheck, a nationally known DNA expert, outlined four proposals for lawmakers to consider this legislative session. He advocated providing for post-conviction DNA testing, improving representation for indigent defendants,

See Ochoa, A7

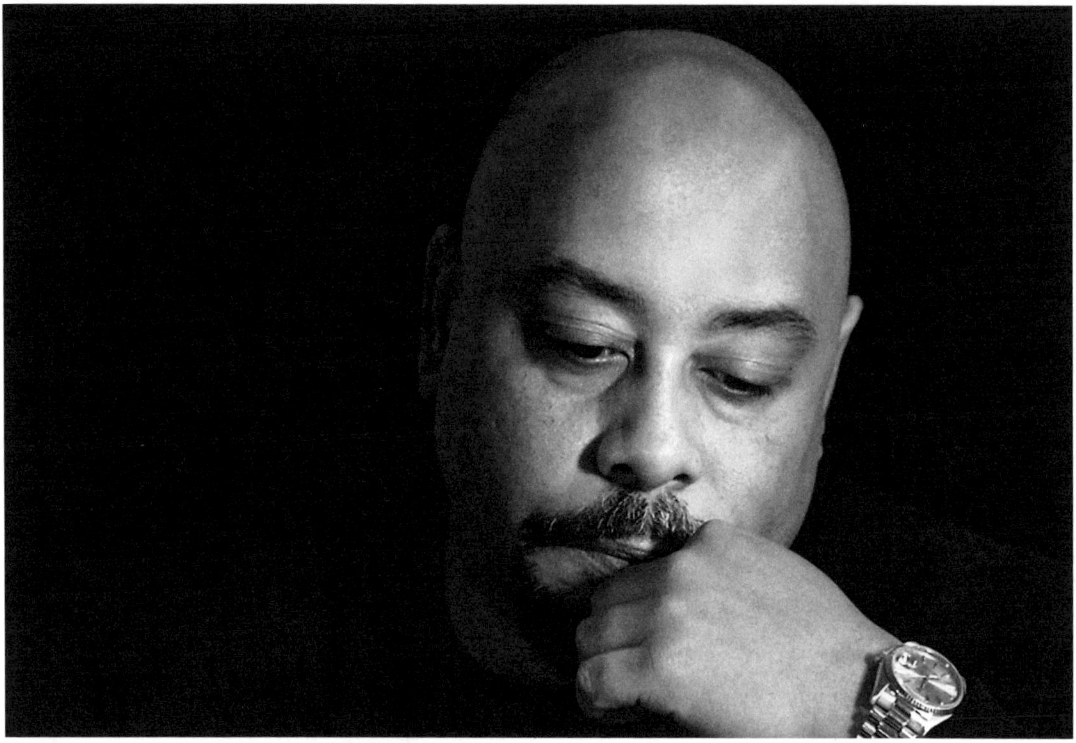

Raymond Santana **Convicted 1990, Age 15** **Exonerated 2002, Age 27**

In April 1989, fourteen-year-old Raymond Santana was interrogated by New York City police detectives for more than fifteen consecutive hours before confessing to a crime in which he played no part–the rape and assault of a young female jogger in Central Park. Santana's grandmother, a small woman who spoke no English, was present during the interrogation. The officers questioned Santana in English and translated the conversation into Spanish for her.

At least three times, different officers called Santana's grandmother out of the interrogation room for varying lengths of time. While she was gone, the detectives yelled at Santana, pounded on the furniture, whispered violent threats in his ear, and physically lunged at him. Gradually, Santana came to believe that if he did not tell the officers what they wanted to hear, neither he nor his grandmother would leave the police station unharmed.

Terrified, Santana implicated himself and two others. He was convicted and sentenced to five to ten years in prison. Twelve years later, Matias Reyes, a convicted murderer and rapist, admitted that he alone had attacked the Central Park jogger. DNA testing confirmed Reyes's involvement. His confession, along with the DNA evidence and the absence of any direct link to Santana, led to Santana's exoneration.

Judge throws out convictions in 1989 rape of Central Park jogger

BY SAMUEL MAULL

NEW YORK — A judge dismissed the convictions yesterday of all five men who served years in prison for the 1989 rape and beating of a jogger in Central Park, a crime that exposed the city's racial tensions and made national headlines.

The courtroom burst into cheers and applause as state Justice Charles Tejada announced his ruling.

"Justice was done," said city councilman Bill Perkins, a supporter of the five. "Unfortunately, it took 13 years of tribulations for the Central Park Five, not to mention the years of suffering for their families."

The five men weren't in the courtroom to hear the ruling yesterday. All have finished their sentences, though one was reincarcerated for an unrelated crime.

Sharonne Salaam, mother of defendant Yusef Salaam, said her son was now "beyond anger and he's beyond joy. ... We have to improve this system so that only the guilty suffer."

Mr. Perkins and defence attorney Michael Warren called for an investigation to determine who was responsible for what the councillor called "this miscarriage of justice."

Authorities a year ago began investigating claims by a serial rapist who said he attacked the 28-year-old woman as she jogged in Central Park on April 19, 1989. DNA testing showed semen samples from the scene belonged to Matias Reyes.

The primary evidence in the case had been confessions that the five, all black and Hispanic boys ranging in age from 14 to 16 at the time, had made to detectives. Supporters argued that the statements were coerced. Prosecutors also had no forensic evidence to link any of them to the crime scene.

The five, now ages 28 to 30, completed prison sentences ranging from 5½ to 13 years on their convictions. They are considering lawsuits.

At the time of the attack, authorities said a roaming gang of youths was in the park for a night of "wilding" — randomly attacking anyone who came into their path.

The jogger, a white investment banker, was found near death in a puddle of mud and blood in the north end of the park. She was in a coma for 12 days, but eventually recovered.

The five were also convicted on allegations they attacked and harassed other people in the park that night.

Raymond Santana, Antron McCray, Kevin Richardson and Kharey Wise confessed on videotape. A detective testified at trial that Mr. Salaam made incriminating admissions to him but never on videotape.

Prosecutors earlier this month asked the court to void the convictions on the basis of the evidence against Mr. Reyes, including a semen sample that proved through DNA that he had assaulted the jogger. Mr. Reyes, 31, is serving time for murder and rape.

The Associated Press

The National Registry of Exonerations reports that between 1989 and 2024, 13 percent of all exonerated individuals in the United States were wrongfully convicted because of a false confession.[1] A disproportionately high number were people of color.[2] Registry data, case files, and investigative reporting reveal that many of these false confessions were obtained through psychologically coercive interrogations.

Those who confessed falsely were often isolated by their interrogators in stress-inducing environments; aggressively confronted with accusations of wrongdoing; prevented from asserting their innocence; denied access to counsel; lied to about evidence; subjected to polygraph exams and then lied to about the results; and physically threatened or intimidated. They eventually found the experience so unbearable that they admitted to crimes they had not committed simply to make the ordeal stop.[3]

Coercive interrogation methods—both psychological and physical—have been used by law enforcement personnel in the United States for generations. That such methods can and do produce false confessions has been long recognized. When subjected to enough pain, even if just psychological, people can be persuaded to say almost anything.[4]

In 1692 and 1693, the Salem witch trials in colonial Massachusetts were among the first recorded instances of coercive interrogations producing false confessions in what would become the United States. At least fifty-five people falsely admitted to practicing witchcraft during prosecutions now understood to have been fueled by mass hysteria. Most of these confessions were the product of threats of execution, inhumane detention conditions, and physical torture.[5]

Two hundred and forty years later, in 1931, the first nationwide study of interrogation techniques revealed that Salem-type tactics were still in use throughout the country and continuing to produce false confessions. A report published by the National Commission on Law Observance and Enforcement, entitled *Report on Lawlessness in Law Enforcement,* documented widespread use of sensory deprivation, psychological pressure, deplorable detention conditions, threats of physical harm, and physical brutality by state and local police,[6] and cited numerous criminal cases in which these methods had produced false confessions.[7] The report sparked national outrage and calls for reform.[8]

In 1936, the US Supreme Court issued its first decision prohibiting the use of physically coercive interrogation tactics by state and local law enforcement. In *Brown v. Mississippi,*[9] the Court overturned the convictions of three Black tenant farmers who had falsely confessed to killing a white landowner after having been physically brutalized by local law enforcement. Two confessed after severe beatings and the third after having been whipped and hanged by the neck from a tree limb. Noting that the US Constitution's Fifth Amendment guarantees those accused of criminal wrongdoing the right to remain silent while being questioned, the Court ruled that state law enforcement officers who physically abused suspects into confessing violated the Fifth Amendment, rendering the resulting confessions inadmissible as evidence at trial.[10]

In the 1940s and '50s, in response to the National Commission's report and Supreme Court rulings, state and local police agencies began promoting interrogation techniques that relied solely on psychological—as opposed to both physical and psychological—coercion.[11] Over time, however, courts and experts recognized that for certain groups—including young people, individuals with intellectual disabilities, those suffering from mental illness, and people who naturally defer to authority figures—psychological manipulation could be as traumatic and coercive as physical abuse, and equally likely to produce false confessions.[12]

In its 1960 decision in *Blackburn v. Alabama,*[13] for example, the Supreme Court overturned the conviction of a Black mentally ill World War II veteran who had confessed to robbery after nine hours of questioning in a room measuring just four by six feet, with up to three police officers present. The Court found that police officials had impermissibly coerced him into confessing. Because of his mental illness, the veteran likely found the prolonged interrogation, without the support of friends or family, akin to physical abuse.[14]

Six years later, in *Miranda v. Arizona* (1966),[15] the Supreme Court imposed safeguards designed to ensure that confessions obtained through psychological manipulation were not wrongfully coerced. Before interrogating suspects in police custody, officers must inform them of their constitutional right to remain silent and to consult with an attorney during questioning. A confession could be used at trial only if the prosecutor demonstrated that the suspect understood and voluntarily waived these rights. These protections became known as "Miranda warnings."

However, as the cases in this book—and research by the National Registry of Exonerations and others—demonstrate, these safeguards have not prevented coerced false confessions. The reasons are numerous. Miranda warnings are not required during non-custodial interrogations, allowing police investigators to freely question suspects before formally taking them into custody. Some courts do not consider certain forms of psychological manipulation, such as deception or lying, to be legally "coercive." And, importantly, many suspects fail to fully understand their Miranda rights. They may not grasp the legal concepts underlying their right to remain silent or their right to counsel, leading them to believe they have no real choice but to talk.[16]

In recent years, law enforcement agencies—largely outside the United States—have promoted alternative interrogation methods to minimize false confessions. One such method, developed by the British police and known as the PEACE model (Preparation and Planning, Engage and Explain, Account, Closure, and Evaluation), emphasizes rapport-building and trust, as opposed to psychological manipulation, to elicit accurate accounts. Early studies indicate that PEACE yields confession rates comparable to coercive tactics but with fewer false confessions.[17] The approach is now used in some European countries and is slowly gaining attention in the United States.[18]

1. National Registry of Exonerations, https://www.law.umich.edu/special/exoneration/Pages/detaillist.aspx.

2. *Id.*

3. *See, e.g.,* National Registry of Exonerations, https://www.law.umich.edu/special/exoneration/Pages/detaillist.aspx; Innocence Project, Cases, https://innocenceproject.org/all-cases/; Northwestern University, Pritzker School of Law, Blum Legal Clinic, Center on Wrongful Convictions, https://www.law.northwestern.edu/legalclinic/wrongfulconvictions/issues/falseconfessions/; falseconfessions.org, https://falseconfessions.org/exonerated/; Hurubie Meko, "3 Young Men Exonerated in New York, 30 Years after False Confessions," *New York Times* (August 24, 2023), https://www.nytimes.com/2023/08/24/nyregion/false-confessions-wrongful-conviction-nyc.html; Debra K. Weiss, "Illinois teen was coerced into false confession, family says; was unique law violated?," *ABA Journal* (February 28, 2022), https://www.abajournal.com/news/article/illinois-teen-was-coerced-into-false-confession-family-says-was-unique-state-law-violated#google_vignette; Jan Ranson, "3 Detectives Obtained a False

Murder Confession. Was It One of Dozens?" *New York Times* (February 18, 2021), https://www.nytimes.com/2021/02/15/nyregion/3-detectives-obtained-a-false-murder-confession-was-it-one-of-dozens.html.

4. *See, e.g.*, Allan Fong, "Interrogations and False Confessions: How the Innocent Are Made Guilty," *Southern California Review of Law and Justice* 30, no. 2 (Spring 2021): 363–89, https://gould.usc.edu/students/journals/rlsj/issues/assets/docs/volume30/spring2021/Fong.pdf; Shane O'Mara, "The Captive Brain: Torture and the Neuroscience of Humane Interrogation," *QJM: An International Journal of Medicine* 111, no. 2 (February 2018): 73–78, https://doi.org/10.1093/qjmed/hcx252; Karl Roberts, "Police Interviewing of Criminal Suspects: A Historical Perspective," *Internet Journal of Criminology* (2012), https://www.fair360.com/media/2019/10/fefeb-899b707418864e1ffef7898cf0cd353.pdf; Richard A. Leo, "The Third Degree and the Origins of Psychological Interrogation in the United States." In Interrogations, Confessions, and Entrapment. Perspectives in Law & Psychology 20, edited by G.D. Lassiter, 20:37–84. Boston, Mass: Springer, 2004. https://doi.org/10.1007/978-0-387-38598-3_3.

5. Kristina García, "Possessed: The Salem Witch Trials," *Penn Today* (March 11, 2022), https://penntoday.upenn.edu/news/possessed-salem-witch-trials; Kirandeep Kaur, "Confessions, Convictions and Controversy: An Examination of False Confessions Leading to Wrongful Convictions in the United States Throughout History," *Touro Law School Journal of Race, Gender, and Ethnicity* 9, no. 1 (May 2020): 165–85, https://digitalcommons.tourolaw.edu/jrge/vol9/iss1/13/.

6. "US National Commission on Law Observance and Enforcement No. 11—Report on Lawlessness in Law Enforcement" (US Department of Justice, Office of Justice Programs, 1931), https://www.ojp.gov/ncjrs/virtual-library/abstracts/us-national-commission-law-observance-and-enforcement-report-no-11. *See* Leo, *supra* note 4.

7. US National Commission on Law Observance and Enforcement, *supra* note 6, at 52–83.

8. Leo, *supra* note 4; Brent Snook, Joseph Eastwood, and Wendy Barron, "The Next Stage in the Evolution of Interrogations: The PEACE Model," *Canadian Criminal Law Review* 18 (2014): 219–239, https://www.mun.ca/psychology/media/production/memorial/academic/faculty-of-science/psychology/media-library/research/brl/Snook_et_al_2014_CCLR.pdf.

9. *Brown v. Mississippi*, 297 U.S. 278 (1936).

10. *Id.*, at 286.

11. Leo, *supra* note 4.

12. *See, e.g., Spano v. New York,* 360 U. S. 315 (1959); *Fikes v. Alabama,* 352 U. S. 191 (1957); *Watts v. Indiana,* 338 U. S. 49 (1949); *Turner v. Pennsylvania,* 338 U. S. 62 (1949); *Harris v. South Carolina,* 338 U. S. 68 (1949); *Ashcraft v. Tennessee,* 322 U. S. 143 (1944); *Miranda v. Arizona,* 384 U.S. 436 (1966). *Also* Saul Kassin et al., "Police-Induced Confessions: Risk Factors and Recommendations," *Law and Human Behavior* 34, no. 1 (2010): 3–38, https://pubmed.ncbi.nlm.nih.gov/19603261/; Saul Kassin, *False Confessions: Causes, Consequences, and Implications for Reform*, John Jay College (2008), https://saulkassin.org/wp-content/uploads/2024/06/Kassin-2008-APS-CD.pdf.

13. *Blackburn v. Alabama,* 361 U. S. 199 (1960).

14. *Id.,* at 206.

15. *Miranda*, *supra* note 12.

16. National Registry of Exonerations, *Annual Reports* page, https://exonerationregistry.org/all-reports; Saul Kassin and Gísli Gudjónsson, "The Psychology of Confessions: A Review of the Literature and Issues," *Psychological Science in the Public Interest* 5, no. 2 (November 2004): 33–67, https://journals.sagepub.com/doi/10.1111/j.1529-1006.2004.00016.x; Steven Drizin and Richard Leo, "The Problem of False Confessions in the Post-DNA World," *North Carolina Law Review* 82, no. 3 (2004), https://web.williams.edu/Psychology/Faculty/Kassin/files/drizenl.leo.04.pdf.

17. Mary Catlin et al., "Protocol: Interview and Interrogation Methods and Their Effects on True and False Confessions: An Update and Extension," *Campbell Systematic Reviews* 19, no. 1 (March 2023): e1314, https://doi.org/10.1002/cl2.1314; Snook et al., *supra* note 8; Roberts, *supra* note 4.

18. *See* Catlin et al., *supra* note 17.

False Confessions: A Social Science Perspective

Dr. Sara C. Appleby
Associate Professor of Psychology
College of Liberal Arts and Sciences
Mercer University

Most people believe that they would never confess to a crime they did not commit. Yet, real world stories, like those profiled in this book, as well as a large body of interdisciplinary research dating back to the 1970s, show that standard police interrogation practices frequently can—and do—result in false confessions. This research has identified numerous individual and situational risk factors that increase the likelihood of an innocent person falsely confessing.

Individual Risk Factors

Individual risk factors are things about a person that make them more vulnerable to police interrogation tactics, thus increasing the chance of a false confession. Youthful suspects and people with mental illnesses, substance abuse problems, and neurodevelopmental disorders such as intellectual disabilities and autism spectrum disorder are all at an increased risk of giving a false confession during a standard police interrogation.[1]

For example, youth are overrepresented among exonerees who falsely confess as are people with mental illness or disability. As of 2022, individuals under the age of eighteen at the time of the crime accounted for only 9 percent of all exonerees but 25 percent of false confession exonerees. Similarly, people who had a recorded mental illness or disability at the time of the crime accounted for 6 percent of all exonerees but 32 percent of false confession exonerees.[2]

For juvenile suspects, the ability to reason and evaluate risk is not fully developed. When subjected to a high-pressure police interrogation, they struggle to weigh the long-term consequences of confessing (being convicted of a crime) against the short-term reward of confessing (ending the interrogation). Additionally, youth, people with mental illness, and people with intellectual disabilities show lower awareness of legal processes, higher levels of obedience to authority, and more suggestibility than the typical adult.[3] As a result, when subjected to police pressure and deceptive tactics, these groups of suspects are highly vulnerable.

Situational Risk Factors

Situational risk factors are aspects of the interrogation that raise the chance of a false confession. These include lengthy interrogations, and lying about and misrepresenting evidence and the seriousness of the crime.

Police interrogations often occur in two phases. The first phase is a nonconfrontational interview aimed at determining whether a suspect is innocent or guilty.[4] The path to a false confession often begins during this interview when interrogators erroneously decide that an innocent person is guilty. Unfortunately, police often mistake a suspect's stress and anxiety at being questioned as signs of guilt.[5]

Suspects judged as guilty in step one move on to step two, where they are isolated and subjected to an accusatorial, guilt-presumptive interrogation. The primary goal of this step is to obtain a confession. It is during this step that interrogators may employ the situational risk factors listed earlier. To the extent they do, it is to create an uncomfortable situation that the suspect is eager to get out of.

Interrogation Length: Increasing the length of an interrogation can bring more pressure to bear on the suspect. In the United States, the average police interrogation lasts about 1.6 hours,[6] and popular training manuals advise practitioners not to exceed 4 hours.[7] Legally, however, there is no time limit on interrogations.[8] Basic psychological research shows that prolonged periods of isolation are stressful[9] and can incentivize people to take actions to remove themselves from the source of the stress,[10] even those that go against self-interest like falsely confessing to a crime. Hand in hand with lengthy interrogations is sleep deprivation, which research shows can impair cognitive function and decision-making ability,[11] making it difficult for suspects to resist the social pressures inherent in a police interrogation.

False Evidence: Real world examples of the false evidence ploy include falsely telling the suspect their DNA, blood, or fingerprints were found at the crime scene, falsely telling the suspect they failed a polygraph exam, and falsely telling the suspect there is eyewitness or video evidence. These types of lies increase false confession rates by making suspects feel trapped[12] or causing them to doubt their own memory.[13] In recent years, citing the research on the coerciveness of the false evidence ploy, numerous states have banned lying about evidence to juvenile suspects.

Minimization: Interrogators who downplay the seriousness of a crime are engaging in a practice called "minimization." They try to change the suspect's perception of the consequences of confessing by minimizing the harm to the victim, emphasizing how common the crime is, or shifting the blame away from the suspect to the victim and others.[14] Minimization creates an impression of leniency, which, in turn, leads suspects to believe that the consequences of confessing will not be as bad as they had originally assumed, lessening the anxiety associated with confession. While the United States Supreme Court has ruled that police interrogators cannot promise leniency, it has ruled that they can fake enough sympathy to imply leniency.[15]

Apart from individual and situational risk factors, a suspect's innocence can also be a risk factor for false confessions. Innocent people think and behave differently from guilty people.[16] For example, believing they have nothing to hide and that their innocence will be obvious to investigators, innocent suspects are more likely to waive their Miranda rights and agree to speak with police.[17] Ironically, the knowledge of one's own innocence often leads innocent suspects to inadvertently place themselves in harm's way.

In addition to the substantial body of research on the causes of false confessions, there is a similar body of research on the consequences of false confessions. That research shows that the implications of false confessions made during a police interrogation are widespread and devastating. Even if retracted immediately, confessions can bias police, forensic scientists, alibi witnesses, eyewitnesses, and judges against the innocent suspect.[18] Mock jury studies show that confessions have a greater impact on verdicts than other types of evidence, and that people do not adequately discount confession evidence even when taking individual and situational risk factors into consideration.[19] Moreover, false confession convictions are more difficult to overturn,[20] and, once exonerated, false confessors are often viewed as less worthy of financial compensation or government support.[21]

In sum, not only does a confession increase the likelihood of conviction, but it also continues to haunt the innocent person upon exoneration. That is why understanding the causes and consequences of false confessions is a key step toward ensuring that the legal system renders results that are fair and reliable.

1. Saul M. Kassin et al., "Police-Induced Confessions, 2.0: Risk Factors and Recommendations," *Law and Human Behavior* 49, no. 1 (February 2025): 7–53, https://doi.org/10.1037/lhb0000593.

2. "Table: Age and Mental Status of Exonerated Defendants Who Falsely Confess," The National Registry of Exonerations (April 2022), https://www.law.umich.edu/special/exoneration/Documents/Age%20and%20Mental%20Status%20FINAL%20CHART.pdf.

3. Kassin et al., *supra* note 1; Saul M. Kassin, "False Confessions," *Policy Insights from the Behavioral and Brain Sciences* 1, no. 1 (October 2014): 112–21, https://doi.org/10.1177/2372732214548678; Richard A. Leo, "False Confessions: Causes, Consequences, and Implications," *Journal of the American Academy of Psychiatry and the Law* 37, no. 3 (September 2009): 332–43, https://jaapl.org/content/37/3/332.

4. *See* Fred E. Inbau and John E. Reid, *Criminal Interrogation and Confessions* (5th ed., 2013): 3–7.

5. Aldert Vrij, *Detecting Lies and Deceit: Pitfalls and Opportunities* (2nd ed.), Chichester: Wiley (2008); Aldert Vrij, Par Anders Granhag, and Stephen Porter, "Pitfalls and Opportunities in Nonverbal and Verbal Lie Detection," *Psychological Science in the Public Interest* 11, no. 3 (December 2010): 89–121, https://doi.org/10.1177/1529100610390861.

6. Saul M. Kassin et al., "Police Interviewing and Interrogation: A Self-Report Survey of Police Practices and Beliefs," *Law and Human Behavior* 31, no. 4 (August 2007): 381–400, https://doi.org/10.1007/s10979-006-9073-5.

7. Inbau, *supra* note 4.

8. *See id.* ("The length at which an interrogation approaches the level of duress associated with an involuntary confession is individually defined."); Kassin et al., *supra* note 1.

9. Kassin et al., *supra* note 1.

10. *Id.*

11. Yvonne Harrison and James A. Horne, "The Impact of Sleep Deprivation on Decision Making: A Review," *Journal of Experimental Psychology: Applied* 6, no. 3 (January 2000): 236–49, https://doi.org/10.1037/1076-898x.6.3.236; June J. Pilcher and Allen I. Huffcutt, "Effects of Sleep Deprivation on Performance: A Meta-Analysis," *Sleep* 19, no. 4 (June 1996): 318–26, https://doi.org/10.1093/sleep/19.4.318.

12. Jennifer T. Perillo and Saul M. Kassin, "Inside Interrogation: The Lie, the Bluff, and False Confessions," *Law and Human Behavior* 35, no. 4 (August 2011): 327–37, https://doi.org/10.1007/s10979-010-9244-2.

13. *See* Robert Horselenberg, Harald Merckelbach, and Sarah Josephs, "Individual Differences and False Confessions: A Conceptual Replication of Kassin and Kiechel (1996)," *Psychology, Crime & Law* 9, no. 1 (January 2003): 1–8, https://doi.org/10.1080/10683160308141; Allison D. Redlich and Gail S. Goodman, "Taking Responsibility for an Act Not Committed: The Influence of Age and Suggestibility," *Law And Human Behavior* 27, no. 2 (January 2003): 141–56, https://doi.org/10.1023/a:1022543012851; Saul M. Kassin and Katherine L. Kiechel, "The Social Psychology of False Confessions: Compliance, Internalization, and Confabulation," *Psychological Science* 7, no. 3 (May 1996): 125–28, https://doi.org/10.1111/j.1467-9280.1996.tb00344.x.

14. *See* Christopher E. Kelly et al., "On the Road (to Admission): Engaging Suspects with Minimization," *Psychology, Public Policy, and Law* 25, no. 3 (August 2019): 166–180, https://doi.org/10.1037/law0000199; Saul M. Kassin, "False Confessions," *Policy Insights from the Behavioral and Brain Sciences* 1, no. 1 (October 2014): 112–21, https://doi.org/10.1177/2372732214548678; Saul M. Kassin et al., "Police Interviewing and Interrogation: A Self-Report Survey of Police Practices and Beliefs," *Law and Human Behavior* 31, no. 4 (August 2007): 381–400, https://doi.org/10.1007/s10979-006-9073-5; Richard A. Leo, "Inside the Interrogation Room," *The Journal of Criminal Law and Criminology (1973-)* 86, no. 2 (Winter 1996): 266–303, https://doi.org/10.2307/1144028.

15. *See* Timothy J. Luke and Fabiana Alceste, "The Mechanisms of Minimization: How Interrogation Tactics Suggest Lenient Sentencing Through Pragmatic Implication," *Law and Human Behavior* 44, no. 4 (June 2020): 266–85, https://doi:10.1037/lhb0000410.

16. Saul M. Kassin, "On the Psychology of Confessions: Does Innocence Put Innocents at Risk?" *American Psychologist* 60, no. 3 (April 2005): 215–28, https://doi.org/10.1037/0003-066X.60.3.215.

17. *See* Timothy E. Moore and Karina Gagnier, "'You Can Talk if You Want To:' Is the Police Caution on the 'Right to Silence' Understandable?" *Criminal Reports* 51, no. 6 (2008): 233–49, https://www.glendon.yorku.ca/timmoore/wp-content/uploads/sites/222/You-can-talk-if-you-want-to-CrimRep.pdf; Saul M. Kassin and Rebecca J. Norwick, "Why People Waive Their Miranda Rights: The Power of Innocence," *Law and Human Behavior* 28, no. 2 (April 2004): 211–21, https://doi.org/10.1023/B:LAHU.0000022323.74584.f5.

18. *See* Saul M. Kassin, Itiel E. Dror, and Jeff Kukucka, "The Forensic Confirmation Bias: Problems, Perspectives, and Proposed Solutions," *Journal of Applied Research in Memory and Cognition* 2, no. 1 (March 2013): 42–52, https://doi.org/10.1016/j.jarmac.2013.01.001.

19. *See* Linda A. Henkl, Kimberly A. Coffman, and Elizabeth M. Dailey, "A Survey of People's Attitudes and Beliefs about False Confessions," *Behavioral Sciences & the Law* 26, no. 5 (September 11, 2008): 555–84, https://doi.org/10.1002/bsl.826; Allison D. Redlich, Simona Ghetti, and Jodi A. Quas, "Perceptions of Children During a Police Interview: A Comparison of Alleged Victims and Suspects," *Journal of Applied Social Psychology* 38, no. 3 (February 2008): 705–35, https://doi.org/10.1111/j.1559-1816.2007.00323.x; Saul M. Kassin and Holly Sukel, "Coerced Confessions and the Jury: An Experimental Test of the 'Harmless Error' Rule," *Law and Human Behavior* 21, no. 1 (February 1997): 27–46, https://doi.org/10.1023/A:1024814009769.

20. Kyle C. Scherr and Christopher J. Normile, "False Confessions Predict a Delay Between Release from Incarceration and Official Exoneration," *Law and Human Behavior* 46, no. 1 (February 2022): 67–80, https://doi.org/10.1037/lhb0000479; Emily West and Vanessa Meterko, "Innocence Project: DNA Exonerations, 1989–2014: Review of Data and Findings from the First 25 Years," *Albany Law Review* 79, no. 3 (December 2016): 717–95, https://www.albanylawreview.org/article/70125-innocence-project-dna-exonerations-1989-2014-review-of-data-and-findings-from-the-first-25-years.

21. Jeff Kukucka and Andrew J. Evelo, "Stigma Against False Confessors Impacts Post Exoneration Financial Compensation," *Behavioral Sciences & the Law* 37, no. 4 (April 2017): 372–87, https://doi:10.1002/bsl.2403.

Citations to Screen Captures from Videos of Interrogations That Produced False Confessions

Front Cover: Altered still from a video recording by the Sheriff's Department of Cherokee County, Georgia, of its 2002 interrogation of Roberto Rocha, a twenty-year-old with intellectual disabilities. Segments of the video recording, including the one from which this still was extracted, were previously available at ABC, "Primetime: False Confession Documentary from 2006 - Saul Kassin," YouTube, April 25, 2020, 36:00. During the interrogation, Rocha falsely confessed to involvement in the murder of a fifteen-year-old girl in Cherokee County. Law enforcement officials later determined that he could not have been involved because he had been out of the country when the murder was committed. Robert Perske, "False Confessions From 53 Persons with Intellectual Disabilities: The List Keeps Growing," *Intellectual and Developmental Disabilities* 46, no. 6 (2008); 468–79, https://doi.org/10.1352/2008.46:468-479.

Page 13: Altered still from a video recording by the Escondido Police Department, Escondido, California, of its 1998 interrogation of fourteen-year-old Michael Crowe. Segments of the video recording, including the one from which this still was extracted, are available at CentreDivide, "Miscarriages/Travesty of justice-Michael Crowe Case-Coerced Confession-Part 2 of (3)," YouTube, August 23, 2010, 14:53, https://www.youtube.com/watch?v=yJcqjPxtIXc. During the interrogation, Crowe falsely confessed to the murder of his sister. One week before his case was to go to trial, the charges against him were dismissed after DNA evidence implicated someone else. In 2012, a judge ruled that Crowe was factually innocent. See Mark Sauer, "Michael Crowe Found 'Factually Innocent' In Sister's Murder," KPBS, May 22, 2012, https://www.kpbs.org/news/public-safety/2012/05/22/michael-crowe-found-factually-innocent-sisters-mur.

Pages 14–15: Altered still from a video recording made by the Denver Police Department, Denver, Colorado, of the 2000 interrogation of fourteen-year-old Lorenzo Montoya. The segment of the video recording from which this still was extracted is available at CBC Docs (@cbcdocs), "In the U.S. police are allowed to lie about evidence. And this can lead people to confess to crimes that they didn't commit," Facebook, January 3, 2019, https://www.facebook.com/watch/?v=356328598480468. During the interrogation, Lorenzo Montoya falsely confessed to murder. He was wrongfully imprisoned for thirteen years before being exonerated by DNA evidence. See Amy Schneider, "Lorenzo Montoya - Celebrating 10 Years of Freedom," Polansky Law Firm, June 28, 2024, https://www.polanskylawfirm.com/blog/lorenzo-montoya-celebrating-10-years-of-freedom/.

Pages 16–17: Altered still from a video recording made by the Fontana Police Department, Fontana, California, of the 2018 interrogation of fifty-three-year-old Tom Perez. Selected segments of the video recording, including the one from which this still was extracted, are available at CNN, "Police pressured him to confess to a murder that never happened," September 6, 2024, video, 6:35, https://www.cnn.com/2024/09/05/us/fontana-pressured-murder-confession. During the interrogation, Perez confessed to murdering his father. Days later, police officers discovered that Perez's father was alive and well. See Caroline Blair, "Thomas Perez Jr. Falsely Confessed to His Father's Murder After a 17 Hour Interrogation – but His Dad Was Alive the Whole Time. Inside the Disturbing Case," *People*, December 6, 2025, https://people.com/thomas-perez-jr-murder-interrogation-11862514.

Pages 148–49: Altered still from a video recording made by the Fontana Police Department, Fontana, California, of the 2018 interrogation of fifty-three-year-old Tom Perez. Segments of the video recording, including the one from which this still was extracted, are available at CNN, "Police pressured him to confess to a murder that never happened," September 6, 2024, video, 6:35, https://www.cnn. com/2024/09/05/us/fontana-pressured-murder-confession. See *supra* pages 16–17.

Pages 150–51: Altered still from a video recording made by the Denver Police Department, Denver, Colorado, of the 2000 interrogation of fourteen-year-old Lorenzo Montoya. Segments of the video recording, including the one from which this still was extracted, are available at Film Independent, "False Confessions movie trailer," YouTube, August 23, 2018, 1:47, https://www.youtube.com/ watch?v=6Jc2WZLkl1A. See *supra* pages 14–15.

Pages 152–53: Altered still from a video recording made by the Escondido Police Department, Escondido, California, of the 1998 interrogation of fourteen-year-old Michael Crowe. Segments of the video recording, including the one from which this still was extracted, are available at National Geographic, "Interrogation or Child Abuse?" YouTube, March 5, 2008, 5:01, https://www.youtube.com/watch?v=WkLHXKHb1Vc. See *supra* page 13.

Acknowledgements

This project grew out of my work as an attorney in the National Legal Department of the American Civil Liberties Union. I spent twenty years designing and implementing campaigns to reform the American criminal justice system. I came to view that system as deeply flawed, prioritizing expediency and finality over justice. Meaningful change will only occur if the public knows and cares about the system's deficiencies.

I wish to extend heartfelt thanks to exonerees Jeffrey Deskovic, Vanessa Gathers, Byron Halsey, Eddie Lowery, Christopher Ochoa, and Raymond Santana for sharing their stories. A special thanks to Jeffrey Deskovic for his support and guidance. Jeff is now a practicing lawyer, having graduated from law school in 2019, and is the founder and executive director of the Jeffrey Deskovic Foundation for Justice. At the Foundation, Jeff works to free the wrongfully imprisoned while pursuing policy changes aimed at preventing wrongful convictions. Visit deskovicfoundation.org to find out more about his work.

I also wish to thank Amanda Marchand; Yolanda Ferraloro and Suzanne Coffman of Music Rightz; Dr. Sara Appleby; Caleb Cain Marcus; Michael Featherstone; Caleb Featherstone; Lisa Cahill; Richard Dahlberg; Brian Kelley; Hayden Maynard; Ted Maynard; Eve Mykytyn; and Nicole Rosenthal for their valuable contributions—and the many others who reviewed the numerous drafts that preceded this publication.

R. D.

Texts: Sara C. Appleby, Robin Dahlberg
Copyediting: James Copeland, Rachel Weinick
Reprint and Photo Clearances: Yolanda Ferraloro and Suzanne Coffman (Music Rightz)
Project Management: Kehrer Verlag (Pauline Vollpert)
Creative Direction: Luminosity Lab (Caleb Cain Marcus)
Image Retouching: Alejandra Jiménez
Image Processing: Kehrer Design (Patrick Horn)
Production Management: Kehrer Design (Hannah Antes)

Bibliographic information published by the Deutsche Nationalbibliothek
The Deutsche Nationalbibliothek lists this publication in the Deutsche Nationalbibliografie; detailed bibliographic data is available on the internet at https://dnb.dnb.de.

Printed and bound in Germany
ISBN 978-3-96900-222-3

Kehrer Verlag Heidelberg
www.kehrerverlag.com